EDWARDIAN AND VICTORIAN

LONDON

First published in Great Britain in 1999 by Brockhampton Press
a member of the Hodder Headline Group
20 Bloomsbury Street, London WC1B 3QA

ISBN 1-86019970-4

A copy of the CIP data is available from the
British Library upon request.

Designed and produced for Brockhampton Press
by Keith Pointing Design Consultancy.

Reprographics by Global Colour
Printed and Bound in the UAE

EDWARDIAN AND VICTORIAN
LONDON

A·R· HOPE MONCRIEFF

BROCKHAMPTON PRESS
LONDON

NELSON'S COLUMN AND PORTICO OFF ST MARTIN'S-IN-THE-FIELDS

INTRODUCTION

MANY BOOKS HAVE been written about London but this one offers a unique insight to the world of late Victorian and early Edwardian London seen through the eyes of a well seasoned man-about-town – a certain Mr A.R. Hope Moncrieff. Born in Edinburgh in 1847, he studied for the Scottish bar but found this too limiting, went into teaching and finally took up writing, producing over 200 books on travel and history. He died in 1927.

This book was first published in the Edwardian era, 1910, when London was still the epicentre of an empire, the British Isles were still one entity, and the British pound dominated international trade. There was little sign of the tumultuous changes which were shortly to engulf the world, brought about by the two world wars. Mr Moncrieff was blissfully unaware that entire sections of the city would be destroyed by the heavy bombing of the second world war. However, it should be noted that most of the landmarks illustrated in his book are still in evidence today. Although what was then he calls *the suburbs*, we now call *inner London* and the much of the local *countryside* are now the suburbs. A city is a product of its history, which he understood well. Using reminiscences and anecdotes, he brings to life the everyday experiences of a Victorian gentlemen — he passes Benjamin Disraeli (1804-1881) in the street, and witnesses William Gladstone's (1809-1898) windows broken in Harley Street during a riot. He also brings to life London's past with extracts from the famous writers and poets of his time such as Dickens and Thackeray. The fictional *Sherlock Holmes* was in his prime, walking around London pipe in mouth. Sir Arthur Conan Doyle's first Holmes book, *A Study in Scarlet* came out in 1887. *The Hound of the Baskervilles* in 1902 and the last *The Casebook of Sherlock Holmes* as late as 1927, three years before the authors death in 1930.

Mr Moncrieff dips in and out of London's past. So it may help to give a potted history, taking us right up his era. There are many ideas as to the origin of the name *London*. Some say it came from the old British words *Lyn-Din*, meaning 'the fortified hill on the lake', *Lyn* being the Celtic word for a broad sheet of water. In the days before the first Roman invasion of Britain, London was likely to have been a stockade entrenchment, possible standing on a higher ground were now stands the Bank of England in the heart of the financial sector in the city. It would have been surrounded by forests and above the marshes and the lower ground which would have been flooded at high tides. The Romans called it *Londinium* when they came in 43AD. The wall which they built to protect the city continued to survive, right through to the medieval time. Even today when foundations are laid for a new building in the city, evidence of the Roman past is often being uncovered.

The Romans built outer walls of the city which extended over two miles and enclosed an area of about 500 acres. Strong towers seem to have been placed at intervals. When the Romans withdrew and after the days of Hengist and Vortigen, Ambrosius captured it and his nephew Mordred was crowned about the year 530AD. Various fires and plagues besieged the city during the time of the Saxons and the Danes often laid the town to waste. After the reign of King Canute it seems to increased in power until the invasion of William the Conqueror, who granted London its charter and he made it his capital.

Throughout the Middle Ages, London was the largest city, political centre, and chief port of England. New palaces replaced the Tower (which became a prison) as the royal residence moved across town, most notably to Westminster, Whitehall and St. James's. The royal court was located in London much of the time, and the city became a great cultural centre. It was during the reign of Queen Elizabeth I that London reached a new level of preeminence. William Shakespeare's plays were performed in the Globe theatre, book publishing began, and London became the centre of England's newly emerging foreign trade.

In the 17th century the city had become crowded, was largely built of wood and sanitation, as we know it, did not exist. When plagues came in 1625 and again in 1665 more than 75,000 lives were claimed. The fire of London in 1666 consumed much of the city. Sir Christopher Wren rebuilt St Pauls Cathedral and more than 50 city churches.

The original St Pauls Cathedral and Westminster Abbey were founded between the years 608 and 616. The Abbey was founded by Sebert, King of the East Saxons; it was destroyed by the Danes and rebuilt by King Edgar in 958 and again by Edward the Confessor in 1065. Pope Nicholas II decreed it "a place of inauguration" of the English monarchs. Henry III rebuilt it from ground and Henry VII added the magnificent chapel at the east end.

By the 18th century London had again expanded. Elegant housing began to appear to the north and west of the old city often built speculatively. The literary and theatrical societies also grew in stature.

The industrial revolution in the 19th century brought radical changes, such as easier travel by train. Industrial suburbs were built to service the new factories. Robert Peel, in 1829 introduced the world's first police force and in 1890 the world's first electric underground railway was opened. Mr Moncreiff's London was capital of a country whose technology had changed the world.

The book is illustrated with numerous paintings from those times, capturing foggy London with a sentimental charm. To our eyes they can evoke the cosy world of Walt Disney's *Mary Poppins* but these paintings were collected by Royalty and the aristocracy of the day. In many respects they exemplify the complacency which many late Victorians viewed their world.

Some artists had access to the highest being collected by the then Prince and Princess of Wales and were commissioned to paint their children. The book's images show evidence of affection for the city and the world captured by these pictures is a

CROMWELL ROAD

wealthy one. Those to whom this book was intended, even by todays standards, would have had a comfortable life: almost all of whom would have had several domestic servants.

London then was undoubtedly more visually homogeneous, without today's consumer clutter. The skyline was just church spires, steeples and chimney pots without interruptions by awkward high rise towers blocks. Fog and mists gave great atmosphere to the city but, of course, the reality was less romantic to sufferers of chest complaints. Thousands fell victim to London's smog each year, and continued to so do right up to when the clean air act in the 1950's.

Some of the authors attitudes and turns of phrase can appear a little shocking to today's politically correct ear, but these views reflected his times. In many respects he did live in more enlightened times when compared to the earlier 1800's. He vividly relates for example, with considerable disapproval, the horrors of when public hangings were seen as an entertainment.

Overall Mr Hope Moncrieff and the artists give a fascinating view to a bygone world. Even Londoners should find some aspect of his considerable knowledge illuminating.

Charles Bullen 1999

THE CROSSING, HYDE PARK CORNER

WHAT LONDON IS

WE ALL KNOW that London stands on the Thames, that it is the capital of an empire on which the sun never sets, and that it has the right to call itself the largest and richest city in existence, perhaps the greatest congregation of human beings to which history ever had a chance of preaching on that old text, the rise and fall of so many a Babylon. We ought to know how it measures at least a dozen miles in length and breadth, and how it contains five millions or so of people, to which some half as many must be added if we take in its outer area. We can learn that it counts a million of houses; that its myriads of streets, if set on end, would reach across Europe; that it includes some sixteen thousand acres of open spaces; that yearly it lays twenty miles of fresh pavements, and adds new inhabitants enough to make a country town, while it is always swallowing some old village in its insatiable maw. Those who have an appetite for such figures may further be instructed that every year its port harbours more than twenty thousand vessels of all flags, that every day nearly nine thousand trains run into its stations, and that every hour about ten million gallons of water are drawn for its various needs, flushing out in subterranean channels more than one cares to count or measure. The above are but samples from an imposing stack of statistics, that might be drawn upon by way of helping the imagination to realise what London is. Unimaginative and uninstructed eyes have long been content to leave the matter thus: "The cities of London and Westminster are spread out to an incredible extent. The streets, squares, rows, lanes, and alleys are innumerable. Palaces, public buildings, and churches rise in every quarter." I am using the pen of Miss Lydia Melford, whose first sensation in those thronged thoroughfares was like that of the fabulous Scot, at a later date found waiting shyly up an entry in Fleet Street, as he explained, till the people had come out of church.

But next arises the question, *What is London?* — one to be less readily answered. Not every Londoner could say off-hand whether Hampstead, for instance, belongs to his hive, nor in what sense it includes Norwood or Kew. London was once a walled city about the mouth of two small brooks flowing into the Thames; then, escaping from this confinement, like the genius released by a fisherman in the *Arabian Nights* it quickly spread itself over the surrounding heights and flats, till, from an area of some square mile or so, it had expanded more than a hundredfold. Sovereigns in

HAMPSTEAD HEATH

vain bade its growth come to a stand, their procla-mations as idle as Canute's commanding the waves. Not less vainly lords cried out against the citizens who presumed to neighbour their parks and gardens, sooner or later to be ploughed up by streets. A century ago sociologists of Cobbett's stamp vituperated that "wen" whose bulk seemed a danger to national health; and by the end of the century the tumour was swollen five times as great. Not that it has grown so much out of proportion to the general body, if we may accept Mr. Matthew Bramble's indignant calculation, made several gen-erations back, that "one-sixth part of this whole extensive kingdom is crowded within the bills of mortality." That is much the same ratio as London proper now bears to England, its own thicker out-skirts and the rest of the United Kingdom being eliminated, which, if brought into the sum, would make it work out in favour of the capital's increase.

When we come to boundaries and definitions, we are met by the truly British want of system, symmetry, regularity, through which London was allowed to straggle and struggle up into a confused rough-cast conglomeration of materials stuck together by chance or by rule of thumb, cross-divided for different purposes, to be managed by divers and sometimes overlapping authorities. There are citizens who, till the consid-eration be brought home to them by rate-collectors or other call to civic duty, do not care to know in what parish, borough, Poor-Law union, Parliamentary division, or what, they have their home; and on the edge of London some may be hardly clear what right they have to call themselves Londoners. The City, as it is styled, *honoris causa*, forms an independent core, round which strangers must be taught to distinguish between the County of London, by law established, and the wider circle that has come to be known as Greater London.

At the end of last century a new

organisation was brought about by the London Government Act, dividing the County of London into twenty-eight boroughs, exclusive of the City, which clings to its time-honoured jurisdiction and privileges, keeping good order within its bounds by a police of its own, and having its own learned judges to supplement the rough-and-ready justice administered by Lord Mayor and Aldermen. Each of the boroughs has now its corporation, wanting nothing of dignity but age; each of them is divided into wards, electing their quota of representatives on borough councils that replaced a hugger-mugger administration of vestries and local boards; and all these are knit together under the municipal parliament of the London County Council. The new boroughs usually take their titles from some parish of note Kensington, Paddington, St Pancras, Shoreditch, and so on — while certain familiar quarters of London have had their fame slighted in this division, as Brixton swallowed up in Lambeth, Sydenham invisibly rent between Lewisham and Camberwell, and half a dozen smaller names lost in that of Wandsworth. Something was then done to round off the county area, as by dragging in South Hornsey, and turning out into Kent the "hamlet" of Penge, with its 23,000 people; but, after all such adjustments, the boundary seems a most zigzag one, which leaves Ealing and Edmonton outside of London, but takes in Woolwich and Hampstead. When one goes out the Edgware Road, beyond Maida Vale he has on his right hand the London borough of Hampstead, stretching on to the "Spaniards" at the farther end of its Heath; but the left side of the road is mere Middlesex, where Willesden would fain change its humble style of urban district for the title of borough, being, indeed, populous as half a dozen boroughs. On the Finchley Road the frontier is at present marked by a loose end of tramway, which haughty London will not admit into her bosom. In less genteel quarters the limit may be betrayed at night by a rush across it of thirsty suburbans, whose public-houses shut earlier than those of the roistering County. On the east side, its manifest boundary is the Lea, beyond which some half-million of people live in Essex boroughs that belong to London as Salford does to Manchester. For certain purposes, indeed, these outskirts may dovetail into London, or be cleft within themselves; thus the south part of Willesden, above mentioned, holds fellowship with the London drainage system, while the north side of the parish has the more expensive lot of discharging its refuse from the Brent watershed.

Beyond the invisible border-line of the County come more or less thickly clustered the county boroughs, municipal boroughs, urban districts, and rural districts, that go to make up Greater London. The boundaries of this area, indeed, are well marked only to official spectacles. The London Postal District has a radius of several miles, stretching beyond the County limits, while excluding its south-eastern corner. A wider sweep is that of the Metropolitan Police District, taking in all parishes within fifteen miles of Charing Cross, among them independent towns like Bromley, Croydon, Epsom, Kingston, Barnet, and Barking, in a province not far short of 700 square miles. A quarter of a century ago, a friend of mine who undertook to walk round London, made it a matter of sixty miles: a round hundred would be nearer the present mark. Mr. Frederick Harrison laments that one must now go forty miles out to secure the rustic peace in which his youth was passed within sight of the dome of St. Paul's.

But even this huge space does not give room for all the monster's limbs and tentacles, ever stretching outwards to drag green countrysides into its gullets of brick. The multiplication of railways and the extension of tram-lines help well-to-do citizens more and more to make their homes far out of the smoke and din, amid which their work lies, so that many thousands of families living an hour or two's journey from the City can count themselves as Londoners after a sort. A ring of old towns now studs the girdle of the Metropolis, that makes up to them in prosperity what they lose in dignity by their dependence — Romford, Brentwood, Epping, Hertford, St.Albans, Watford, Uxbridge, Staines,

CHAUCER'S TOMB

Woking, Guildford, Dorking, Sevenoaks, Gravesend; and still further afield appear fringes and tassels of this still growing capital.

It will be seen, then, how various measurements might be taken of London's bulk, imposing by any definition. One visible boundary, that seems novel and practical, is suggested by Mr. Ford Madox Hueffer (*The Soul of London*).

"We may say that London begins where tree-trunks commence to be black, otherwise there is very little to distinguish Regent's Park from Penshurst, or Wimbledon from Norwich. This tree-trunk boundary is, however, defective enough; in many parts of Epping the wood is so dense that boughs and boulders are as green, as brown, as mossy, or as lichened as at Fontainebleau. The prevailing winds being from the south and from the westwards, again, the zone of blackened trunks extends farther than is fair towards the north and the east. But judge I by this standard, London, as far as I have been able to observe, is bounded by a line drawn from Leigh in Essex, half-way through the Epping Forest, to the north of Hendon, to the west of Brentford, the south-west of Barnes, well to the south of Sydenham, well to the east of Bromley, and so up to Leigh again. Other observers will no doubt find this tree-trunk limitation a little faulty; but it takes in at least nearly all the looser elements of the sphere of London influence. And, as the invariable and bewildering exception to this, as to all rules, it may as well be set down that the most "Londony" of all London trees has a bark that is never uniformly black. The plane-tree grows best of all in London, because it sheds its bark continually; getting rid of its soot, it clears the pores of its skin and flourishes — if I may be allowed an image that appears frivolous but that is sober enough — a perpetual emblem to the city of the morning tub. In the suburbs the plane yields first place to the flowering almond, in the parks to the thorn, but it is the tree of intimate London. Elms, however, are the trees most noticeable on the roads into London, and their trunks blacken perhaps soonest of all. Nine Elms, Barn Elms, and how many hotlier "Elms"? greet us on the run into town; and the feathery outlines of how many of these trees close the vistas of those new suburban streets that are for ever drilling little pathways into the ancient "estates" of the home counties!"

It might be fancifully put that this giant spreads not only over the earth, but mounts to the very sky, aglow for leagues above the lights of London. Too often, indeed, that pillar of fire becomes by hidden daylight a cloud of smoke; and another mark of London would be its obscuring breath. The London fog is one of its darkest reproaches, yet even through this seeing eyes can catch glimpses of weird charm, as vistas among the grimy walls frame fine sky-effects, toned and coloured by the emanations of its crowded life. The true lover of London admires her most in her coy, not to say sullen, moods, when her smiles have to be won by patient courtship. Summer and sunshine tempt him to faithlessness, suggesting charms that are not her native characteristics. If it be not false heraldry to quote again from a rival *or* upon *argent* — I will own there is much in what Mr. E. V. Lucas says in his *Wanderer in London*. "Although London beneath a May sun is London at her loveliest, it is when signs of winter begin to accumulate that to me she is most friendly, most homely. I admire her in May, but I am quite ready to leave her; in November I am glad that I shall not be going away for a long time. She assumes the winter garb so cheerfully and characteristically. With the first fog of November she begins to be happy. 'Now,' one seems to hear her say, now I am myself again. Summer was all very well, but clear air and warmth are not really in my line. I am a grey city and a dingy: smoke is the breath of my life; stir your fires and let us be comfortable and gloomy again.' "This writer's beloved Charles Lamb would surely have agreed with him. "O, never let the lying poets be believed, who 'tice men from the cheerful haunt of streets!" Johnson thought that a man might as well be tired of life as of London. And James Smith bluntly puts the creed of those to whom all but London are "rejected addresses," declaring this "to be the best place in summer, the only place in winter."

At all events, our fog cannot be held deadly, when London, long one of the healthiest capitals in Europe, has, by the sanitary care of the last generation, come down to, or up to, a death-rate of some fourteen in the thousand. Moreover, the Metropolitan counties of Middlesex and Essex were lately reported the healthiest in England, while their suburban quarters, surprisingly, had a lower mortality than some more rural districts. It seems only in unstatistical ages that poets bring death with equal pace to mansion and hovel; so London's death-rate, covering the inner circle, varies, of course, according to the conditions of life and work in different quarters, as does the birth-rate, regrettably highest among those least able to bring up a large family under favourable circumstances. Too many sickly and crippled children are born and kept alive by the medical skill and multifold charity at work to counteract ignorance and improvidence. But in general, the Cockney is healthy enough, where even his stunted average of stature seems an adaptation to the environment. Very manifest is the energy with which he takes to games and athletic exercises under difficulties, often beating yokels at sports that might hardly be expected to thrive under the smoke of a thronged city. That nickname, dubiously interpreted as derived from the idea of a cock's egg, or from the lubberland of Cockayne, apparently implies some rustic gibe at a softness or slackness quite belied by fact. The Londoner is said still to make a good soldier; and in old times he proved his martial spirit in train-bands always ready to turn out for any popular cause, a city militia represented by more than one regiment's origin, most clearly by the Honourable Artillery Company, that in its Finsbury headquarters boasts to be the oldest military corps of the kingdom.

Cockney blood, to be sure, seems to run thin in the stress of this life. It is said, though scarcely proved, that, outside the class which gains fresh force by contact with mother earth, few Londoners can claim three generations of London origin. But if the giant be always wasting his strength, he is constantly recruited from the country far over which flare the lights of London as beacon to streets that too often turn out hardly paved even with silver and copper, and only here and there with gold, for those who can find it beneath the mud. Fresh-faced servant-maids and stalwart policemen are won from the country to mate in London, which naturally attracts ambitious and enterprising craftsmen of every kind. Unfortunately, too, many are attracted being masters of no craft in demand here, nor always willing to play the Gibeonite with effect, so that a spoilt rustic often makes a feckless Londoner, to whom "back to the land!" is cried in vain, once lie has known the allurement of lights, and company, and spectacles, and the charitable funds that breed as much poverty as they relieve.

For citizens of other lands also, London has of late years proved more and more attractive. How far their visits be due to admiration makes a difficult point, when cultured Britons themselves are not at one about the charms of our capital, which has at least developed a late consciousness of need for aesthetic improvement. Foreigners have been apt to shrug their shoulders over its architecture, its art, its want of sweetness and light ; but some strangers within our gates appear now better disposed to tickle John Bull with a flattery he does not much trouble to bestow on himself. One of our recent visitors, the lady styling herself Pierre de Coulevain, in her *L'Ile Inconnue,* presents a description worth quoting for its manifest effort to be fair, even to our fogs.

"London appears beautiful or ugly, according to one's turn of mind. For me it has an actual fascination. I feel its immensity, its power, its multitudinousness. Its low sky, its rayless sun, its yellow fog, give it an aspect of full north which charms me particularly. The fogs, so much abused, soften its lines, tone down its uglinesses, and afford an admirable grey tint. They have, besides, striking effects: often

NELSON'S COLUMN IN A FOG

THE PAVILION AT LORDS CRICKET GROUND

they veil a whole side of the horizon; a light breeze opens them out to let a Gothic cathedral emerge, a monumental bridge, high factory chimneys; then, if a strong wind scatters them roughly, the panorama of a city is unrolled before one's eyes. . .

London is an ant-hill — yes, but gigantic and marvellous. I see endless lines of small dwellings with "guillotine" windows, some imposing houses, then here and there more lofty structures of six, seven, nine storeys, overcharged with ornament, particularly ugly, and too much trenching on the low sky. I see wide arteries, narrow and grey side-streets, an immense meeting of ways — Trafalgar Square, separating two centres of different activity — openings where vehicles of all sorts cross each other, green spaces, flowery parks, fine trees, bits of meadow with cows on them, and even sheep. I see the Thames spanned by monumental bridges; the Thames now become a river of business, its dark waters bearing heavy cargoes and struggling against the tides. I see several great whirlpools of life: the

Docks, where physical strain is at its highest, the City, the Strand, Piccadilly, Bond Street, Hyde Park. And dominating this mighty mass with thought and beauty, I see Westminster Abbey, the Houses of Parliament, Gothic edifices, cathedrals, churches, royal palaces, St. James', Buckingham.

From these lines my eye turns to the expression of London. It seems to me severe and dull, but full of vigour. As to its moral atmosphere, that is singularly heavy and dry. I feel that it wants many higher elements. Thought and youth are away in the University towns; art is here in very small, almost invisible quantity; the churches are shut six days in the week. In general, its features are marked externally by money cares, ambition, pride, snobbism, powerful energies, force of will and of character, brutal passions, sufferings of a life and death struggle. London is a trading city, greedy for gain, where everything has its price, where the Golden Calf is fabricated and worshipped. In this merchant City, however, one is aware of a soul of Gothicism, of spirituality, of Bible faith, which ennobles it, gives it a higher distinction, perhaps, than it gets from the royal and imperial flag under which it works and trades. It is to this soul, if I am not mistaken, that it owes its true grandeur."

The material greatness of London is unquestionable. Its moral grandeur should be not less imposing, though hardly realised by most Londoners, paled as it is by the pride of Paris, *ville de lumière*, shadowed by the fame of Rome, mother of arts and faith, thrown into relief by the decay of Delhi and Peking, done homage to by the envy of capitals that hope to be what London is now. There is no city with so many inhabitants for whose sayings and doings all the world is agog. At Florence I once met a damsel hailing from some Hugginsville or Mugginsopolis in the centre of Uncle Sam's dominion, whom I vaguely remember as a most conceited, ignorant, and bumptious young person; but it was so many years ago that she has had time to learn better. She took no notice of me till she found out how I lived in London, whereupon, without preface or apology, she demanded my aid in discharging a commission given her by the *Hugginsville Eagle*, or suchlike local organ, to write her impressions of London, well spiced with "personal items" drawn from its " prominent citizens." The idea, as I understood it, was that I must go about with her to knock at the doors of the prominent citizens, and expose them to the pen of this confident interviewer. When I modestly declined such an enterprise, she dismissed me with republican rudeness, such as I hope she herself had not to encounter among our prominent citizens. We have since seen presumptuous Englishwomen go into paroxysms of scratching, screaming, and slapping policemen's faces when they are not allowed to waste the time of laborious statesmen with petitions and addresses that might be sent under a halfpenny stamp, after becoming known by heart to every newspaper reader. Do such foolish virgins recognize what manner of men are London's prominent citizens, for whom honest John Bull has not often been wanting in regard and respectful curiosity?

This is a city, a congregation of cities, where at any turn you may meet a sovereign prince, a modern Crœsus, a statesman whose name is sterotyped in every civilized language, a thinker whose influence goes out to all ends of the world. One has sat beside Ruskin in a bus, and John Bright in a Metropolitan railway carriage; one has seen Herbert Spencer, Huxley, Dickens, Tennyson, Carlyle, walking the streets unnoted by the common herd; one has come upon Disraeli meditating before the statue of John Stuart Mill in the dusk of the day it was unveiled; one has had a casual glimpse of Gladstone hurrying back from a momentous interview at Windsor; one has stared at Emperors, Kings, and Presidents paraded in turn for London's greeting, and at a whole galaxy of such potentates in their finest array, on occasions of festal ceremony that concerned half the royal families of Europe. Our own Princes, the cynosure of so many eyes, one may catch on foot in Pall Mall, or taking a hansom in Piccadilly. These are sights I myself have seen by chance, who am not one to put myself out of the way hunting for them, as is the sport of some Londoners.

There is a work of national reference called *Who's Who*, in which, taking a couple of pages at random, I find, among a score of more or less distinguished Britons, only one-third who seem not to have at least a *pied-à-terre* in London, and some half of them altogether Londoners. So a chronicler of King Stephen's time tells us that then "almost all the Bishops, abbots, and magnates of England, are in a manner citizens and freemen of London City." But even if its living citizens were a mere mass of nonentities, London might still take pride in its dead generations. Whatever be its merits or demerits in the way of beauty, stateliness, and comfort, at least our Metropolis is rich in famous scenes and world-familiar associations. A visitor must be ignorant indeed to pass by the "things of fame that do renown this city," as no more interesting than the sky-scrapers of New York or the shambles of Chicago, whose smart citizens sometimes undertake to cream the sights of London in a

BROMPTON ROAD, LOOKING EAST

couple of days. I have met an American tourist proud of having "done" all Europe, with Egypt and the Holy Land, in three weeks. But the stranger who has time to indulge a visionary mood, may see our streets full of ghosts often invisible to their descendants in the flesh. Here are courts trodden by the feet of Lamb, Johnson, Goldsmith; houses in which Macaulay, Byron, Pitt were at home; walks known to Addison and Swift; spots consecrated by memories of Milton, Shakespeare, Chaucer; and tombs of many a world famous name. If our foreign visitors turn away from monuments of Wellington, Nelson, or Marlborough, they may be lied to reminiscences of their own celebrities — where Louis Napoleon lived and died in exile, like other rulers of inconstant France; where Mazzini took sanctuary to brood over the regeneration of his people; where Swedenborg died and was buried; where Alfieri fought a duel, and Voltaire had to repent a rash challenge; where Benjamin Franklin worked as a printer, and William Penn scandalised his family as a Quaker; where Peter the Great drank like a Tartar; where Philip of Spain could not make himself at home; where Erasmus visited Sir Thomas More; where Vandyck and Holbein left their best work, like many another foreign craftsman — but these are only extracts from a catalogue of *mémoires pour servir*, to be kindled into life by ready imagination.

To the most stolid eye can be shown the very rooms in which Queen Victoria played as a girl; the palace of the Georges; the park where Charles II. fed his ducks; the hall where Charles I. took his trial, and another whence he stepped on to his scaffold; the water-gate at which Elizabeth was ushered to her barge for Greenwich or Richmond; that other Traitors' Gate under which so many of England's best and bravest passed to their doom; the chamber where the most loved of our Henries assumed the crown from his dying father; the church before whose altar James I. of Scotland was married, to breed a longer line of kings than Shakespeare foresaw; the City playground where Richard II. parleyed

with his rebels, an arena once deified by the ashes of martyrs and by the blood of Wallace among more ignoble victims; a tower built by William the Conqueror; a chapel worn by the knees of Edward the Confessor; streets through which Canute and Alfred have passed; fragments of walls on which Roman soldiers kept watch, and stones that may have been stained by Druidical sacrifices. Looking down the long vista of our history, we can thus turn to London as a great gallery of illustration, where shadowy pictures of long ago are not wholly lost in the light of common day.

London has no pretentious show of newly-conscious pride, like the Sieges Allée of Berlin; no elaborate architectural display, like the Ring of Vienna; not much effect of official taste, like the boulevards of Paris. In this City, that grew grand with little shaping but from Nature and circumstance, one has the excitement of searching out its various interests, sometimes of surprise at coming upon its titles to renown where least expected. Its scattered shrines and relics, for the most part preserved by happy accident, are set in relief among its trite features of daily life. Too thoughtlessly have many of its monuments been slighted and swept away, till the spirit of our time awoke to save the past from the hasty needs of the present. Now it may be taken for granted that our new authorities are alive to the duty of guarding London's soul as well as her body; and whatever scandal may be said of other municipal bodies on both sides of the Atlantic, whatever reproach may be clamoured back between its own factions, London's local parliament has to do its best for a city that should set an example of public spirit, as of wealth and power, to the world that has known no greater capital.

Next, let us see what London was, from days long before books began to be written about it.

THE ROYAL EXCHANGE

THE CITY

ONCE UPON A TIME the lower reaches of the Thames trickled sluggishly through a wilderness of marsh and moorland, swamped by tides from below and floods from above. Such names as Moorgate and Moorfields are to be taken, not as suggesting the "bonnie heather" sung by northern bards, but in the southern sense of puddled flats, as *moor* is still used on the undrained outskirts of Hindhead. This dank waste was the resort of countless wild-fowl, also of wild beasts splashing through its thickets, among them huge mammoths and other extinct "dragons of the prime," whose bones have been turned up along with the rude flint weapons of their exterminators, when their old haunts came to be tamed by drain-pipes. Men of science can carry their vision back through dark centuries, from which poets strive to catch distant echoes:

> Rumour of battle, noises of the swamp
> The gride of glacial rock, the rush of wings,
> The roar of beasts that breathed a fiery air,
> Where fog envelops now electric light.

All history has to say is that she knows not when, if she can guess how, the first human inhabitants began to pick up a living here. Their earliest dwellings were perhaps raised above the water on piles and wooden platforms, as in the lake village unearthed near Glastonbury. But to the founding of a firmer camp nature herself had invited by throwing up along the riversides a bank of such gravel as still makes the choicest building-sites of London, where the name Chelsea, for instance, has been said to imply a miniature *chesil* beach, like that piled along the Dorset coast, while a more round-about derivation grinds its name down from *Chalkhythe*.

Sooner or later a town arose whose rude citizens seem to have banked in the river to make a port about the creek of a little tributary afterwards known as the Walbrook. When we are first introduced to our forefathers by Cæsar, they were not all so bluely naked as they have sometimes been painted. They had coins, chariots, tools, and weapons, implying long elaboration from the flint flakes of savage ancestors; and it is clear that already some of those Britons carried on commerce with the Continent. Ancient tracks led from various quarters to Londoner, rather, to an island two miles above, where the silt of another tributary formed a ford, by which traders' caravans could cross the river, making for one of the open seaports. It is remarkable that Cæsar seems not to have heard of London when from Kent he marched on to pass the Thames some way higher up, at Brentford or at Walton, or elsewhere, according to contesting theories. But old chroniclers will have it that then London was already a noted place of trade; and legend tells of a King Lud, who has left his name here, nay, of one Brute, descended from Aeneas and Venus, who, landing at the mouth of the Thames, built a new Troy older than Rome. Such tales we must leave in the same obscurity as hides the origin of the name. The commonly received derivation, scouted by the high authority of Dr. Bradley, is *Llyn-Dun,* such a "lake-stronghold" as rose where every high tide turned the river reaches into a wide lagoon, till, either by the Romans or before them, stream and tide were confined between embankments like those that still protect the Essex marshes.

Under the name of Londinium, this town comes authentically to view in Tacitus, who speaks of it as full of goods and traders. Besant very reasonably argues that in its early days London may have been not so much a town as a fair, held only in the summer months, when the inland roads were most serviceable: that might account for its being passed by in Caesar's time. At all events, after the firmer conquest for which Claudius took credit, the Romans adopted the place, sought to dignify it by the title of Augusta, and set about improving its structure and communications. They also occupied the Thorney Island, about which Westminster was destined to grow in dignity, while its commercial importance would be drained away to the developed port below.

The young settlements were almost uprooted by an insurrection under Boadicea, "bleeding from the Roman rods," who fell in a great battle, of which the supposed scene ranges from St. Pancras to Colchester. It may have been after that British mutiny that the conquerors built a strong fortress to safeguard London. A more difficult work of theirs would be the bridge across the Thames, to which, by way of Oxford Street, was diverted the old road afterwards known as Watling Street, a

branch sucking traffic aside from the ford at Westminster. London became the radius of half a dozen paved roads leading to the Roman colonies in different directions; and "London Stone," let into a wall opposite Cannon Street Station, is believed to be the mother of British milestones. The City wall, of which sturdy fragments remain, seems not to have been built till a late period of the occupation, and then in haste, as protection against some sudden peril, for its materials include fragments of sculptured monuments and other ruins of a stately city. The wall measured some two miles, the little circus behind Tower Hill marking one of its first bastions, from which it ran to Aldgate, there turning to Bishopsgate and on to Cripplegate, beyond which, before finally bending south to follow the course of the Fleet to the Thames, it made an angle about Aldersgate, explained by Besant as probably half enclosing an amphitheatre, outside the wall. Later on, in Norman times, the fortification became strengthened by a ditch, which, on one side, was ready-made in the Fleet valley.

The belated building of this wall hints how the power of Rome might be shaken by rebellion, or by the civil wars of rival aspirants to the purple, half a dozen of them distracting this distant corner of the empire. Finally the Romans withdrew, leaving Britain to be subdued by another race, more at home in ships than in cities. Perhaps London was then almost deserted; at all events a long century of darkness falls upon its history, lit only by such glimmering legends as that of Vortigern calling to his aid the foes who were to overwhelm him, and by tapers of controversy as to how far Roman or Teutonic influences are found at the base of London's municipal institutions. By-and-by the sea-traders, who in that age had need for hearts of oak, ventured back to the port of London, reviving its export of metals, hides, wool, corn, cattle, and slaves, a trade again checked by the Viking pirates, that under the name of Danes came to be known as chronic invaders and half-conquerors of England. The original port at the Walbrook mouth had been supplemented by another at Billingsgate, a name

The White Tower

said to be corrupted from that of Belinus, the Roman engineer of a road leading from the bridge through Billingshurst in Sussex; but a plain Saxon Billing, or family of Billings, is also put forward as godfather. The additional quay at Queenhithe, higher up, got a clearly Saxon name. Soon after the Saxons accepted Christianity, London became a Bishop's seat, and its importance was recognized by Alfred, who may be called its refounder after a long spell of Danish ravage.

Its walls having been repaired by this great King, when for a time he quelled the Danes, the City again grew so prosperous as soon to be expanding beyond its fortifications. Its trade brought flights of peaceful strangers, French, Flemish, German, to settle at a port that at times would be closed by battles about it on land and sea. The Saxons left no such solid traces of themselves as the Roman works; but how fully they adopted London is shown by the names of its streets and churches. St. Magnus and St. Olaf, however, point to a period when more than once it was held by the Danes, who, for further sign of their temporary domination, have left us the word *hustings,* originally meaning such popular assemblies as the Saxon folk-mote. Canute, a fragment of whose supposed house at Southampton claims to be the oldest structure in England, is also said to have founded the palace at Westminster, which was certainly the seat of Edward the Confessor. Then came the Norman Conqueror, to whom the now much mixed population of London would not open its gates till he had granted them the first of its charters, foundation of its power to foster our national liberty — a document still extant in the Guildhall, five lines on half a dozen inches of parchment, making a curt contrast with the verbosity of later laws:

"William, King, greets William, Bishop, and Gosfrith, Portreeve, and all the burghers within London, French and English, friendly; and I make you to wit my will that ye be all law-worthy that were so in King Edward's day. And I will that every child be his father's heir after his father's day. And I

will not suffer that any man offer you wrong. God keep you."

William appears to have kept word with the citizens, whose good-will, however, he did not trust without fortifying his power in two strongholds overlooking their walls-the Montfichet Tower, at the western end of the City wharves; and at the eastern corner the White Tower, on a site where tradition puts a citadel of Alfred and one of the Romans. This eastern keep, designed for such a *Zwinger* as raised angry suspicion among William Tell's compatriots, grew in following reigns into a palace fortress, where Norman Kings were sometimes fain to hold themselves close. But the most notable service of the Tower came to be as a State prison in later days, when sovereigns could dwell at more ease in gardened mansions like Hampton Court and Greenwich.

How many of England's princes and peers have been brought through the Traitors' Gate, the edge of the axe turned towards them, never to leave this Bastille, unless for the scaffold on Tower Hill, now worn down to the level commonplace of our own times! Tower Hill has been turned into a garden; but no grass grows on a spot blighted by the blood of royal or noble victims like Anne Boleyn, Katherine Howard, and Lady Jane Grey, who met their fate within the walls. Their execution place was beside the chapel of St. Peter ad Vincula, where so many headless bodies are buried without memorial, beyond a modern record of their names ; the monuments here are those of their gaolers. The head of the Duke of Suffolk, Lady Jane Grey's father, a waif from those bloody times, used to be preserved at Trinity Church in the Minories; and I understand that the grim relic may still be seen at St. Botolph's, Aldgate, with which that other parish was lately amalgamated.

The Tower, guarding its relics and survivals of quaint ceremony, has now come down to be a Guards' barrack, and a show for visitors, who do not fail on days when admission is free. At once they get a hint of Tudor times in its ornamental warders, the Yeomen of the Guard, whose quaint costume, indeed, *formosa superne,* falls off below the waist into mere trousering. The entrance is by the Lions' Gate, a name reminding us how, before its living crests of the monarchy were set up in Regent's Park, the Tower served the office of a "Zoo," to which Charles Lamb's schoolfellows had once prescriptive right of free entrance. But the crowd finds still many attractive sights, in the historic buildings more or less restored, in the dazzling display of Crown jewels, in the great collection of old armour, in rusty hints of torture and touching inscriptions left on their dungeon walls by prisoners waiting for death. Among trophies and vouchers of a storied past, the latest is that plain gun-carriage on which Queen Victoria's body passed across London, after a long reign throughout which no blood was shed on English soil for political offences.

The last State execution here was Lord Lovat's, that lifelong trickster, whose doublings in the '45 did not save his grey head from a fate little lamented; when —

Pitied by gentle minds, Kilmarnock died,

The brave, Balmerino, were on thy side.

But of Lovat, "true to no King, to no religion true," Horace Walpole reports that at least he "died extremely well, without passion, affectation, buffoonery, or timidity"; and, indeed, at his age one might welcome such an effectual cure for the gout that crippled him when he played the fugitive, end of his many parts.

The Tower's last prisoner of anything like dignity was Sir Francis Burdett, father of Lady Burdett-Coutts, the Radical reformer who spent a fortune in winning a seat in Parliament, which he held through the life of a generation, till his zeal had grown so much cooler that he could be twitted with a recant of patriotism. But in 1809, when he made the figure-head of Hampden clubs and the mouth-piece for repressed Radicalism, his championship of free speech was so bold as to be condemned by an unreformed Parliament as breach of privilege. For several days he stood a siege in his house in Piccadilly, protected by a mob of sympathizers, by allies like Lord Cochrane, and by one of the Sheriffs of London; but in the end he was haled out upon the Speaker's warrant, and hurried off to the Tower under an escort of cavalry. The riots over this imprisonment cost not only much breaking of glass, but some bloodshed. As soon as Parliament was prorogued the popular hero had to be released, and the same disorders were threatened in a demonstration of welcome, which Sir Francis had the good sense to avoid by slipping off across the river to his villa at Wimbledon.

This brings us to an age when Parliament might try its hand at a tyranny which had slipped out of the grasp of Kings. But it was the King's Government that let the terrors of the Tower fizzle out in farce, by committing to it some obscure and crack-brained agitators of Burdett's following. The last prisoners confined here were the melodramatic gang headed by a dissolute ex-officer named Thistlewood, whose Cato Street conspiracy in 1821 aimed at seizing London with a score or two of ill-armed and penniless desperadoes, after murdering the Ministers assembled at a dinner-party. The plot was blown upon by informers; then these hot-headed rapscallions, posing as patriots, found themselves treated to dungeons in the Tower, but were more fitly transferred to Newgate for sentence and execution.

The battlements of the Tower might tempt us to a wide outlook over England's history, but let us come back to the story of a City whose famed municipality grew up beside the walls once threatening to overshadow it. There may be some doubt as to whether a model was taken from continental communes, or how far the City's constitution arose in our own unsymmetrical fashion upon use and opportunity. It appears that during Richard's robustious wanderings, the oppressions of his Chancellor set the citizens on dealing with John or a measure of self-government; but London had already a magistracy of its own, when, towards the end of the twelfth century, Fitz Aylwin was

Bow Church, Cheapside

appointed the first Mayor, holding his office for twenty-five years. Masterful Kings proved naturally jealous of this enhancement on the older office of Portreeve. Once at least the mayoralty was arbitrarily reduced to the humbler rank of *custos*, or warden; and not without question was the right of free election established, sometimes to be suspended by royal usurpation, down to the time of Charles II.

There were factions within the City itself, disputes between masters and men, struggles between an aristocracy of rich citizens and a turbulent democracy. But organization of municipal government went on apace: the old quasi-religious guilds took shape as the City companies; the barons of manors changed into aldermen of wards, more or less openly elected; the Lord Mayor became head of a Court of Common Council; and the Corporation grew to such strength as to stand up against the Crown, which its voice would go far to confer. London lent a hand to wring Magna Charta from John; then, again, it sent a contingent of 12,000 men to the Barons' War, after which its Mayor, bold beyond his time, pardoned the humbled sovereign in what seemed presumptuous words: "So long as unto us you will be a good lord and King, we will be faithful unto you."

Richard III. was not the first King to seek a title in the acclamations of London citizens, whose support established the House of Lancaster, till its weakness turned over their influence to the stronger line of York; and all along the wealth of this City weighed heavily against the splendour of the throne. Medieval London must have made a formidable power by its population alone, to be guessed at from the fact that it contained more than six score parish churches, many of them at first chapels of manor-houses enclosed within the walls. Some of the parishes, indeed, were no more spacious than a mansion and its precincts; people packed close in days when retainers and underlings had to be content with as narrow room as sailors on board ship. And this mass of men had not grown unwarlike in an age when every citizen must be ready to defend his life and goods. The lords of the City bore arms

in a double sense; Mayor and Aldermen kept watch and ward; the craftsmen were trained to use weapons as well as tools; a proclamation of Edward III. denounces such unprofitable games as football, bowls, and quoits, whereas young men ought rather to be making records in archery. Besant, aware of the value of story-tellers as witnesses to manners and customs, shrewdly points out that the Old London 'prentice heroes were not such as came to be glorified by Dr. Smiles; no successful merchants like Whittington, but youths of their hands going forth to win fame by bold adventures. He cites an Elizabethan book — *The Nine Worthies of London,* all of them legendary fire-eaters, who slew wild boars, fought foreign champions hand to hand, or came to be knighted on a stricken field for exploits that might well lead to marrying their masters' daughters. One legend gives this good fortune, in reward of an adventure at home, to Jack Osborne, apprentice of a pin-maker on London Bridge, whose daughter falling into the river, the gallant youth plunged to her rescue; then, in due time, came about a wedding which the Duke of Leeds looks back on as the origin of his house.

Yet the City always had a clear eye to business; and it was in times of peace that it prospered as a great hive of industries and trades, each localized in its own quarter, as is still recalled by such names as Bread Street and Ironmonger Lane, Cornhill, and Fish Street Hill, the Poultry and the Vintry. Let us look at Besant's lively picture of it in those old days.

"Wherever one walked there arose the busy hum and mingled sounds of work: the melodious anvil rang out from a court; the cry of the 'prentices sounded in Chepe; the song of those who retailed wares was heard about the street; the women who sold fish cried aloud; the man who carried water also cried his wares; and so did the baker who took round the loaves. In the broad streets, Chepe and Cornhill and Bishopsgate Street, the knights and men-at-arms rode slowly along; perhaps a great noble entered the City with five hundred followers all wearing his livery; broad-wheeled waggons heavily rumbled; the Queen was carried along in her cumbrous but richly decorated carriage or her horse litter; the Mayor rode down the street accompanied by the Sheriffs and the Aldermen on the way to a City Function; a trumpeter, a drummer, and a piper preceded a little procession, in which the principal figure was a man tied on a hurdle with a whetstone round his neck to show that he was a liar and a cheat; thus was the attention of the people called to the culprit, and they were invited to assist at his pillory, and were admonished of the punishment meted out to offenders. And all the time from every shop and stall and sold the voice of the 'prentice was uplifted, crying, "Buy! buy! buy! What d'ye lack? what d'ye lack?" Above all, and all day long, was heard the ringing of the bells in the hundred and fifty churches and chapels of the City. They sounded all together for early mass, and all together for Angelus; at other times for the various services in the Religious Houses; even at midnight they sounded, when the monks were summoned from their warm beds to Matins. It was a noisy, bustling City, full of life and animation; the people were always ready to fight, always dreading fire, famine, and plague, yet always hopeful; and the City was always young as befits a City continually at work."

As often as it was free to stick to prosperous work, London went on growing, extending itself beyond its walls and gates, at first over the outer area of its "liberties," marked by "bars" on the main roads, then straggling out to embrace surrounding hamlets, which by that time were mainly in the hands of the Church, while all Middlesex had been in a sense granted to the City whose officers still replace royal sheriffs in this Metropolitan county. Its first great outswelling seems to have been along the road to Westminster, and on the north-west side round Smithfield and Clerkenwell. The population at various unstatistical periods can only be guessed, like that of certain Chinese cities down to our own time, claiming to surpass it in numbers which have shrunk under critical examination. Ghent and

Bruges were larger even after Edward III. ordered English wool to be woven at home, no longer in Flanders. In the middle of the fourteenth century, when the Black Death swept over Europe, destroying half the people of some countries, more than 50,000 corpses are said to have been huddled into the field on which the Charterhouse now stands, a burial-ground opened when the many churchyards were already gorged with infection. This figure, even allowing for panic-stricken arithmetic, suggests at least 100,000 to give such a tale of dead. The City watch paraded before Henry VIII. some 15,000 strong; and in the Armada crisis London furnished 10,000 men for service. But surely Fitz Stephen drew a laudatory long bow in boasting that for King Stephen it could turn out 20,000 horse and 60,000 foot! Let us hope that the same monkish chronicler spoke by the book in declaring the London citizens already distinguished above other townsfolk by the refinement of their manners dress, meals, and conversation.

Under Elizabeth, an Italian writer classes London among Naples, Lisbon, Prague, and Ghent, with an estimated population of 160,000. In the same reign Sir Thomas Gresham, after experience of raising foreign loans for several of our sovereigns, took a hint from Antwerp to build the Royal Exchange, which founded London's credit as the commercial centre of Europe; and now it was that its Chartered Companies began to open channels of adventurous trade in other continents. As money merchants, the Jews had been supplanted by Lombards, their name preserved by one of the headquarters of banking ; then this business passed to the Goldsmiths, whose street, at the end of the sixteenth century, was admired by a German traveller as the finest in the City; but from Goldsmiths' Row they transferred themselves, under the Stuarts, to Cheapside and Lombard Street. In recurrent fits of jealousy against alien traders, a census of them was sometimes taken, that under Elizabeth more than once numbered several thousand foreigners, chiefly Dutch and French refugees.

In the next century the population seems to

have rapidly increased. At Charles I's. accession it is taken to have been over 300,000; then, at the end of Charles II.'s reign, two English statisticians differed in their estimates as between 696,000 and 530,000. By this time, at all events, London began to count over Paris as the largest city in Europe. The first official census (1801) showed a population of over 860,000 — no such great advance on the rough estimates of a century back, for now were included suburbs that then had been independent villages.

This growth had all along had its ups and downs: crushing calamities came on the heels of triumphal pageants, and the prosperity of the City waxed and waned with the national fortunes. Several disastrous fires are recorded; and in a town largely of crowded wooden or half-timbered buildings they must have been frequent, as were visitations of pestilence. Again and again, the epidemics bred by filth and ignorance took tribute of victims, often by thousands; almost year by year the City might be appalled under outbreaks either of the plague or of the more deadly sweating sickness that once carried off two Lord Mayors and six Aldermen in a few days. The memory of former visitations is eclipsed for us by the Great Plague of 1665, when in full light of history, London for the last time lost nearly 70,000 lives; but twice already in the century there had been outbreaks almost as deadly in proportion to the population.

Through that sweltering summer the bills of mortality grew from hundreds to thousands weekly, till the chills of autumn checked the seeds of death, and by the mournful Christmas time scared citizens could come home to whole rows of empty houses and closed shops. Imagination still sees on the ancient front of Staple Inn the red cross marking a stricken abode, from which a familiar picture shows a naked figure being lowered in a blanket, no rag allowed to spread contagion from within. It is a well-known tale how the plague was carried from London in a box of clothes to the Derbyshire village of Eyam, famed by its share in that awful infliction. In the City it spread steadily from west to east,

dying down in one quarter as its ravages came to a height farther on. The living were forbidden to stir out at night, lest they should meet the dismal torches that made a warning of the death cart's round. Yet so many had to be buried, that by daytime, too, the work went on; and it was hard to prevent thoughtless people, in whose ears the death-bell had grown habitual, from crowding to the gruesome spectacle of funerals. Decent burial was the rule, but some corpses long lay exposed, "this disease making us more cruel to one another than we are to dogs," as moralizes Mr. Pepys, who from his refuge down the river ventured back to find grass growing in the court of Whitehall, and fires blazing in the streets by broad daylight.

Hard upon such a curse followed the Great Fire of 1666, a blessing in disguise, since it cleared off the too cramped dwellings and purified the soil poisoned by centuries of intramural burials. On a September Sunday morning the fire broke out at a baker's in Pudding Lane, a row of old wooden houses, close to warehouses full of combustible materials. Fanned by a strong east wind, it soon spread; and when people should have been going to church, they found the streets full of terror and confusion. Organization and authority were wanting to fight a peril always to be feared. The waterworks of the time proved inefficient, their supply rnnning short after a spell of dry weather; and hands that should have helped were too busy in panic-stricken efforts to save their own property or in plundering amid the hot hurly-burly. The scene has been described by several eyewitnesses, by John Evelyn for one:

"Here we saw the Thames covered with floating goods, all the barges and boats laden with what some had time and courage to save, as on the other the carts carrying out to the fields, which for many miles were strewed with movables of all sorts, and tents erecting to shelter both people and what goods they could get away. Oh, the miserable and calamitous spectacle! Such as happily the world had not seen the like since the foundation of it, nor be outdone till the universal conflagration of it. All the sky was of a fiery aspect, like the top of a burning oven, and the light seen above 40 miles round for many nights. God grant mine eyes may never behold the like, who now saw above 10,000 houses all in one flame: the noise and cracking and thunder of the impetuous flames, the shrieking of women and children, the hurry of people, the fall of Towers, Houses, and Churches, was like a hideous storm, and the air all about so hot and inflamed that at last one was not able to approach it, so that they were forced to stand still and let the flames burn on, which they did for near two miles in length and one in breadth. The clouds also of smoke were dismal and reached upon computation near 56 miles in length. Thus I left it this afternoon burning, a resemblance of Sodom, or the last day. It forcibly called to my mind that passage *non erim hic habemus stabilem civitatem:* the ruins resembling the picture of Troy. London was, but is no more."

For three days the conflagration raged almost unchecked, till dockyard men, under the Duke of York, were set to work pulling down and blowing up houses, as might have been sooner done had the civic rule been effective to meet such a bewildering emergency. It was brought to a stand at St. Dunstan's, Fleet Street; and though it broke out again next day in the Temple, this fresh blaze was luckily got under. As it began in Pudding Lane, its furthest point northwards, at the Pie Corner of Smithfield, did not fail to yield some half jocose hint of a judgment on what might be taken for the citizens' besetting sin. It ravaged almost all the City up to the wall; but the north-eastern corner about Bishopsgate was spared, leaving Gresham College to be turned into temporary municipal headquarters, along with St. Helen's Church, and its tiny neighbour, St. Ethelburga's, one of the oldest in London, passed by many who hardly notice its entrance squeezed in among shops. Several fine old buildings were then saved, to vanish in our own time, like Sir Paul Pindar's house in Bishopsgate, a victim of the Great Eastern Railway, but its fine timbered front is

treasured in the South Kensington Museum. The Hall of Crosby Place came to be demolished only the other day, after being used as a Presbyterian church and a restaurant; and it is now to be reerected at Chelsea as a students' settlement. This was at one time, as Shakespeare shows, the house of Richard III. built (1466) by the sumptuous Alderman Sir John Crosby, whose tomb, with that of Sir Thomas Gresham and others of note, is in St. Helen's Church, which, secluded in its quiet old nook, makes one of the City sights.

Paternoster Row had vainly sought to save its stocks by storing them in the crypt of St. Paul's. The Tower proved a safer depository, for not only was it to windward of the fire, but its gunners did not stick at battering down blazing houses about it. Half the dwellings that cumbered London Bridge were burned before the fire could be checked on its way to Southwark. Here and there it appears to have swept over some houses or groups of houses without licking them up; and gutted walls must have in part escaped total destruction, for bits of old structure have been found incorporated in rebuilt churches. More than 13,000 houses were destroyed, with nearly 90 churches, in some 400 streets, from which at least 200,000 people were hurried out homeless, for the most part to bivouac in the open fields, turned into camps as far as Hampstead Heath, whence awestruck eyes looked down upon a glare that realized their conceptions of the Judgment Day. The damage was reckoned at over ten million pounds; but little loss of life came to be reported, while, indeed, many persons may have disappeared without being accounted for in the widespread confusion.

The ashes of the fire are said to have been carried as far as Windsor, and at Oxford the sky was seen dimmed by that awful eclipse, which spread consternation all over the country. On recovering from their stupor, the people soon began casting about on whom to lay the blame of a calamity that any day might have been brought about by some drunken man in the rotten old houses beside the Thames. Foreign incendiaries were at first

GROCERS HALL

suspected, and Frenchmen and Dutchmen had a bad time of it in London. Next, some of Cromwell's old soldiers were executed for an imaginary conspiracy. Then, in his angry mood, Protestant John Bull took Papistry as scapegoat. A Frenchman named Hubert, who seems to have been insane, was hanged on his own confession, full of contradictions as it was, that he had set the flames a-going with a fire-ball put into his hands by an accomplice. The Monument erected at the starting-point of the fire was furnished with an inscription recording a prelude to the Popish Plot; but this "tall bully" no longer "lifts its head and lies," its groundless libel having been wiped off in 1830. It has been the Monument's fate not to be taken very seriously once that scare of Catholic conspiracy had died out. In the beginning of the eighteenth century, Ned Ward jokes about it as a gymnasium for young tavern waiters to practise activity by running up and down its steps. While it now seems a little thrust aside, the Monument then stood opposite the end

of London Bridge, the footway to which ran through a passage by St. Magnus' Church.

The rebuilding of the City was pushed on in haste. It is a pity that advantage of the clearance was not taken to adopt plans offered by Wren and Evelyn for a new London more regularly and openly built. But the citizens were too much set on keeping to their own sites, in some cases being able to use the old foundations, so that the new streets sprang up on much the same lines, though on a larger scale and with more solid architecture. Wren's design was a pattern of straight streets opening into piazzas, in the largest of which a ring of public buildings was to enclose the Royal Exchange. Now disappeared even the opening of Cheapside, where jousts and games had been held before the ground became so valuable as building sites. The name tells how West Cheap was a marketplace, in which stood an ornate cross, near the famous church of St. Mary-le-Bow, so called from the arches of the Norman crypt upon which it was rebuilt, that also gave a name to the ecclesiastical Court of Arches once held here; and this still asserts a primacy among London churches by being the scene of the confirmation of Bishops in the province of Canterbury. To be born within the sound of Bow Bells is a proverb for a Cockney, those very bells heard by Dick Whittington calling him back from Highgate Hill to be Lord Mayor of London. But one brood of born Cockneys lost their birthright, since the ringing of Bow Bells had a few years ago to be suspended while certain repairs were carried out, or, as exaggerating newspapers put it, for fear of wrecking Wren's beautiful steeple, that bears aloft the dragon emblem of the City.

The City, rebuilt in a few years, had suffered other than material loss. The few nobles who still kept mansions there would take the opportunity of removing; as did citizens, who, after the Plague and Fire, thought of building houses in opener suburbs. Shopkeepers of Cheapside and Ludgate Hill, without waiting for new premises, set up in Covent Garden and the Strand, where the West-end grew upon the misfortune of the East. That scorching east wind had blown good to other proprietors, notably to those of the New River Company, which, opened early in the century, began by drying up the means of its promoter, Sir Hugh Middleton; but now so many wells had been choked by the débris of the fire that its waters became a Pactolus for future generations of shareholders. But, indeed, so far back as Henry III., London had filled its conduits by pipes laid from the Tyburn.

Now may be marked the gradual change that made the City no more than part of a Greater London. About the same time also, its social position was going down. Hitherto its apprentices had come from the upper class as often as not, trade being no discredit to good blood, even in the far back days when to have made three perilous voyages across the sea gave a trafficking adventurer the rank of thane. Besant, examining a list of some six score mayors and magistrates in the century before the Fire, finds that half of them are recorded as sons of country gentlemen, and that in the Stuart reigns

apprenticeship fees had rapidly risen to a figure of tens or even hundreds of pounds. In the Jacobean play "Eastward Ho!" the two young "Flatcaps" who may have given Hogarth a hint for his industrious and idle apprentices, can both claim gentle birth. Pepys' father was a tailor, while he had a lord for cousin, a connection bulking in his diary above memories of the shop. At that period Lord North sent one son to the Temple, another to the City as apprentice to a Turkey merchant. Lords in the olden days were not ashamed to buy and sell; and even Kings would do a turn of trade in their high-handed style, debasing the coinage being an "operation" always open to them. The Flatcaps of Fleet Street might well be gently born, though called on to perform menial offices in their master's household, at a day when pages and scholars, too, passed through a stern school of humility. But about the time of the Fire began a slump in the demand for a business career among scions of aristocracy. Under Queen Anne the *Spectator* saw a gulf opened between Court and City: "The inhabitants of St. James's, notwithstanding they live under the same laws and speak the same language, are a distinct people from those of Cheapside, who are likewise removed from those of the Temple on one side, and those of Smithfield on the other, by several climates and degrees in their way of thinking and conversing together." Yet, as the *Tatler* lets out, there would be always aspiring cits rebellious against "the order and distinction which of right ought to be between St. James and Milk Street, the Camp and Cheapside."

The eighteenth century shows the citizens an isolated class, content to live by themselves in solid comfort, to be looked down on by fine gentry at the other end of the town, to be caricatured by out-at-elbows authors, and to bring up their sons with no ambition but that of becoming "warm" men by sticking to the counter. This depreciation lasted down to the days of Thackeray, since when we have seen City stocks much risen in the Vanity Fair market. But always the prosperous Newcomes had a good chance of finding noble husbands for their daughter; and ex-Mayors, worth a "plum," would realize it to buy land in the country, where three generations or less made as good a gentleman as any in the land.

Meanwhile the pressure of room and the growth of the suburbs more and more set citizens on living away from their business, not only when they were able to retire for good to

Suburban villas, highway-side retreats,
That dread the encroachment of our growing streets.

Some properous traders could now afford to have two homes, hibernating in town till May stirred them to dream of "meadows trim with daisies pied" and "hedgerow elms on hillocks green," such as still cluster close to London outskirts. Defoe tells us how the chalk heights of Sutton had in his day already had in his day already become a favourite site for such retreats, and how Middlesex was dotted with not less than three thousand houses, for the most part genteel enough to have stabling for their own coaches. The fields covered by our crowded Tower Hamlets were then to London much what Hampton or Chislehurst is to our generation. The roomy old Georgian mansions still fringing Epping Forest had not always to abate their rents because cut off from the City by a wilderness of mean streets.

So in time came about the further revolution by which the City ceased to be a place of residence, except for a garrison of watchmen or caretakers, its life every morning flooded by a tide pouring in from outside to ebb strongly back at evening in crowds eager to get home, by a journey that may take them fifty miles and more, or to suburban outskirts reached by various wheels of fortune, or only to some shabby purlieu still within reach of a walk. Few of us, indeed, can afford to live in an area where sites may fetch fifty pounds per square foot, and where every tall block of buildings fetches rent enough to hire a dozen Venetian palaces or castles in Tyrol. The City becomes a mere workshop to those who know it only in business hours, their

affections and amusements and private interests being planted out from Hornsey to Norwood, from Berkhamsted to Brighton, or yet further afield. While Greater London has been growing by miles and millions, the inhabitants of what was once walled London have decreased by a hundred thousand souls in a century or so, now to be counted at little more than a score of thousands, swollen nearly twenty-fold during business hours.

The City churches, as rebuilt by Wren, though then reduced in number, soon became too many for their shrinking congregations, who also found other folds in chapels or wandered shepherdless in a glacial age of faith. Half a century ago the work of abandoned pastors had been mainly reduced to what is profanely "called eating their heads off." There used to be a joke about a City incumbent's stereotyped speech at an annual dinner, which gave him, as he put it, a welcome occasion of once a year meeting a considerable number of his parishioners. Some of these officiants themselves live in distant suburbs, travelling by train to what duties they can contrive for their stipends. Some City parishes have been amalgamated, and the sites of certain churches sold to build others where they are more wanted. But with the revival of Church energy our generation has seen various efforts at turning the empty churches to use. Gifted preachers succeed in attracting from other parts of town congregations fit, if few, to break the Sabbath quiet of their idle parishes. Several of the City churches are now kept open on weekdays, some of them inviting sightseers by their old memorials or fine architectural features, like the domed interior of St. Stephen's, Walbrook, a miniature of St. Paul's, or the graceful spire of St. Dunstan's-in-the-East; and at some, short daily services, addresses or organ recitals are given at hours convenient for busy men. Certain curious functions are provided for by bequest, as the "Lion" sermon at St. Katherine Cree, instituted by an early African adventurer in commemoration of his escape from a lion, scared off when he knelt down to pray in face of a danger against which modern travellers keep their powder dry. The "Flower service" at this church is also a notable function. A truly Christian use of certain places of worship is opening them in the morning as refuge for workers who, having come to the City by cheap early trains, might else have to hang about the streets for an hour or two, in wet or cold, before being due at their places of business. In more than one church a small library is kept for the use of involuntary idlers. But on Sundays, for the most part, many bells ring here in vain, calling citizens to prayer. "These citizens hear no more the pious call. Along the leafy lanes of Weybridge, on the breezy *chaussée* of Hampstead Heath, over the turf of Wimbledon, across the furzy common of barnes, everywhere — all round London — they are moving churchwards, obedient to the harsh tinkle of the little bell in the perky new suburban church: þut the loud tongue of the sonorous City bell strikes not upon their ears."

After the churches, we must notice the halls of the City Companies, several of them worth visiting for their show of portraits and plate, not to mention the good cheer set forth in them, upon-occasion, for fortunate guests. Like the churches, these buildings and their owners no longer play such a part as once in City life, though certain companies still exercise important functions, as the control of Billingsgate Market by the Fishmongers, and the hall-marking of plate by the Goldsmiths. Of the old trade societies in London, once flourishing by scores, some are now extinct, some represent crafts no longer carried on, and all of them contain many members who might be puzzled to teach the mysteries which they are supposed to profess. Princes and nobles are honoured by nominal membership. An Archbishop is a Skinner: a Field-Marshall a Goldsmith: the late King of Belgium was a Turner; the new King of Norway is a Draper. Our late sovereign made an honarary member of half a dozen companies, and had his sons in partnership. Peers, parsons, doctors, artists, soldiers, country gentlemen, living in all parts of the kingdom, have become entitled to call themselves Haberdashers, Grocers, Leather-sellers, or what not, keeping up a perhaps

hereditary connection with such trades, sometimes as a matter of sentiment as well as of interest, while many real City men do not concern themselves about the "freedom" without which at one time they would have been barred from its business.

Freedom of the City through membership of one of the Companies is gained in various ways: by patrimonial inheritance; by "servitude," now for the most part nominal; or by purchase, in which the payment of a lump sum is taken for title enough. Besides chances of advantage from the common property, these initiates have in their hands the separate government of the City that is such an eyesore to municipal reformers, for since 1475 the Lord Mayor and Sheriffs have been elected by the liverymen of the City, and the Mayor must be a member of one of the twelve great Companies, distinguished among three times as many in all.

The wealth of the great Companies is proverbial. Exact accounts in each case are not always open to outsiders, but the richest are understood to be the Goldsmiths, the Fishmongers, the Mercers and the Drapers — this last through the sale of Drapers' Garden, an oasis that bloomed in the City till it grew to be worth a king's ransom for building sites. Their property in some parts of the country has been enhanced by time, as, for instance, a bequest of £9,000 to the Haberdashers' Company for the foundation of a school and almshouses at Monmouth in 1641, part of which was invested in a farm at New Cross and now brings in an income of something like £15,000 a year. In the City itself, Threadneedle Street (properly *Threeneedle*) must be a gold-mine to its landlords, the Merchant Taylors. Part of such wealth is ear-marked for trust purposes; part has been taken into the hands of the Charity Commissioners; but the rest is spent at the discretion of the members, acting through a Court of Master, Wardens, and Assistants, who come to power in rotation by attending to the business of their Companies. An old reproach was their superabundance being spent on too much eating and drinking, and on the entertainment of guests brought in from highways and byways. In our time, at all events, the Companies have shown a liberal public spirit, spending nobly on educational and other institutions, even without any direct claim on them, as in the case of the Drapers' benefaction to Oxford. They still keep up their traditional name for sumptuous hospitality; but the scenes of gorging and gormandizing satirized by Thackeray are as much out of date as the armour in the Tower, and City banquets now invite to a more refined conviviality, cheered by good music, if sometimes rather oppressed by undigested oratory.

An invitation to such a feast gave me a curious experience a generation ago. I was writing an account of scientific progress, in which it was desirable to mention a certain inventor, whose name had fallen a little into the background, since his most notable addition to our resources went to be "made in Germany," the chimneys of its original factory at this day standing idle. I could not find out whether he were still alive; I looked into books of reference in vain: I consulted scientific friends who had no certain knowledge; still uninformed, I had to give up the search, when the hour drew nigh for keeping my engagement in the City. There, of all persons in the world, I met the very man, all alive as Master of the hospitable Company. But this perfunctory president at our feast had so far strayed from the tradition of the elders as to be a vegetarian and teetotaller, a regime that kept him going to a good age, for he died only a year or two ago. Not long before his death scientific brethren testified their esteem for him at the banquet, where every possible display was made of mauve, a colour introduced by his experiments; but I fear that honoured guest have also had to look on red and white wine. As a master of revels when I sat his guest, he proved a little of a wet blanket, his principles being so strict that he would not allow the loving-cup to be handed round.

Everybody in London knows the Mansion House, that eighteenth-century capitol of the City; if not everybody has entered it as a fortunate guest or an unfortunate culprit. Almost everybody in Europe has heard of the Lord Mayor, this palace's tenant, about whom it was said of old:

> No lord of Paris, Venice, or Florence,
> In dignity or honour goeth to him nigh.

Foreigners are supposed to take an exaggerated view of the Lord Mayor's place in the State, but, indeed, he plays a part greater than is borne in mind by all Englishmen, as appears by his presence at such national functions as the proclamation of a new sovereign, for which he has once and again been mouthpiece. More than once he has withstood a monarch to the face, as when Beckford made George III. flush to be addressed with uncourtly frankness. Within the City no man is greater than he, where the King's troops may not pass through but by his leave; while only certain regiments march here with fixed bayonets and colours flying in sign of old connection with London. To his favoured ear is daily trusted the watchword of the King's own Tower. Yet this potentate is merely the "first best" citizen of character, means, and standing, who has taken the trouble to qualify himself to hold such an office in turn; and all the more plainly does it show the average common-sense and public spirit of the citizens that their figure-head, drawn by his team of permanent officials, seldom does discredit to what is hardly a choice.

The richest, and perhaps the ablest, men in the City may not care nowadays to put themselves in the way of such a burden; some are even inclined to despise the rather ludicrous pomp exhibited in the circus procession of the Lord Mayor's Show, to the annual delight of the vulgar and of children. At the last Mayoral inauguration, it may be mentioned, the time-honoured display was turned into a quasi-military demonstration, which showed the City keeping up with the times. Till little more than half a century ago the Lord Mayor progressed by water in the City barge, as became the Admiral of the Thames. There was a time when prudent citizens often paid a heavy fine to escape from honourable duties that were like to be perilous as well as

THE TOWER

burdensome. Nowadays the City offices are sought by a class of men put into training for them by playing minor parts in civic life, and working their way up to that crowning year of greatness. The election of Lord Mayor is usually a matter of cut-and-dry routine; yet not always, for in our time there has been at least one instance of a popular Alderman rejected by the sober civic fathers as unworthy to fill the chair, by reason of a weakness that might have passed for a qualification in more roistering days. The rule is for the two senior Aldermen who have not "passed the chair" to be presented by the Liverymen to the Court of Aldermen, by whom the first will be chosen as a matter of course.

The Lord Mayor is called on for prudence, dignity, industry. Some eloquence is desirable; a good digestion must be prayed for; but what seems most absolutely necessary is the special product of City life, since the official salary of £10,000

scrimply meets the expenses of his year of office. He has to entertain statesmen, princes, sometimes sovereigns: no foreign potentate's reception in England is hall-marked without a City feast. He has to act as Grand Almoner of the nation, collecting and distributing vast funds to alleviate disasters, both at home and abroad. His petty duties as a police magistrate seem of small account among those manifold functions. A proud man must he be who first puts on that robe, and a weary man when he puts it off, unyoked from the round of duties, banquets, and ceremonials, as souvenir of which he should carry away a baronetcy on the top of the knighthood he is like to have won as Sheriff; but never again, in town or country, will lie sit in such a blaze of lordliness as for a year threw his own name into shade.

The Guildhall, standing back from main thoroughfares, is less well known to strangers than the Mansion House, deserving, as it does, to be better known. This council-house of the City has had to be rebuilt more than once; but part of its walls stood through the Fire; and the other day was disclosed the stonework of two of its fifteenth-century windows, long blocked up and forgotten till suspected by the City surveyor's keen eye. It is used not only for City business and public gatherings, but in part as an extensive library and a museum preserving a collection of Roman and other remains of ancient London. Here also is the art gallery of the Corporation, that cannot, indeed, vie with those of Liverpool and Manchester, but contains some pictures of interest as showing what London was in former days, and also occasional loan exhibitions. Not the least of the sights is the great hall, with its fine timber roof and Gothic windows, and at one end the huge effigies of Gog and Magog, whose monstrous absurdity is half-masked in their legendary renown. These works of art are only two centuries old, but they represent older figures once carried in the Lord Mayor's procession as somehow symbolizing the greatness of the City when other cities, indeed, were proud to possess similar Palladia. Who the mysterious Gog and Magog were I cannot say, which our irreverent age has made bold to rename Gammon and Mammon, as fit patron saints for much that goes on in the City.

Another sight for strangers is the Royal Exchange, whose open court, with its central statue of Queen Victoria, under whom it was rebuilt, is to be surrounded by fresco panels representing famous scenes in the history of the City. More than half of them are already in place, as Mr. Stanhope Forbes's picture of the Great Fire, Mr. Ernest Croft's "Opening of the Exchange by Elizabeth," and Mr. Seymour Lucas's" Granting of London's Charter by William the Conqueror," with more than one but indirectly connected with London, like Leighton's "Phœnicians trading on the Coast of Cornwall," and Mr. Gow's "Nelson leaving Portsmouth" for victory or Westminster Abbey. There is still some formal business done in the Exchange, that might seem at most times a mere lounge for idlers, but at certain days and hours — notably about three in the afternoon — it may be found a scene of dealings, many of which are now specialized in the Coal Exchange, the Corn Exchange, and other separate buildings, while in the *coulisses* of the Royal Exchange are housed the transactions of Lloyd's, that rose from a coffee-house to be a commercial institution. More astir with bargaining is the adjacent "House" of speculation, whose activity even overflows into the street. But the Stock Exchange, with its mysteries of the "Kaffir Circus" and the "Jungle," and its cryptic worship of "Berthas," "Doras," and such-like, stands by no means open to the public, for one of the schoolboy tricks of its roistering members is a rough handling of any uninitiated visitor who presumptuously or unwarily may have made his way into their sacred precincts. Hardy youth, with a pencil cocked in its ear and a counterfeit air of familiarity, sometimes accomplishes the adventure unscathed.

The Bank of England is open to all having business there; and certain introductions will make a sesame charm to unlock its *penetralia* for the exhibition of undazzling treasures of gold and silver, as well as historic curiosities in the form of old bank-notes, one dating from 1699. I have had the satisfaction of holding in each hand a million of money for half a minute, and I was invited to help myself to as many ingots as I could lift — a truly negligible quantity. All the same, I observed that, in visiting such wealth, one was attended by discreetly watchful eyes, a precaution said to have proved not needless in regard to the attendants of certain Oriental potentates treated to a so congenial sight, where sovereigns seem to be lying about as if common as stones, and bricks of pure gold are wheeled along on trucks. What strikes one as the most enchanter-like feature in this treasure-house, is a magical machine for weighing sovereigns, one by one coming down through a spout, to place themselves upon a little button that, after an instant of deliberation, contemptuously tosses them away if they prove a grain too light; then back they go to the Mint that stands beside the Tower, within whose walls its spells were worked till a century ago. The City's financial citadel guards some twenty millions in bullion, besides millions in coin and notes. Its own garrison is over a thousand strong, and at night it is under charge of a party of the Guards, who may be seen marching into the City through the shades of eve; but in wet weather the officer seems expected to pay their fare on the Underground Railway, so one hopes it be true that, at dinner in the Bank, he finds a sovereign beneath his plate. In the Bank parlour, matters of such financial magnitude are settled that one may well tread delicately on its soft carpet and hold one's breath, looking out upon a gardened court that was once the churchyard of St. Christopher-le-Stocks, a parish more than covered by our cathedral of Mammon.

The open space before these institutions is through the day the liveliest scene in London, an exchange of passengers in all directions, some few mere idle visitors, but most of the hurrying throng will be such as "go into the City" on the business of gaining, or losing, money. How this is done I hardly understand, authors being seldom versed in the letters L.S.D.; nor am I qualified to be showman to those bulls and bears who play such clever tricks on this crowded stage. I vaguely conceive the main point to be buying for less or selling for more than the operator judges something to be worth, a game in which someone must be at a loss in the long-run. But this much seems clear to the meanest comprehension, that City speculators cannot always be so selfish as they are represented by impecunious poets and moralists. I am continually getting circulars from firms who inform me that, having a certain chance of making large profits on such and such a concern, they propose to let me share the advantage of their shrewd experience. Not caring to benefit at the expense of so open-hearted philanthropists, I always throw their circulars into the waste-paper basket, along with the lithographed letter of a confiding gentleman who, a total stranger to me, kindly offers to lend me any sum I may require up to ten thousand pounds. Goldsmith was not so trusted, not even by his tailor.

Thus it might strike simple minds. But more cynical observers take a less charitable view of City

DUTCH BARGES NEAR THE TOWER

life, declaring a considerable part of the business done there to be the cheating of fools by knaves. There always were cheats as well as gulls in the City, but in old days, it appears, knaves ran the risk of such rough experiences as standing in the pillory, being whipped at the cart's tail, having some or other brand put upon them for the scorn of honest citizens. Nowadays men hold up their heads in the City of whom it is openly told, not always as a reproach, that their business is reckless gambling with other people's money trusted to them on the score of shameless lying. Such scoundrels, when they have brought their dupes to beggary, still seem to flourish like green bay-trees: as undischarged bankrupts they have somehow the means of living in luxury, and would fain flaunt in society their halo of impudent fraud. Of late years, it is said, unclean birds of prey have grown fatter and bolder than ever in the City, where no sooner has one flock of victims been scandalously plucked than another, blinded by stupid greed, comes fluttering into the traps baited for them, as trustfully as the pigeons that make such tame guests about the Guildhall. If that ravenous breed be allowed to increase, will it not ruin London City as surely as ever did fire, and plague, and pirates? But let us remember how, while advertisement is the breath of life to blaring charlatans, the mass of more or less honest dealers carry on their business quietly and without observation, in offices where gas or electric light are often turned upon a show of dingy ledgers representing the treasures of Aladdin's cave.

One more temple of commerce has yet to be mentioned, and that not the least in importance, whose ministers bring its services to every door. The Post-Office, like the Bank, makes a monument of London's medieval piety, standing as it does on the site of St. Martin's-le-Grand, of old a monastery and collegiate church, one of several that nestled under the wing of St. Paul's. As London has outswollen its nucleus, so this institution has had to split itself into branches, the largest now growing upon the other side of the way, soon to line nearly the whole length of Newgate Street: one rooted apart beyond St. Paul's, another as far off as Clerkenwell, all with suckers and grafts over every quarter of the Metropolis, and filaments thrown out to the farthest ends of the kingdom like the nerves of an organized body. The Post-Office of last generation is already little more than a chief receptacle into whose yawning mouths slides the City's correspondence, singly, by dozens, by hundreds, by sackfuls, at the rate of millions a day or, say, some thousand millions a year but I forbear to overwhelm the reader with statistics, of which one might here make an amazing show, as in the vaults of the Bank of England.

The business of London nowadays has to be done mostly by post, when its wealth is on paper rather than in goods or bullion. A few crafts still linger in its high-rented byways. A considerable part of it, notably on the river-side, where the Custom House, Billingsgate Market, Fishmongers' Hall, and Cannon Street Station are its most monumental institutions, has to handle some of the wares which it exchanges and distributes. But its richest trade is money-making through the buying and selling of credit, carried on chiefly in the quarter between the Mansion House and Bishopsgate. This restricted area, where no cranes swing and no vans rumble unless on their way through Old Broad Street to Liverpool Street Station, is what the financial world knows and reverences as the City, *par excellence*. And in its fullest meaning the City measures only a square mile or so, amid a hundredfold that area now bearing the name of London.

St Pauls

ABOUT ST PAUL'S

"CAN YOU TELL me, sir, what is this large building?" asked a civil fellow traveller of mine on the top of an omnibus; and as soon as I had got over a shock of mild surprise, I was able to let him know that we were passing St. Paul's Cathedral. No Londoner would be so ill-informed, for the dome of St. Paul's makes indeed a City landmark, its crown reared to a level with the brow of Hampstead Heath. Yet St. Paul's is no longer so familiar to the citizens as when in every sense it was the centre of London life. On special occasions it draws together huge congregations from all over the metropolis, as for ceremonies of national thanksgiving, or when a roistering multitude gathers about it to hail the first stroke of the New Year; nor do its ordinary services waste their sweetness on a stony void. But to most Londoners this is a monument rather than a fane; and among the throng of Mammon worshippers that hurry by it, but a small proportion find time to enter the doors unless for a peep of curiosity.

Hereabouts is the highest point of the City, as recorded on an old stone preserved in the rebuilt walls of Panyer Alley, leading from the east end of Paternoster Row into Newgate Street. It is supposed that a Roman temple stood on this site, succeeded by a Christian church. The first authentic church of St. Paul's dates from Ethelbert, in the beginning of the seventh century, built and rebuilt, till medieval art produced a Gothic Cathedral larger than the present one, topped by what was then the tallest spire of Christendom, and adorned, no doubt, with sumptuous ornament as with monuments that seem to have fallen into decay before they were swept away by the Great Fire. This Cathedral swallowed up the parish church of St. Faith's at the east end. Several times it had been destroyed or damaged by fire; and its spire was ruined by lightning in Elizabeth's reign, a disaster taken by zealots of the old faith for a judgment. St. Paul's had then come to be an open lounge as well as a place of worship. At certain pillars lawyers were wont to hold consultations with their clients. Ladies and their gallants kept assignations here. Porters carried loads through the church as a short cut. Servants stood waiting to be hired. One aisle, known as Duke Humphrey's Walk — from some memorial of that Duke of Gloucester, Henry IV.'s son, who was, however, buried at St. Albans — grew notorious as a haunt of bankrupts, beggars, and other penniless idlers; hence the proverb "to dine with Duke Humphrey," who need never want guests even in this richest city of the world.

It was outside, at the north-east corner, that the famous Paul's Cross pulpit stood, about which

Latimer drew crowds by his homely eloquence. "There is one that passeth all the other, and is the most diligent prelate and preacher in all England. And will ye know who it is? I will tell you. It is the devil. He is the most diligent preacher of all other; he is never out of his diocese; he is never from his cure; ye shall never find him un-occupied; he is ever in his parish; he keepeth residence at all times . . . He is no lordly loiterer from his cure, but a busy ploughman, so that among all the prelates, and all the pack of them that have cure, the devil shall go for my money. For he still applieth his business. Therefore, ye unpreaching prelates, learn of the devil to be diligent in doing of your office. Learn of the devil. And if you will not learn of God nor good man, for shame, learn of the devil." This pulpit is now to be restored, as a matter of sentiment rather than of utility, one supposes, since there is not much room for an open-air congregation in the corner of the Churchyard where shops and offices wall in a gardened oasis of rest.

Protestant preaching, it is to be feared, did not foster reverence for a sacred building. At that time St. Paul's seems to have been allowed to fall into sad disrepair. Under Charles I. began a restoration, soon interrupted by the Civil War, that let the Cathedral serve as a stable for troopers' horses. Then came the Great Fire, from the ashes of which arose Wren's masterpiece, begun 1675, and not completed till Queen Anne's reign, as commemorated at the entrance by a statue of that sovereign, restored in our time. Behind this, at the foot of the steps, an inscription marks the spot where the aged Queen Victoria offered the thanksgiving of her Diamond Jubilee.

Wren's Cathedral blends some Gothic features with the classical style he had mainly in view for a nobly massive structure, whose dome but gathers fresh dignity from its grimy environment. Fancy how the white fretwork of Milan, or the colour of St. Mark's, would have borne the smoke of London! Had Wren had his way, he would no doubt have gained an opener space to display the proportions of his masterpiece, too much pressed upon by the hasty

rebuilding of the City. In internal ornament, also, his design was starved, a reproach which our time labours to wipe away. At first, the effect of the interior must have been rather austere, and it was long before cold Georgian piety ceased to be suspicious of decoration. In vain the Royal Academy offered to consecrate its establishment by contributing religious paintings. The first statues introduced were those of Howard the philanthropist and Samuel Johnson, guarding the entrance to the Choir in classical scantness of costume, which has caused inconsiderate visitors to mistake them as St. Peter and St. Paul, the more readily for the emblematic prison-key put in Howard's hand. This was the statue on which Charles Lamb, "saving the reverence due to Holy Paul," would willingly have spat, because the reformer of prisons had recommended solitary confinement for runaway Blue-coat boys. Of the old monuments, the only one saved — apart from fragments preserved in the Crypt-was that of Dr. Donne, which now stands on the south side of the Chancel, opposite the bronze effigy of Dr. Mandell Creighton.

Once monuments were admitted, the long French war supplied a good show of them, and the aisles are lined with memorials of military and naval heroes, whose whiskered and uniformed effigies sometimes make an absurd contrast with the allegorical figures that seemed appropriate in their Philistine age. The most imposing is Alfred Stevens' grand monument to Wellington, not yet topped by the equestrian statue that was part of his design, a feature as to which architects and artists appear to be at variance. This is on the north side of the Nave, near the recumbent effigies of Lord Leighton and of Gordon, that mark an altered taste. Nelson stands on the other side, at the corner of the transept.

> O saviour of the silver-coasted isle,
> O shaker of the Baltic and the Nile,
> If aught of things that here befall
> Touch a spirit among things divine,
> If love of country move thee there at all,
> Be glad because his bones are laid by thine!

CLOTH FAIR

The monuments here are only cenotaphs: for the actual tombs we must descend into the Crypt, where impressive gloom shrouds the sarcophagi of Wellington and Nelson in the central space. Next to this, the most interesting spot in the Crypt is the north-east aisle, known as Painters' Corner, from a cluster of artists' graves, among them Sir Joshua Reynolds, Turner, Landseer, Millais and Leighton. Here, too, a quite modern note is struck by a group of memorials to warcorrespondents, whom Wellington might have hanged. In this corner is the plain tomb of Wren with its famous motto *Circumspice,* afterwards displayed more worthily over the north door. He got little enough gratitude or honour from his own generation, his plans thwarted, scrimped, or marred, his salary at one time docked, and his enemies even went so far as to indict him for delaying the work in his own interest, a charge from which he was easily cleared. Under the Hanoverian Government, his post of Surveyor-General was taken away. But he lived to see the structure finished, and for a dozen years longer in retirement at Hampton Court, whence, till his death at the age of 91, he made an annual pilgrimage to his great monument.

In our æsthetic time much has been done to light up this great fabric by colour and gilding. The Chancel is now closed by an elaborate reredos of white marble, with sculptured panels and niches at which sound Protestants may shake their heads. Behind this the apse has been finely decorated as a Jesus Chapel in memory of Canon Liddon. The most discussed ornament is Sir W. B. Richmond's mosaic work of coloured glass, which glows so smoothly as seen from below that one might not guess what a rough surface it presents close at hand. Such a show of colour has been severely criticized as out of keeping; but it seems that Wren had something of the kind in view, and other judges hope to see it extended from the domelets of the Choir till all the ceiling is thus enriched. A recent addition is a replica of Holman Hunt's *Light of the World,* hung on the south side of the nave in presence of the venerable painter, who unhappily could no longer see

his own work. Older ornaments are Thornhill's dome paintings of scenes in the life of St. Paul, and Grinling Gibbons' carvings in the Choir. So now St. Paul's presents a fair presentment of the Anglican Church in its double character — at one end solid, spacious, rather cold, decked with hints of the world and the State; at the other toned into harmony with a revival of Catholic forms of worship. Few visitors carry away such an unfavourable impression as Mr. W. D. Howells, to whom "St. Paul's always seemed a dispersed and interrupted St. Peter's in its structure and decoration, and a very hard, unsympathetic, unappealing Westminster Abbey in its mortuary records." But, indeed, the heroes here commemorated beneath ponderous Fames and Britannias, belong to an age that no longer appeals to the ancestral pride of Americans.

The services also have been warmed and brightened for our generation, and now, at certain times of the day, there are as many worshippers as sight-seers, while Sunday and special festivals bring crowded congregations. Even sightseers tread more reverently than half a century ago, when a charge of twopence was made at the doors, and the vergers kept a sharp lookout for tips. Did the reader ever come across a curious little book called "John Wardle's *Pilgrim's Progress* from a Devonshire Valley to the Temples of the Metropolis," under the personage of a simple-minded and self-taught peasant preacher giving a slyly satirical account of regulations that should have moved Sydney Smith to ridicule? There is still a table of money-changers, at which one pays sixpence for going down into the Crypt, and as much for ascending to the "Whispering Gallery" with its curious trick of acoustics, and on to the "Stone Gallery" on the roof. One may climb farther for a higher fee, into the Golden Gallery and even the Ball. But the Stone Gallery is high enough to give a broad view over Wren's thirty towers and steeples, rising above a sea of roofs, often strangely distorted in the struggle to add a new dimension to space round "streaming London's central roar." Ground is so precious here that St. Paul's Choir School has been

CHILD FEEDING BIRDS SALT AT ST PAULS

fain to make its playground on a fenced-in roof, whereas the greater St. Paul's School, before removing to a roomier site in West Kensington, had to *prendre ses ébats* below the schoolrooms.

Overshadowed among closely-packed warerooms lie the Deanery and the Canons' houses, that at night may enjoy congenial peace; and the labyrinthine openings around bear names such as Ave Maria Lane, Amen Corner, Chapter-House Court, Creed Lane, to show how they belonged to sacred precincts. Doctors' Commons is no longer a place of much legal business, as in David Copperfield's day; but couples are still licensed to be happy at Dean's Court; and Godliman Street leads to the headquarters of heraldry, whose rites may still be taken seriously by their ministrants. Most famous of these purlieus is Paternoster Row, renowned seat of a power that in our time usurps that of the pulpit. This narrow street, though figuratively taken as a centre of the publishing trade, has much changed

its character since Mr. Arthur Pendennis was here entertained by his publisher. Mr. Bacon comes to business from his residence at Kensington, and Mrs. Bungay drives out from her villa at Hampstead or Putney; while the garrets of their authors are no longer in Grub Street, now dignified as Milton Street and occupied by more profitable crafts. In our time the large publishing firms have been moving their offices and warehouses to the West-end. But still some long-known names stick to the "Row," which is much occupied by religious bookshops of diverse doctrine, fostered under the shadow of the Cathedral. The oldest house here seems to be the Longmans', set up in the Row at the sign of the "Ship and the Black Swan" so far back as 1726, soon after which date it published a *Chambers's Cyclopædia* that took from its author a title afterwards transferred to the enterprise of a Scottish firm grafted in Paternoster Row.

The twin printing and publishing trades

VIEW OF ST PAULS FROM ACROSS THE RIVER THAMES

were cradled by Caxton at Westminster; but they soon betook themselves to the height of St. Paul's, where Stationers' Hall became their nursery. "True Paul's bred" is Ben Jonson's description of a bookseller; and generations afterwards the Chapter coffee-house made an Exchange for publishers and authors. At one time the trade spread into Little Britain, so called from a residence here of the Dukes of Brittany, as Scotland Yard got its name from a lodging of Scottish kings on their visits to London. Still farther from St. Paul's was Cave's office, the scene of Johnson's servitude, occupying the rooms above St. John's Gate, near the Charterhouse, a fragment of the old Priory of the Knights of St. John, now restored to possession of the modern brotherhood that has revived that name. It was only the other day that "Sylvanus Urban" dropped off from the survey of men and manners for which this old-world nook long made an observatory.

From St. Paul's Churchyard, which now houses rather the drapery trade, let us turn aside as far as Little Britain, which seems still a "heart's core of the City," not altogether, indeed, so "ready to tumble down" as when an American amateur of antiquity drew it in his *Sketch Book,* and found it even then deserted by the booksellers. As we enter it from Aldersgate Street, we may note one quite modern feature: the churchyard of St. Botolph's has been laid out as a garden, nicknamed the Postmen's Park, where, under shadow of the G.P.O. buildings, a little arcade displays tablets recording deeds of contemporary heroism, placed here by G. F. Watts,

48

whose own works adorn so many statelier galleries. This end of little Britain is being rebuilt; and as it curves round beside St. Bartholomew 's Hospital, it shows little more picturesque than a grimy air of having seen better days, in memory of which the farther end reassumes the old name, after being disguised as Duke Street, that seems an enhancing of Duck Lane. But apparently Washington Irving had also in view Cloth Fair, converging with Little Britain at St. Bartholomew's Church; and here may be found a nest of quaint old houses, once lordly family mansions, now fallen into decay about the "Old Red Cow" that has drawn beer for more than a dozen generations. In this narrow lane, with its narrower side-courts and alleys, American visitors will still come upon the sort of house they cannot see at home; but they should make haste about it, as nothing but artistic sentiment can keep such slums cumbering a valuable site. Bartholomew Close, on the other side of the Church, where Hogarth lived and Benjamin Franklin worked as a printer, is already half rebuilt. The fine archway opening from the Churchyard into Smithfield was lately marked for destruction; but has been rescued by a company of subscribers. As for the great Hospital opposite, that is bound to be rebuilt, picturesqueness and sanitary science being seldom on good terms.

The early Virginian settlers gave the name of Smithfield to their first playground by the palisades at Jamestown, a hint of what it was to Londoners in their day. It seems hard to realize that this cramped opening of London was once a suburban nook, when the "Smooth Field" here had not the best of reputations as a swampy common outside the walls, such as we might now look for in the Hackney or Tottenham Marshes. Here were held races and horse fairs; tournaments, too, that could be witnessed from London Wall, and infamous executions, as when Wallace was butchered to make a London holiday. Here Wat Tyler, or one of the rebels bearing that name, was stabbed by Lord Mayor Walworth, whose effigy stands not far off on Holborn Viaduct. The most illustrious victims of Smithfield were the Protestant martyrs, from Anne

Askew onwards, a tale of nearly three hundred sufferers, among whom three are noted by name on a tablet let into the wall of the Hospital, close to where the stake is believed to have stood. Less noble Smithfield victims suffered in the pillory, a most barbarously unfair punishment, as depending for its severity on the temper of the mob, that sometimes cheered the criminal and sometimes pelted him to death, when officers of the law might be driven away from the scaffold in fear of their own lives. After public butcherings and roastings had gone out of date, Smithfield's chief fame was for its cattle-markets, and for the annual orgies of Bartholomew Fair, not put down till 1855. In Washington Irving's time, he could tell us how still —

"The late quiet streets of Little Britain are overrun with an irruption of strange figures and faces; every tavern is a scene of rout and revel. The fiddle and the song are heard from the taproom, morning, noon, and night; and at each window may be seen some group of boon companions, with half-shut eyes, hats on one side, pipe in mouth, and tankard in band, fondling and prosing, and singing maudlin songs over their liquor. Even the sober decorum of private families, which I must say is rigidly kept up at other times among my neighbours, is no proof against this Saturnalia. There is no such thing as keeping maid-servants within doors. Their brains are absolutely set maddening with Punch and the Puppet Show ; the Flying Horses; Signior Polito; the Fire-Eater; the celebrated Mr. Paap; and the Irish Giant. The children, too, lavish all their holiday money in toys and gilt gingerbread, and fill the house with the Lilliputian din of drums, trumpets, and penny whistles."

Certain foreign writers have it that to this market John Bull could legally bring his wife for sale, a halter round her neck. But one sees no show of such chattels, now that Smithfield is swept and garnished, its centre laid out as a patch of garden, and its meat-trade housed under a row of spacious

VIEW OF ST PAULS FROM FLEET STREET.

roofs at the north end, where a great congregation of vans keeps up the horsey connection of the place. With the stomach of a horse, one might get an appetite for dinner by walking through its galleries of still life, or descending to the catacombs of frozen carcasses underground. The liveliest sight here seems the rubicund and shining faces of the butcher boys, whose suety hair could not well stand on end at the apparition of that Spectre Pig famed by O.W. Holmes. Smithfield is in its glory under the patronage of Father Christmas, when his time-honoured rites demand such hecatombs of beasts and birds; but "endless prospectives of sides, fitches, quarters, and whole carcasses, and fantastic vistas of sausages, blood-puddings, and the like artistic fashionings of the raw material," may on some of us have the effect of object lessons in vegetarianism. This market has at least a certain moral beauty of its own, as representing the organization of London's food-supply, and the modern municipal activity that swept away a chaos of small marts like that of Newgate, breeding vermin and infection under the old muddle of metropolitan government.

The shrine of æsthetic pilgrims here is the Church of St. Bartholomew the Great, half blocked up by that "squalid knot of alleys" between Smithfield and Aldersgate. St. Bartholomew the less stands within the adjacent Hospital, that also had for pious founder one Rahere, who lived so long ago as the reign of Henry I., and was minstrel, jester, or hanger-on about his Court. Little is known of his early life but that he gained favour with the King, and must somehow have come to be better off than is the lot of most minstrels and merry-makers. But good fortune did not harden his heart; and the religion of the age sent him on its well-beaten course of a pilgrimage to Rome. There falling ill with fever, like so many another ancient and modern *roamer* in those parts, he had a vision of St. Bartholomew, to whom he vowed the founding of a hospital as ransom for his life. His life was spared, and the price was paid in the Hospital that has since grown and thriven to be one of the richest of such institutions, Lord Mayor Whittington having been

one of its many benefactors. Every London doctor, after putting his own school first, will own "Bart's" as the second metropolitan hospital, which, for all the well earned increment of its wealth, is now fain to ask further aid from our generation.

Rahere was better than his vow, for, at another prompting from the Saint, beside the Hospital he set up a Priory, of which — apart from the lately restored Canonbury Tower, that near Islington made a country retreat for the Canons, and the park bearing their name at Edgware — nothing remains but the eastern half of the monastery church. This became a parish church, spared by the Great Fire, to be so scurvily treated in our whitewash period of religion, that its Lady Chapel was turned into a factory, and one of the transepts served as a smithy. About half a century ago the work of redressing such wrongs was seriously begun, parts of the church being bought back to sacred use, its sides cleared from darkening obstructions, and the whole fabric, except the lost nave, restored with a reverent eye upon its early fifteenth-century structure, for then it had been almost rebuilt. There is still room for restoration; but this rescued fane, with its ancient monuments and sumptuous tombs of Rahere and of Mildmay, founder of Emmanuel College, makes "the noblest medieval monument left to London," haunted by artists as well as sight-seers.

An offshoot of St. Bartholomew's, as founded by the first master of Rahere's Hospital, was St. Giles, Cripplegate, on the farther side of Aldersgate, where it will be found at the junction of Jewin Street, Fore Street, and Red Cross Street, overshadowed by blocks of trim warehouses rebuilt ten years ago after a conflagration from which St. Giles escaped more narrowly than from the Great Fire of 1666. This Church also stood without the Wall, a considerable fragment of which comes to view in its Churchyard. Its chief fame is as the parish church of Milton, whose statue has recently been erected outside. His bust within recalls that he was buried here, along with Foxe the martyrologist and Frobisher the Arctic voyager; and here Oliver Cromwell was married. Such a shrine does not lack pilgrims, well worth seeing for itself and for its memorials, among them a quaint one to the daughter of Sir T. Lucy of Charlecote, that brings Shakespearian associations in touch with the tomb of Milton.

Bunhill Fields, not far away on the City Road, made a noted burying-ground of Dissenters, where lie Bunyan, Isaac Watts, Defoe, and the mother of the Wesleys, John Wesley himself being buried at his chapel, close at hand, and George Fox either in the Bunhill cemetery or beside the Friends' meeting-house in Roscoe Street. But these Nonconformist shrines may seem too far a digression from the Cathedral round which we are wandering. So along the Barbican let us seek Aldersgate Station, whence Long Lane leads us shortly and straightly back into Smithfield.

Behind the meat-markets is soon found the pleasant opening of Charterhouse Square, where the building that first strikes the eye is a smart modern hotel. Beyond this an archway gives entrance to what Besant declares "the most beautiful and most venerable monument of old London," the Charterhouse or Carthusian monastery, built by Sir Walter Manny upon a burial ground of victims to the Black Death. After the Dissolution, the property passed to less austere owners, and was finally bought by Thomas Sutton, a rich and benevolent merchant, who in James's reign turned it into an almshouse for eighty old men linked with a school for forty boys. The Almshouse is famous as that where Colonel Newcome said *Adsum* for the last time; and many broken-down authors have found sanctuary from misfortune or improvidence in this noble refuge, with its time-mellowed courts, its great Hall and ancient Chapel containing Sutton's tomb, shown to strangers on application at the porter's lodge. A little farther on one gets through the gate a peep into the green playground of Thackeray's old school, affectionately remembered by his contemporaries as "Smiffle," though its discipline then seems to have been of the roughest, and though its most celebrated modern scholar might have said of his school-days, "I learne song; I

know but small grammere." But the boys playing here to-day are no longer the sons of Thackeray's *alma mater*. The schoolrooms were acquired by another old City school, that of the Merchant Taylors' Company, when the Charterhouse transferred itself with some of its more portable monuments to a height above Godalming. There it thrives afresh in more airy scenes, cherishing its memories of Addison, Steele, and Wesley, with its relics of later pupils like John Leech; and its last hero is General Baden-Powell, who all over the country has raised such a miniature army of boy-scouts.

Across Smithfield, we reach the site of another renowned foundation, the Blue-coat Hospital, that has also swarmed into the country, and its yellow-legged bees, now hived near Horsham. are no longer so familiar dots of colour in the London streets. This, too, was housed in a monastery, the old Grey Friars, which Edward VI. gets the credit of turning into a charity school; but he seems to have done little more than hand over the buildings robbed from the Church, to be equipped and endowed by benevolent citizens. Such a home for foundlings, as it was at first, grew to be no common school, rearing a long line of illustrious scholars, three of whom, Coleridge, Charles Lamb, and Leigh Hunt, helped to make it famous by their reminiscences.

Another account of Blue-coat school life, less well known, deserves to be better known, in the *Wayside Thoughts* of Professor D'Arcy Wentworth Thompson, once a master at my own school, where his initials tempted us to nickname him "Pennyweight." This wise and witty book is really a plea for educational reform, but makes an oasis among the rather dry writings commonly devoted to that subject. The second chapter deals with the author's boyhood, from the day that, in a coachful of other seven-year-olds, he was sent off to the Hertford nursery of the school, "all weeping — going, as it were, to the funeral of our respective childhoods." With dismay the neophyte found himself "encased in an imitation horse-hair shirt, yellow

CLOTH ALLEY, SMITHFIELD

worsted stockings, fustian knee-breeches, a yellow hearthrug petticoat, and a long blue gown; a red leathern girdle went round my waist; a pair of parson's bibs hung down from my neck, and my hair was cut so short that I think I might have been used, with a little inconvenience to the user and myself, as a hair-brush. I cannot say what my poor dear Mother thought of the grotesque-looking article before her. She was bewildered in the midst of her sorrow. I think she looked upon me as a ridiculously small parody upon John the Baptist, bound for years of sojourning in the wilderness and of feeding there on locusts and wild honey." In France I have known a Blue-coat boy's mother condoled with on her son's precocious monkhood. Sydney Smith's humour threw out a mock theory identifying the Blue-coat as the larva of the Quaker. "At a very early age young Quakers disappear; at a very early age the Coat-boys are seen; at the age of seventeen or eighteen young Quakers are again seen; at the same age the Coat-boys disappear . . . Dissection would throw great light on the question. . . . I have ascertained that the Blue-coat infants are fed with drab-coloured pap, which looks very suspicious.

D'Arcy Thompson is quite sure that he was fed at school mostly on mere locusts of grammar and parsing, and that only in the upper forms did he taste the honey of what long seemed an educational wilderness. There is an earnest purpose in his humorous retrospect of ill-managed classes, of wasted school-hours, of dreary Sundays, of tyrants and bullies, of hardy games and severe discipline. Among his experiences was that of a mutiny, a Comus rout soon quelled by waving of the headmaster's wand, who threatened to flog a dozen of his rebels if they did not go into school, and when they did go, flogged three dozen of them. "One very knowing beadle had mingled with the noisy crowd, pretending great enjoyment of the fun; but unobservedly he had put a little chalk mark on the coats of the most obstreperous; and the owner of every coat so chalked was now singled out for execution." It was a rough-and-tumble life, that sometimes crushed weak spirits.

When I look back upon the condition of the school in these years, I seem to have before me a picture in little of old medieval and older heroic days. In the Hellenists I see the studious and exclusive searchers after a Latin-and-Greek philosopher's stone. In the Brassers (bullies) I recognize the Barons of the middle ages, who had all the half-pence going in their days; and in the little ones I see the burghers who paid the piper, the retainers who did the dirtier work, and the general rabble who came in for the kicks and cuffings. How I should like a return of the old feudal times, if I were only sure of being a baron! How I should like to fight round windy Troy, if I were only the son of a goddess, and could scurry the poor Trojan fellows like locusts into the river, without one of them having a chance of grazing my royal and semicelestial shins! How splendid it must have been for a great chieftain, gifted specially of Heaven with superhuman shoulders, indefatigable hips, and an impenetrable hide, mounted on a light car drawn by divine steeds, his sword upon his thigh, his shining shield in front, and a great tree of a lance in his terrible hand, to rush careering in among a crowd of leather-clad trembling louts, and prog and pierce and skewer and stab and slash until at length he ceased from very exhaustion, and doffed his helm, and with the fringe of what may be called his frock-coat wiped the sweat from off his steaming forehead in the middle of a great slaughter-house of groans and glory!

I know a schoolfellow of this satirist, who cannot name him without solemn reprobation. "He has reviled his old Hospital!" But all D'Arcy Thompson did was to point out how the resources of a magnificent institution were squandered by clumsy routine, and his half-serious resentment shows kindly feeling, too, for a school where his time could not have been all wasted. That is the way with all the Blue-coats; beaten, bullied, and half-starved mentally and bodily, as they might be, they seldom are found failing in loyalty to a scene of mingled memories. Coleridge expressed gratitude

ST BARTHOLOMEW'S HOSPITAL

that he had been flogged, "wisely as I think, soundly as I know." Leigh Hunt wept bitterly on leaving the stony cloisters. Charles Lamb, though in one of his two accounts his humour is to be critical, kept always a soft heart for that "play-place of our early days." And if thin-skinned authors let old sores heal so kindly, it can be imagined how the average stolid Johnny Bull cherishes a bigoted affection for the spot where he learned, if little more, to suffer in silence, whose customs, rude survivals, and its very abuses seem worthy of veneration in our "dear conservative, wilful, pigheaded old England."

No doubt the school is better managed in its new quarters, where still it clings to the quaint costume of Tudor days; nor do its scholars omit their annual visit to the Lord Mayor, to receive an all-round tip, ranging from a guinea to a shilling. Their old home is now being transformed by the new buildings of the Post-Office, behind which part of the site will be over-spread by St. Bartholomew's Hospital. In the course of this clearing there has been unearthed a bastion of the Roman wall, that

for centuries lay unsuspected beneath the feet of those young Latiners. Christ Church still stands, whose huge gallery served as chapel for the school; but even Londoners will soon forget the lively cloister into which they till lately could peep through the Newgate Street railings; and strangers must be content with such a description as Leigh Hunt's:

Christ Hospital (for this is its proper name, and not Christ's Hospital) occupies a considerable portion of ground between Newgate Street, Giltspur Street, St Bartholomew's, and Little Britain. There is a quadrangle with cloisters ; and the square inside the cloisters is called the Garden, and most likely was the monastery garden. Its only delicious crop, for many years, has been pavement. Another large area, presenting the Grammar and Navigation Schools, is also misnomered the Ditch ; the town-ditch having formerly run that way. In Newgate Street is seen the Hall, or eating-room, one of the noblest in England, adorned with enormously long paintings by Verrio and others, and with an organ. A portion of the old quadrangle once contained the library of the monks, and was built or repaired by the famous Whittington, whose arms were to be seen outside; but alterations of late years have done it away. In the cloisters a number of persons lie buried, besides the officers of the house. Among them is Isabella, wife of Edward the Second, the "She-wolf of France." I was not aware of this circumstance then; but many a time, with a recollection of some lines in "Blair's Grave" upon me, have I run as hard as I could at night-time from my ward to another, in order to borrow the next volume of some ghostly romance. In one of the cloisters was an impression resembling a gigantic foot, which was attributed by some to the angry stamping of the ghost of a beadle's wife!

D'Arcy Thompson, too, has hints of juvenile superstitions that grew rank within those old walls. In his day, and oftener in Hunt's, the boys might still shudder to hear the tolling of St. Sepulchre's bell, close at hand. This church, in which doughty John Smith of Virginia lies buried, had the office of ringing a knell for criminals hanged at Newgate, its gloomy walls separated by little more than a street's breadth from that barrack of hearty boyhood, where, on nights before an execution, ears were strained to catch the hammering at the scaffold, and bold truants sometimes contrived to slip out for a peep at the gruesome spectacle. How often did the bellman of St. Sepulchre have to recite his doggerel homily below barred windows

All you that in the condemned hold do lie,
Prepare you, for to-morrow you must die!

Round the corner of Newgate Street, we turn down by the Old Bailey, where a few years ago Newgate came to be rebuilt in more cheerful style, crowned by a statue of Justice, not so blind or befogged as she once showed herself here. This is still the Central Criminal Court, but no longer a place of imprisonment and punishment, of torment rather, in which felons and debtors were herded together, innocent men among the guilty, some even acquitted of all offence but poverty, yet

detained for a grasping gaoler's fees. We have many pictures of old Newgate, where authors, and publishers too, often pined for libel, if not for debt. Laudators of good old times must find it hard to excuse the stupid heartlessness of our forefathers, before Howard began the work of prison reform, when hundreds of wretches were pent up so foully that their executioner was often the "gaol fever" with which judges, jurymen, lawyers, and witness might be infected while putting the rope round the neck of victims who now would get off with a few weeks' imprisonment. It takes all the aromatic herbs and pungent essences of romantic sentiment to sweeten the law's sickening cruelties in the past.

The sternest function of Justice was till lately carried out here, when the bell of St. Sepulchre's boomed in the ear of one

Who shall hear the stroke of eight,
But not the stroke of nine —

and the hoisting of a black flag proclaimed that a murderer had been done to death with impressive secrecy. But living men still remember how the Old Bailey was the theatre of public hangings, to fill it with a crowd of sight-seers and seekers after morbid excitement.

There are many accounts of that ghastly spectacle, from different points of view, for one that of Ingoldsby's Lord Tom Noddy, who fell asleep after sitting up all night. J. T. Smith, in his *Book for a Rainy Day,* tells how he was admitted into Newgate to see Governor Wall pinioned and led trembling to the gallows amid the execrations of the very felons; and how, on coming out, he found one of the officials already selling off the fatal rope at a shilling an inch. This case shows our law at least no respecter of persons. Joseph Wall, an Irish officer, was governor of Goree in Senegal, where he had a sergeant flogged to death by the hands of black slaves, as seemed to some the most atrocious feature of the case. Harsh as was the military discipline of the day, this act of drunken brutality roused vengeful indignation. Taking refuge on the

FLEET STREET

Continent, Wall eluded Nemesis for twenty years; then, in 1801, when he hoped the feeling against him might have died down, he surrendered to take his trial. Convicted and sentenced to death, he had strong influence brought to bear on his behalf; but the Government durst not gainsay the popular verdict, and he was hanged before an exulting mob. Forty years later, Thackeray attended the execution of another famous criminal, Courvoisier, the Swiss valet who murdered his master, Lord William Russell; then the novelist's spectacles of playful cynicism were dimmed by an emotion that did not let him look to the end.

"As the clock began to strike, an immense sway and movement swept over the whole of that vast dense crowd. They were all uncovered directly, and a great murmur arose, more awful, bizarre, and indescribable than any sound I had ever before heard. Women and children began to shriek horribly. I don't know whether it was the bell I heard; but a dreadful, quick, feverish kind of jangling noise mingled with the noise of the people, and lasted for about two minutes. The scaffold stood before us, tenantless and black, the black chain was hanging down ready from the beam. Nobody came. "He has been respited," someone said; another said, "He has killed himself in prison." Just then, from under the black prison-door, a pale, quiet head peered out. It was shockingly bright and distinct; it rose up directly, and a man in black appeared on the scaffold, and was silently followed by about four more dark figures. The first was a tall, grave man; we all knew who the second man was. *That's he — that's he!"* you heard the people say, as the devoted man came up. I have seen a cast of the head since, but, indeed, should never have known it. Courvoisier bore his punishment like a man, and walked very firmly. He was dressed in a new black suit, as it seemed his shirt was opened. His arms were tied in front of him. He opened his hands in a helpless kind of way, and clasped them once or twice together. He turned his head here and there, and looked about him for an instant with a wild imploring look. His mouth was contracted into a sort of pitiful smile. He went and placed himself at once under the beam, with his face towards St. Sepulchre's. The tall, grave man in black twisted him round swiftly in the other direction, and, drawing from his pocket a night-cap, pulled it tight over the patient's head and face. I am not ashamed to say that I could look no more, but shut my eyes as the last dreadful act was going on, which sent this wretched, guilty soul into the presence of God."

Dickens, in his more tub-thumping manner, preached on the same text in a letter to the *Times* in 1849, written while he still shuddered from the sight of such a popular spectacle; this letter is sometimes, though erroneously, quoted as having rung the knell of public execution.

"When I came upon the scene at midnight, the shrillness of the cries and howls that were raised from time to time, denoting that they came from a concourse of boys and girls assembled in the best places, made my blood run cold. As the night went on, screeching and laughing, and yelling in strong chorus of parodies on negro melodies, with substitutions of "Mrs. Manning" for "Susannah," and the like, were added to these. When the day dawned, thieves, low prostitutes, ruffians, and vagabonds of every kind, flocked on to the ground, with every variety of offensive and foul behaviour. Fightings, faintings, whistlings, imitations of Punch, brutal jokes, tumultuous demonstrations of indecent delight, when swooning women were dragged out of the crowd by the police with their dresses disordered, gave a new zest to the general entertainment. When the sun rose brightly — as it did — it gilded thousands upon thousands of upturned faces, so inexpressibly odious in their brutal mirth or callousness that a man had cause to feel ashamed of the shape he wore, and to shrink from himself, as fashioned in the image of the Devil. . . . I am solemnly convinced that nothing that ingenuity could devise to be done in this city, in the same compass of time, could work such ruin as one public execution; and I stand astounded and appalled by the wickedness it exhibits."

The hanging that called forth this burst of indignation was at Horsemonger Lane Gaol in Surrey; but Dickens was well acquainted with Newgate, as readers of *Barnaby Rudge* do not need to be reminded. The gaol burned by the Gordon rioters was replaced by the one described in *Sketches by Boz*, who there saw more than a score of men under formal sentence of death, among them a boy below fourteen, not that on all of these would the extreme penalty be carried out. Nobody in his day did more than Dickens to rebuke the absurdities and brutalities of "old father antic the law." By that day considerate parents and teachers no longer sent young folks to witness an execution as an edifying example; but to be inveterately familiar with the gallows was so much John Bull's humour, that not till 1868 was an end put to such demoralizing spectacles. Since then I note how an Italian observer of our manners reports that hanging and flogging are done every Monday at Newgate, "and no dog barks." As a matter of fact, a murderer is now hanged at the gaol in which he awaits his trial. When Newgate prison came to be demolished, a gruesome question arose what to do with the bones or half-decomposed remains of the latest stratum of criminals buried here. Some were for cementing up these dishonoured graves and leaving their occupants to rot in peace, like better men. Sanitarians suggested cremation to finish the work imperfectly done by quicklime. Finally it was decided to give the bodies fresh burial in the City cemetery at Ilford.

Close to Newgate, almost under the shadow of the Cathedral, where now the Congregational Memorial Hall dignifies Farringdon Street, stood another prison of ill-fame, that, also wrecked by the Gordon rioters, was rebuilt to be a scene in Mr. Pickwick's adventures, after housing many a more woeful sight; but the railway epoch made a good riddance of it. This was the Fleet, so called from a little river rising on Hampstead Heath, to flow into the Thames at Blackfriars. Not fully covered over till

half a century ago, this once purling stream had long for part of its course become a noisome ditch, opening out at the *Hollow Bourne* into a canalized tidal estuary on which barges rode up to Holborn in the middle of the eighteenth century, if we may trust a picture of that day at the Guildhall. In the *Dunciad* we learn how its stream was not fit for bathing; and quite unquotable to ears polite is Ben Jonson's description of a voyage through the filth of the Fleet Ditch, on whose banks more than one prison raked in human dregs and offal.

The Fleet Prison was specially for debtors, whose lot might be so harsh that there was at least one case of a prisoner qualifying as a felon to exchange it for transportation. Here were huddied a swarm of bankrupts, ne'er-do-wells, and other unfortunates, sometimes mere victims of the law's stupidity or of pettifogging knavery. Their alleged offence being to have no money, they were given over to the exactions of official harpies licensed to demand fees, perquisites, and bribes from men whose means of livelihood were cut off by the bars that often closed on them for life. Some were able to carry on trades and handicrafts in prison, and thus to support families, else left destitute outside, but sometimes able to pig together with their breadwinner, the innocent gaol-birds going in and out on errands. The Fleet was once found turned into a smuggler's store under the nose of dishonest turnkeys. The greatest rascals of all, those who could pay their debts and would not for one or other reason, might be better off, for, as Mr. Pickwick soon learned, "money was, in the Fleet, just what money was out of it." Private rooms and other luxuries could be had at exorbitant rates by guests for whom, as Besant puts it, the Fleet was no worse than "a very expensive and most uncomfortable hotel." Some lively spirits seem even to have enjoyed the squalid clubbability of the place, in which they could play the games that perhaps had brought them to ruin outside. Most to be pitied were the penniless prisoners on "the poor side," who had to eke out a scanty allowance by charity, taking turns to exhibit themselves in an iron cage to the compassion of passers-by, in whose ears they

The Temple Church

rattled a begging-box. "Pity the poor prisoners!" was a familiar cry in days when legacies were left to plaster the galling sores rubbed by Christian law, and collections came to be made for ransoming captives to the cruel Turk, their lot not always less endurable than that of prisoners at home, as described before Mr. Pickwick's day in *Amelia* and *The Vicar of Wakefield*, or afterwards, with sympathetic retrospection, by Besant. Perhaps our latest authentic glimpse into the Fleet is through the eyes of Mr. Arthur Pendennis, who was also not ignorant of its waiting-rooms in Cursitor Street, where Jewish bailiffs had their gloomy dens.

"Pen had never seen this scene of London life, and walked with no small interest in at the grim gate of that dismal edifice. They went through the anteroom, where the officers and janitors of the place were seated, and passing in at the wicket, entered the prison. The noise and the crowd, the life and the shouting, the shabby bustle of the place struck and excited Pen. People moved about ceaselessly and restless, like caged animals in a menagerie. Men were playing at fives. Others pacing and tramping: this one in colloquy with his lawyer in dingy black-that one walking sadly, with his wife by his side, and a child on his arm. Some were arrayed in tattered dressing- gowns, and had a look of rakish fashion. Everybody seemed to be busy, humming, and on the move. Pen felt as if he choked in the place, and as if the door being locked upon him they never would let him out. They went through a court up a stone staircase, and through passages full of people, and noise, and cross lights, and black doors clapping and banging."

Certain prisoners, *moyennant finance,* got leave to live outside, within the "Rules" of the Fleet, a narrow space bounded by Ludgate Hill, the Old Bailey, Fleet Lane, and the line of the stream. In this disreputable sanctuary, at one time, out-at-elbows parsons could pick up fees by performing summary marriages, as told in Besant's *Chaplain of the Fleet.* Originally the Fleet marriages took place in the prison chapel, at the rate of thousands a year. The Church law had then no hold on those unbeneficed officiants; and after their trade was threatened by legal enactment against marrying in chapels without banns, they set up altars in their own houses or in the Fleet taverns, sending out touts to fetch in might-be happy couples. A special Act of the middle of the eighteenth century was needed to repress this scandal, for which other places besides the Fleet were notorious, Sion Chapel at Hampstead, for instance, and that of Mayfair.

Was it for want of room within prison walls that their boundaries were extended by "Rules"? If so, no small part of London's population must have been in confinement, when the rest of the nation was "Merry England." The gates of a city seem to have been much used as prisons, their connection with justice being as old as Biblical "sittings in the gate." Within a stone's-throw of the Fleet, before London's gates were pulled down, Ludgate had tacked on to it a debtors' prison for City freemen, improved, according to tradition, by a Lord Mayor of Henry VI.'s reign, who had been himself a prisoner there, but when taking his turn "to angle into Blackfriars for brass farthings," this beggar so won the heart of a rich widow, that she set him free, and opened his way to fortune as her husband. That cage of confinement was succeeded by various "compters" and "clinks," replaced in time by the City prison of Clerkenwell, now deodorized as the Parcel Post-Office. Then there were several prisons on the Southwark side, the King's Bench the largest and most celebrated of them, to which, if tales be true, a Prince of Wales was once committed by his father's Chief Justice. Besides all that public accommodation, there were the bailiffs' "sponging houses," detention in which might make the first stage in a rake's downward progress, when Colonel Crawley was liable to be tapped on the shoulder as he left a West-end banquet, and Count D'Orsay, in real life, could not appear at his club till after midnight on Saturday, Sunday being a truce of the law.

Another old prison, near Ludgate, which has not wholly lost its rusty office, became so

St Pauls from the river

renowned that its name made a generic one for a house of correction. This was Bridewell, once a royal palace on the left bank of the Fleet, given by Edward VI., to be a hospital for the clients of the dissolved monasteries and a workhouse for sturdy rogues. After the Fire, it took the form of an institution with miscellaneous purposes, among which came to the front that of punishment, when one of the sights of the town was to see unfortunate women whipped here, screaming "Knock, good Sir Robert, knock!" to the presiding Alderman whose hammer would cut short the tale of stripes. One of Hogarth's illustrations of "The Harlot's Progress" shows ne'er-do-wells, chiefly women, beating hemp at Bridewell under the cane of a keeper, as described also by Pennant: "About twenty young creatures, the eldest not exceeding sixteen, many of them with angelic faces, divested of every angelic expression, and featured with impudence, impenitency and profligacy, and clothed in the silken tatters of squalid finery." But Bridewell, besides a doling of charity, did more wholesome work in training lads to trades and setting them out in life, an undertaking that developed into something like a technical school, still on foot; while at Witley, in Surrey, the foundation has a large boarding school.

Very untoward Blue-coat boys, it appears, might be threatened with being sent to the old Bridewell to be disciplined or taught trades. Its connection with apprenticeship is still shown by the fact, not known to every Londoner, that the City Chamberlain can commit apprentices within his jurisdiction to Bridewell, after a quite paternal and medieval manner. This power is now very rarely exercised; but the modern building, which serves mainly as offices of charities administered by the institution, has also dungeons for unruly youth such as a century ago were sent here to have the offending Adam whipped out of them. The late Rev. E. C. Hawkins, Chaplain of Bridewell, told me, not so many years ago, of its being part of his duty to visit those young prisoners with ghostly counsel, which I am sure took a kindly form. "It generally meant a row with the foreman," was his account of their offence.

Nowadays, to be sure, the City has not many apprentices to imprison; and those are of more orderly behaviour than the Jin Vins and Frank Tunstalls, so impudent and turbulent in Fleet Street when Richie Moniplies exposed himself to their raillery. The 'prentices of that day, "both proper and tall," made an estate of the City's realm by no means modest in their pretensions, heard and seen not only as shouting "What d'ye lack?" to passersby, but, on occasion, by raising the cry of "Clubs! Clubs!" and throwing down their yard-wands or what not, to swell riots that often became serious. In Gay's time he has to tell of 'prentices that their idea of a good joke was to direct inquiring strangers the wrong way, and that they would rush out of their shops to join a mob of street football players. As for Chaucer's 'prentice, "Brown as a berry, a proper short fellow "—

> At every bridal would he sing and hop,
> He better loved the tavern than the shop;
> For when there any riding was in Cheap,
> Out of the shoppe thither would he leap,
> And till that he had all the sight y-seen
> And danced well, he would not come again.

We know how there were industrious as well as idle and bellicose apprentices. Those pages of commerce, gentle or simple by birth, were as much part of their master's household as his squires of a belted knight's; and their servitude was then the honourable initiation to a chosen trade, when the privileges of a freeman were well worth acquiring. But nowadays a draper's or bookseller's apprentices are not too proud of the name or status, while in most crafts carried on in London, apprenticeship, more's the pity, has been dying out through various causes.

St. Mary-le-Strand

ALONG THE STRAND

THE CITY being taken as the heart of London, there are two main arteries by which its blood is put in circulation. One is Holborn, prolonged by Oxford Street and the Uxbridge Road, so as to make almost a straight line through the metropolis, continued eastward from Aldgate along the great Whitechapel highway, in all a distance of some ten miles for a bee that had spare time to measure it from Bow Bridge to Hammersmith. The other, beside the curving bank of the river, has a shorter stretch of a mile or so to the central ganglion where it branches into several veins ; yet its former course may be roughly followed by Pall Mall and Piccadilly, along the Parks and through Kensington High Street on to Kew Bridge. If any thoroughfare is to rank as chief street of all London, it is the Strand, till the other day choked by double tides of business and pleasure, but now opened out more roomily, and its channel seconded by the broad Thames Embankment, on to which a fleet of tramcars has at last broken way. The still raw cut of Kingsway is also drawing traffic into a new current But, as we saunter towards Charing Cross together, we shall follow the Strand as our main line, with peeps of exploration on either side Its name may at least serve us as a text for considering certain aspects of London life, old and new. If a more fanciful title were wanted for this chapter, one might call it "All the World's London."

Beyond Temple Bar, the offices of business merge into a quarter chiefly noted for houses of entertainment. One must not count the Courts of Justice under a head that would seem a mockery to anxious suitors, not to speak of nervous witnesses and impatient jurymen. Yet here are often enacted thrilling spectacles to draw as eager crowds for admission as do any of the Thespian temples neighbouring this modern shrine of Themis, which some aver to be dedicated rather to Æolus, though all its draughts do not clear it of what has been described as "an amalgamated effuvium, a reek of stuff gowns, dog's-eared papers, mouldy parchment, horsehair wigs, imperfectly washed spectators, police constables and witnesses, with a bracing whiff of ammonia from the wood pavement in the Strand outside." What one can say without fear of contempt of court, is that the Strand and its side streets are much given up to theatres, music-halls, restaurant, and hostelries of all kinds, making this the part of London most familiar to strangers, and perhaps to some Londoners.

In the Strand itself it was my chance to meet a young American seeking direction to Furnival's

Inn, where he desired to lodge because Dickens lived in that "hotel." Again I have known another New Englander ready to quarter himself upon the "House" of a celebrated Briton, because he took this title to imply an hotel, as it did in Boston. The Dickens enthusiast was not so far out, since at that time a lodging for strangers was contained within Furnival's Inn, now rebuilt as an Insurance Office by a Company so prudential in its dealings as to have become one of the great landlords of London.

Inns in our fathers' sense, seem to be shrinking out of existence or swelling themselves as "hotels"; but in this part of London there are still "Inns' of much dignity that do not offer accommodation to "transient' guests. The name that began as meaning a large house, is still borne in honour by the Inns of Court, where successful lawyers now have their chambers rather than their homes and would-be successful ones have at least their names on the door to which clients may or may not come. The unsuccessful are not now so "contented to sleep in dingy closets, and to pay for the sitting-room and cupboard which is their dormitory, the price of a good villa and garden in the suburbs"; but some Spartan Templars still spend dusty years in a cramped, rat-riddled garret, perhaps on no sweeter fare than eating their hearts out for disappointment and envy of more fortunate brethren. A. may have been the hopeful glory of his school and college, but he found his laurels soon fade in this smoky air, and has been fain, like George Warrington, to acquaint himself with editors rather than solicitors, while in his chosen career he sees himself passed by the tortoise B., whose first step towards the goal was marrying a "rich attorney's elderly, ugly daughter," or by the once despised C. who brings to this market just the qualities of carefulness, readiness, glibness, unscrupulousness, or what not, that find demand. These old Inns have hid many tragedies of blighted lives, enacted behind the scenes of the legal stage on which not always the best men get the leading parts. I speak feelingly, as one who was to have been apprenticed to this trade, but early deserted to the ranks recruited by many a sucking Solon who

"penned a stanza when he should engross." Looking back to the companions of my own youth, I see how those harnessed to the law have for good or ill not always sped according to promise or expectation. In this career, especially, it seems as if a certain baser alloy were useful in tempering intellectual gold.

The Inns of Court, as we all know, are time-honoured and dignified institutions, each with its Chapel, its Library, and its Hall, through which latter aspirants eat their way to the Bar, now fenced, indeed, by more intellectual ordeals; but the final stage is marked by the ceremony of a call supper, when libation seems the chief rite. The most illustrious of these Inns is the Temple, in which arms may be said to have ceded to the gown. It was the home of that proud, rich, and envied order of Knights Templar, who at the end of the twelfth century moved here from Holborn, like a prosperous barrister rising from Bloomsbury to Belgravia. Hero, in imitation of that of the Holy Sepulchre they were vowed to defend, they built one of their round churches, now owned by a fraternity more devoted to law than to Gospel. The incumbent of this venerable church bears the title of Master, an office shorn of the martial glory that once gave a double halo to the head of priest-warriors, whose swords long ago went to rust, but we cannot be so sure that their souls are with the saints.

One of the darkest puzzles of history is the fate of the Templars, whose crimes, whatever they were, came to be glaringly punished. Their original badge was two men riding on one horse, emblem of a pride that aped humility. By this darling sin of the devil they fell from the height to which they had risen by courage and devotion, waxing so rich and luxurious that their wealth seemed too much to be won honestly, when their Grand Master held his head high as any king. The kings of Europe grew jealous of a power that owned no lord but the Pope, while the arrogance of the Templars made them hateful to great and small. So they had few friends when Philip of France, where their lands mainly lay, cast covetous eyes upon such dubiously

STAPLE INN

earned increment, after he had drained all other resources by adulterating his coinage, robbing the Jews, and even taxing the property of the Church. The haughty Grand Master and sixty of the knights were tortured into confessions that brought them to the stake, like many better men, and some perhaps worse. In England, the Templars had a less cruel ordeal to bear; and there as elsewhere the charges against them were shown to be more or less false. But the Pope seems to have voiced general opinion in abolishing the order by a Bull of A.D. 1312; then some of its members, with part of its property, passed to the rival order of Hospitallers, who, rich as they too had grown, bore a better name, and longer kept their vows in exercise by doughty deeds against the unbelievers.

The Knights of St. John had their own palace in Clerkenwell, a fragment of it now held by the modern brotherhood that has revived their name. The fate of the Templars made a striking lesson for them as to the vanity of wealth; or it may be that, as having no use for the London Temple, they handed it over to the lawyers, a new body in the State, by this time grown independent of the Church clergy. Law made itself at home here so soon that before the end of the century Chaucer could speak of "A manciple of a temple." Chaucer himself is supposed to have had a Temple chamber, when he was fined two shillings "for beating a Franciscan friar in Fleet Street." The Outer Temple, on the western side, indeed, seems not to have been affected by the profession; but the only remnant of this division is its water-gate at the bottom of Essex Street. The rest was partitioned between the two legal guilds known as the Middle and the Inner Temple, separated by barriers not apparent to a layman's eye.

The Temple's quaint and quiet courts make

one of the sights of London, with the old-world gardens blooming among their smoke-grimed walls, green relic of a generation not so hard pressed for choice building-sites. It was in the Temple Garden, according to Shakespeare, that a brawl of noblemen ended in plucking of the red and white roses which became badges for a generation of civil war. The Temple Chambers are mainly occupied by lawyers; yet other occupants have entered under the cloak of a legal tenancy. The name of Johnson's Buildings and the tomb of Goldsmith remind us how authors, too, lived and died here. The Court where Pendennis and his friend Warrington had their rooms, though neither of them appears to have much worn wig and gown, gets its name from the Middle Temple badge of the Lamb and Flag, so freely displayed on these buildings ; but it may well recall the most famous of all laymen lodged in "those bricky towers." Charles Lamb was born here as son of a Bencher's servant or factotum, at a time when a well-to-do lawyer would be content with such snug quarters. Elia, for one, desired no more congenial home of a dreamy childhood.

"Indeed, it is the most elegant spot in the Metropolis. What a transition for a countryman visiting London for the first time — the passing from the crowded Strand or Fleet Street, by unexpected avenues, into its magnificent ample squares, its classic green recesses: What a cheerful, liberal look hath that portion of it which, from three sides, overlooks the greater garden; that goodly pile

Of building strong, albeit of Paper hight,

confronting with massy contrast, the lighter, older, more fantastically shrouded one, named of Harcourt, with the cheerful Crown Office-row (place of my kindly engendure) right opposite the stately stream, which washes the garden foot with her yet scarcely trade-polluted waters, and seems but just weaned from her Twickenham Naïades! — a man would give something to have been born in such places. What a collegiate aspect has that fine Elizabethan hall, where the fountain plays, which I have made to rise and fall, how many times! to the astoundment of the young urchins, my contemporaries, who, not being able to guess at its recondite machinery, were almost tempted to hail the wondrous work as magic! What an antique air had the now almost effaced sun-dials, with their moral inscriptions, seeming coevals with that time which they measured, and to take their revelations of its flight immediately from heaven, holding correspondence with the fountain of light! How would the dark line steal imperceptibly on, watched by the eye of childhood, eager to detect its movement, never catched, nice as an evanescent cloud, or the first arrests of sleep!

> Ah! yet doth beauty like a dial hand
> Steal from his figure, and no pace perceived!"

Rebuilding has of course wiped off some of the mellow bloom of the Temple; but there are still good old buildings enough to keep up its character. The narrow lane by which it is entered from Fleet Street, shows what London streets would be when the Great Fire was luckily stayed beside the Temple Church. At this entrance, facing Fleet Street, is a house that well deserves to have been taken under the protecting wing of the County Council, though its pretension as a palace of Wolsey seems fondly invented. The device of the Prince of Wales' feathers has suggested it as destined for the short-lived Prince Henry, who died in 1612, about the time this house was rebuilt ; and it is also supposed to have been used as an office of the Duchy of Cornwall. Whatever dignity it may have had, it came down in the world, when about a century ago was moved into it the collection of waxworks formed by Mrs. Salmon, a Madame Tussaud of the *Spectator's* time, so that it may at least have housed the counterfeit presentments of kings and princes. For some two generations now it has been a hairdresser's shop, after at one time being a tavern or coffee-house, such as in Don Quixote's country, too, gave a stage for shows and performances.

Before waxworks were thought of, giants, dwarfs, wild men, scaly or bristly children, and the like prodigies, would come to be exhibited at some such house of call, as appears from a British Museum collection of advertisements, among which one strikes me with misgiving whether a forebear of mine were not a seventeenth- century Barnum.

At *Moncreff's Coffee-House* in *Threadneedle Street,* near the *Royal Exchange,* is exposed to view for sixpence apiece a MONSTER that lately died there, being Humane upwards, and Bruit downwards. Wonderful to behold: the like was never seen in England before. . .

And a very fine CIVET CAT, spotted like a Leopard, and is now alive, that was brought from Africa with it.

When there are said to have been two thousand coffee-houses in London, which did not confine their dealings to temperance beverages, several of them sought to draw custom by an exhibition of curiosities, like "Don Saltero's" Museum at Chelsea mentioned in the *Tatler.* I can only guess at that "Moncreff" as a progenitor of Alexander Moncrieff, who in the next century was host of the "Rainbow" in Fleet Street. His grandson, W. T. Moncrieff, became a more notable showman, author of the dramatic version of *Tom and Jerry* and other once popular plays, the profits of which did not keep him from dying a brother of the Charterhouse, as did his fellow dramatist, T. M. Morton, best remembered by the *Box and Cox* that still have their joint home on our stage.

There were many famous taverns about the Temple, from the days when Ben Jonson took his ease at the sign of the "Devil" that did not get its name from any connection with lawyers, but from an orthodox legend in which the adjacent St. Dunstan figured with his tongs. Child's Bank, one of the oldest in London, the "Telson's" of Dickens' *Tale of Two Cities,* has been rebuilt on its site. Of hostelries on the east side of Temple Bar, some are still extant in name or in a rebuilt form, the "Mitre," the "Rainbow," and the "Cock," whose "plump

head-waiter!" stands embalmed in Tennyson's verse. "Dick's," another famous resort here, vanished a few years ago. The most apparent antiquity is claimed by the "Cheshire Cheese," where pressmen of our day seek inspiration and refreshment in rooms, or at least fittings, that may have been known to Johnson and Goldsmith. Westward, at the corner of Arundel Street, opposite Smith's great newspaper distributing agency, stood the "Crown and Anchor," once famed for Radical banquets, afterwards turned into a club-house, which had various names and chequered fortunes. Here we reach the province of modern hotels ; but first let us have done with "Inns" in the older sense. The old City seems to have been shy of harbouring lawyers, kept aloof on her outer skirts ; and this must make my excuse for stringing their havens on the line of the Strand.

Behind the Law Courts, beside Chancery Lane, that was once a "New Street," lies Lincoln's Inn, also displaying a variety of buildings old and new, from the Jacobean Old Hall, and solid fronts of the next century, down to the restorations carried out under Lord Grimthorpe's domineering auspices. Legend has it that Ben Jonson worked with his trowel on an earlier alteration. The Chapel shows the peculiar feature of being borne up on the arches of an open crypt, if that expression be allowable. The noble New Hall, adorned with a large fresco painting by G. F. Watts, stands on the other side. Another modern building of Lincoln's Inn is the Drill Hall of the gentlemen-at-arms, whose nickname, "The Devil's Own," has been attributed to the wit of George III., while a more professional joke gave them as motto "Retained for the Defence." All along, the lawyers have shown themselves ready to take up arms in time of need, as when five hundred of them marched down to guard Charles I. at the outbreak of the Civil War, and when they garrisoned their gates against the Gordon rioters. The Inns of Court gave forty briefless recruits to the gallant band that won its spurs for the volunteer force in South Africa, and their contingent is now promoted as an Officers'

Training Corps under the new model. But not all the students of Lincoln's Inn seem likely to serve in the Territorial army, since it has become favoured by our dusky fellow-subjects, who at the Hall dinner make a mottled show of black and brown among truly British faces.

Lincoln's Inn Fields, entered from Holborn by their "Turnstiles," form the largest square in London, its twelve-acre area, that would hold the Great Pyramid, now turned into a public garden, and its well-worn mansions much given up to solicitors, though they no longer live and die here as did Mr. Tulkinghorn. Another profession is represented on the south side by Surgeon's Hall, with its grim Museum of skeletons, a place of instruction rather than entertainment. On the opposite side lurks an institution not enough known to the public, that is invited to enter gratis. Nearly a century after Sir Hans Sloane's collections became the nucleus of the British Museum, the eccentric architect, Sir John Soane, had the ambition of earning similar credit. Having quarrelled with his son, an author undutiful enough to criticize the paternal taste, he left to the public his house with its omnium gatherum of contents, including many valuable pictures, a dozen by Hogarth, and other works of art and verta. Among them is the great Egyptian sarcophagus discovered by Belzoni, that Herculean Italian explorer who, on an early stage of his career, was found playing the acrobat at Bartholomew Fair. The Soane Museum, too much ignored, is well worth the trouble of writing one's name in the hall, when it stands open most days in summer. And while at sight-seeing, one should take a look about the Square's south-west corner, where a sweeping clearance of slums has as yet spared one house in Portsmouth street that boasts itself to be the original of the "Old Curiosity Shop."

Gray's Inn, on the farther side of Oxford Street, though it keeps its status as an inn of Court, has been invaded by the laity, its rooms let out to all sorts and conditions of men, and women. I have

THE EMBANKMENT

known a young married couple established here very snugly, not so much at the mercy of such a laundress as David Copperfield's. Dr. Kenealy was, perhaps, the last barrister of note to keep chambers here. But Gray's Inn, too, is redolent of legal memories, Bacon's for one, whose essays are dated from it,and he is said to have laid out the gardens, after his own model, planting a now decrepit catalpa tree, the slip of which may have been brought across the Atlantic by Raleigh when this was a chief nursery of learned lawyers. So good Americans must by no means neglect to visit Gray's Inn, where they will see an actual rookery nestled in the grounds of what was once a country house ; and to them, as to Hawthorne, it may have the effect of a spell "to find so much of ancient quietude in the monster City's very jaws, which yet the monster shall not eat up — right in its very belly indeed, which yet in all these ages it shall not digest and convert into the same substance as the rest of its bustling streets." But here, also, some of the most picturesque features have been renovated away, or, again, in part restored from the desecration of a stucco age that defaced the exterior of the beautiful Hall, in which Shakespeare's *Midsummer Night's Dream* is believed to have been first acted before Queen Elizabeth, as the Middle Temple Hall made a stage for his *Twelfth Night*.

In the same once suburban district, just outside the City, and not far off its way to the Courts at Westminster, there are, or were, several smaller "Inns of Chancery" that once made colleges for attorneys; but now that the "lower branch" is fostered by the Incorporated Law Society, these have been tottering down of late years, letting daylight in upon a bewildered multitude of rats. Dane's Inn, no ancient one indeed, is gone. Clement's Inn, where Justice Shallow lay when he heard the chimes at midnight, is smartly rebuilt. Another Inn hard by is hardly remembered except by a street ballad, celebrating a murder that made a great sensation in its day.

They cut his throat from ear to ear,
His brains they battered in:
His name was Mr. William Weare,
He dwelt in Lyon's Inn.

On the opposite side of Chancery Lane, Clifford's Inn stands in imminent peril, at the best, of restoration. Its neighbour, Serjeant's Inn, is down, having lost its *raison d'etre* when the order of Serjeants at Law was abolished in our time, a few survivors pocketing a good solatium in their share of the common property. Mr. Serjeant Cox, the last of the order, had a sharp eye On both worlds; and if not by his Psychical Society enterprises, by the periodicals he owned, the *Field*, the *Queen*, and so forth, he acquired a beautiful seat at Highwood Hill, near Edgware, where the Hall of his Inn was reproduced as a monument. The building itself comes, as I write, to be swept away, like the old houses supplanted by the carefully isolated block of the Record Office, whose not yet blackened walls contain Domesday Book and other treasures of the past. Barnard's Inn, in Holborn, is now full of young life as the Mercers' School; and its neighbour Furnival's Inn, as already mentioned, has been turned into an Insurance Office, while Thavies Inn, near Holborn Viaduct, which seems an *alias* for "Taffy's Inn," could no longer lodge such an ambitious spirit as the ablest member of the firm Quirk, Gammon and Snap. There were others once, which live only in the pages of *Bleak House* and *Pendennis* The "Ancients" of some of these old Inns are reproached with having made too much haste to line their own pockets by selling valuable sites over which custom had given them ownership.

It was not only the rats that were disturbed, when crazy buildings came to be pulled down. Crusty and dusty old bachelors, who had grown long at home in their dark chambers, found themselves driven forth blinking and hooting into raw daylight. I wonder what voice the author of *Erewhon* would have lifted up, had he lived to be evicted from his familiar quarters in Clifford's Inn, apparently the oldest of all, that a century before sheltered Lamb's absent-minded friend, George Dyer. Another friend of mine had the pain of being first burned, then turned out of two successive lodgings in New Inn, a deserted fragment of which stands now awaiting its fall, like a broken back-tooth in the gaping crescent of Aldwych, which the County Council dentists have not yet filled with a new set of structures. My friend, more distinguished in the realm of exact science than in that of imagination, cherishes a romantic belief about both his New Inn sets of chambers, that they were no other than those occupied respectively by Captain Costigan and the Chevalier Strong. Not long ago, he took me over the deserted abode, reconstituting the scene in which one of those worthies bilked his duns by risking his neck to crawl and climb into the friendly neighbour's window, and slip out by an unwatched staircase. Naturally he has no patience with heretics who hold the "Shepherd's Inn "of the novel to have been Clement's Inn in its unregenerate days.

Banished reluctantly from New Inn, this *laudatory temporis acti* found congenial refuge in Staple Inn, a "home of ancient peace," preserved out of sentimental rather than prudential considerations by the Insurance Company that transformed Furnival's Inn, over the way. Outside are the obelisks between which a chain could be stretched to bar the Holborn *octroi* of the City; and the name Staple seems connected with the wool that is believed to have been weighed and taxed in the courtyard of this Inn. Its picturesquely gabled front, now restored, appears the last fragment of Tudor domestic architecture in London, part of it perhaps dating from Richard III. It made one of Dr. Johnson's many residences; in it is said to have been written his *Rasselas,* but he appears to have moved in just as the book was published. It figures among the scenes in *Edwin Drood.* The lawyers have long abandoned it to miscellaneous hermits ; and the fine old Hall, that once no doubt smoked with good cheer, is now taken up by the dry doings of the Society of Actuaries, beneath the bust of a fitting patron saint, the Napier of logarithm memory.

In the great clearance about Aldwych, the rebuilding of which seems to be a little hanging fire, there will no doubt spring up new hostels open to all the world. There was long contention over the christening of this crescent, ended by restoring the old name Aldwych, while the broad road behind leading across to Holborn was loyally dubbed Kingsway, when it began to emerge from a chaos into which had been swept some very unsavoury byways. Quite juvenile Rip van Winkles may wonder what has become of Holywell Street, that shady haunt of old book-hunters, that in its dark back rooms carried on a more dishonest commerce, giving it a reputation it sought to sweeten by re-christening itself Booksellers' Row in its old age. Its original godfather was, of course, the holy well, that springs, I understand, under Gladstone's statue in the now broadened thoroughfare. When this came to be looked into of late, it was found littered with crooked pins and other superstitious offerings such as are still half credulously, half jestingly, cast into sacred fountains from the Land's End to John o' Groat's house.

Holywell Street, a backwater of the Strand, stretched from St. Clement Lanes to St. Mary-le-Strand, both churches now standing well out in the broadened thoroughfare, that at this reach used to be cramped into a rushing strait. St. Mary's, one of the fifty churches called for under Queen Anne to supply the growth of London beyond the City, was built on what had once been a scene of open-air entertainment, for here stood a tall Maypole, carried off, it seems, to Wanstead, where it served a graver purpose, bearing up for the astronomical parson, Dr. Pound, what was then boasted the largest telescope in the world.

Opposite the future site of St. Mary's was the palace built by Lord Protector Somerset, of stone from the slighted Priory of St. John, quarried by gunpowder to that end, a sacrilege that brought no good fortune to the royal Duke. His Somerset House has been replaced by a block of modern buildings, now divided between King's College and various Government offices, best known to the public, perhaps, for the registry of wills. The

THE LAST LAMP, THAMES EMBANKMENT

memory of another princely palace is preserved by the noble Chapel Royal of the Savoy, John of Gaunt's house, burnt by the followers of Wat Tyler. Most of the Strand's side-streets recall how here once stood hotels in the French sense, *entre cour et jardin,* the semi-suburban seats of noblemen and prelates, who, long before the Court occupied Whitehall, built themselves mansions upon the Thames, that was then the best highway to Westminster, or to the Traitors' Gate of the Tower.

> Here Arundel's famed structure reared its frame,
> The street alone retains an empty name. . .
> There Essex' stately pile adorned the shore,
> There Cecil's, Bedford's, Villiers', now no more.

The Water Gate of York House still stands as memorial of the northern Archbishop's palace, afterwards acquired by the Duke of Buckingham. His name and title were long embalmed in five streets beside Charing Cross Station: *George – Villiers – Duke – of – Buckingham – three* of them still in evidence, but George Street became York Buildings and Of Lane was dignified as York Place. Names like Norfolk Street, Southampton Street, and Chandos Street hint at similar beginnings. But John Street, Robert Street and Adam Street record the two builder brothers who left their mark on Georgian London, notably in the riverside terrace christened from them the Adelphi.

The dust of those old Inns once shaken from our feet, we soon come to the quarter of modern hotels. Offices still prevail in the smartened streets leading down from Aldwych to the river; but a little farther west we find the great palaces that have sprung up by the Strand to invite strangers within our gates. The newest of all, that takes the title of "The Strand Palace Hotel," fills the place of Exeter Hall, a place of religious exercises helping to whitewash the old ill-fame of Exeter Street. This institution had followed Exeter Change, about a century ago used as a menagerie of wild beasts,

WATERLOO BRIDGE

which once came near being let loose into the street, when the *must* elephant Chunee struggled to break out of his cage, and after being ineffectually treated with monstrous doses of physic, and of poison, he had to be killed by unskilful hands, the soldiers on guard at Somerset House called in as well as the police; then it took a bombardment of over an hour to lay him low with more than a hundred bullets in his thick hide.

The Strand Hotel now dominates and dwarfs an older hostelry, squeezed up into a corner of it, Haxell's, the *ci-devant* Exeter Hall Hotel, which has a special interest for me, since here I slept my first night in town, or did not sleep till mornng, kept awake through the small hours by the amazing rattle of cabs and the rumble of market waggons. I am glad to see that my first London lodging still holds out, while other old landmarks have been destroyed or removed, like Rimmell's the perfumer's, which blooms afresh a few doors off, but

used to stand at the corner over the way, exhaling such an advertisement, that a Strand boy, asked the way to Exeter Hall, could say "Keep straight on till you come to a smell, and it's just opposite." On the same side of the street, also, has been rebuilt Simpson's, which had a name for solid English fare, along with an incongruous fame as resort of cosmopolitan chess-players to its "Cigar Divan," a refuge of clubless youth in days when cigars were not smoked everywhere. An old picture shows the name of *Simpson* nestling under Exeter Change, with the inscription *Billiard Room* at the corner, so I suppose it had been moved across the Strand before my time. Not far off are good old-fashioned hotels, like the "Tavistock" and the "Bedford," that laid themselves out for bachelors, waited on by discreet and familiar attendants like the old John who received Major Dobbin, after ten years' absence in India, without the least surprise: "Put the Major's things in twenty-three, that's his room."

No modest Major could expect to be greeted thus in the new palace hostels of the Strand, where the guest gets a sense of his own insignificance as No.666 or what not, and mine host becomes a Joint Stock Company, Limited, while the snuffy old waiter, once good enough for John Bull, is translated into a legion of mainly alien menials. Of the army of 10,000 or so who man our London hotels, some three-fourths are estimated to be foreigners. The prosperity of such international caravanserais, whether in the way of cause or effect, implies London's rising in the world as the resort of strangers. Good Yankees, when they died to Broadway or Beacon Street, used to go to Paris; now their Elysian fields seem rather to be sought on the Thames Embankment, where even French tourists come to be familiar figures of late years. It is Transatlantic custom, I take it, that has chiefly made demand for the luxurious accommodation affected by simple-minded republicans away from home. One understands that the sky-scraping hotels of New York look down even on our latest Babels as "back numbers"; but wherever he goes, Uncle Sam is content with nothing but the best to be got; and till he took to visiting us so freely, the best we had to offer him in this sort showed indeed much room for improvement.

Has anyone ever written a complete history of English hostelries, from the "Coldharbours" that supplied only bare shelter for man and beast, like an Eastern *serai*, down through the age of the "Boar's Head" taverns and the "Garters," where Falstaffs "sat at ten pounds a week, " but did not always settle the bill? In my youth, little progress had been made; we old fogeys can remember the Mid-Victorian hotel, at which still lingered the tradition that a traveller's main business was drinking for the good of the house. "Waiter, have you anything to while away the time till dinner?" asked *Punch's* guest, and was promptly answered: "Yes, sir, wine or spirits, sir?" The "Georges" and "Dragons" in country towns are often little developed out of this state, with their cheerless coffee-rooms, their bare bedrooms, their stuffy smoking-rooms, their liveliest apartment the bar parlour used as a club by local sons of Belial; and their choice of cold meat or bacon and eggs for ordinary fare. Cycles and automobiles, of course, have stirred up many roadside inns; while some still remain as dismal as they are depicted by the satirist who, a century ago, wrote so amusingly on *The Miseries of Human Life*. But we remember how, in London, the "Grosvenor" and the "Langham" made a new departure in this enterprise, soon followed by hotels that were not ashamed to take their titles from adjacent palaces, and by big ones tacked on to railway terminuses. Then arose Northumberland Avenue with its "Grand" and "Métropole" that set a copy heading in the matter of hotel names, these soon cast into the shade by others still more pretentious; and the cry is still "They come," even though original shareholders drop off flaccid and drained.

The population of the big hotels about Charing Cross, at their full season, must be equal to that of a small town. All the world and his wife may be seen taking their ease in the dining-rooms and lounges, where they try to look quite at home. One cannot help speculating how many of the gentlemen and ladies, here waited on by liveried menials, are accustomed to other ministrations than those of some neat — handed Phyllis. According to Mr. G. R. Sims, in his *Mysteries of London*, some hotel guests, for all their fine clothes and manners, might be more fitly lodged in a cell of Holloway or Brixton. No doubt the management of such a house of universal call has to keep a detective eye on certain customers, as to whom strange stories could be told. Princes and noblemen may be mixed with the throng; I have stayed at an hotel with a live king, and never knew it till one day I thought of asking why a couple of footmen stood always in waiting by a certain corridor. But most of the people one sees are no doubt mere well-to-do citizens of some kingdom or republic; and I sometimes wonder if many of them would not be more at home in an hotel that provided the essentials of homely yet not inelegant comfort, without such a show of palatial grandeur.

The American guests to whom this "high-toned" style of accommodation recommends itself, used to cause scandal and grudges by neglecting the palm-oil with which such elaborate machinery is greased. Perhaps there are still some stalwart republicans who stand out against paying a cent beyond what is in the bill. In their country, a generation ago, I have known gratuities indignantly refused by social inferiors, if there are any such persons across the Atlantic; and in my own country, north of the Tweed, I have had the same experience, as in no other civilized land. I shall never forget James Russell Lowell's indignation when I asked if I should tip anyone at an American hotel — "Niggers and foreigners, if you like, but an American, never!" Now, if all tales be true, things are so much changed in a generation that the tipping of American hotel life might almost be called blackmail.

However this may be, it seems that in Britain, of late years, tipping has increased, is increasing, and ought to be diminished. It is an old story that at taverns, as in law-courts, even in church services, officiants were paid by fees, not always exactly fixed, though a rough scale would be understood on each side. Some of us can remember how an attempt was made to do away with this unsatisfactory system, when hotels took to charging for "attendance." What happened was that the landlord pocketed the extra charge, while the guest soon found himself expected to pay the servants as before. For this bad custom both parties are to blame. The servant, such is human nature, prefers the excitement of uncertainty; and sometimes, indeed, finds more to be expected of casual generosity than on a strict calculation of the value of his services. The tipper, also human, is apt to enjoy playing the sixpenny or twopenny patron, a most pitiful ambition, and one to be reformed altogether in a truly democratic state, where no man has the right to put his fellow-citizens to an abased attitude of looking out for gratuities.

The case of flunkeys seems past praying for, though the "vails" of old days became a tax that provoked radical reform. One would like to see a revolt against extortionate tyrants of the menial world, such as gamekeepers, who turn up their noses at silver fees, and expect to be bribed by five-pound notes. The evil has its root in the snobbery that has grown so rank in our generation, which does not see self-respect increasing along the rate of wages. In one field this weed has sprung up within quite recent recollection. Hairdressers now, it seems, expect to have a trifle given them, as *dustoor* on the charge for their ministrations. It is, of course, the sheepish public's own fault that it lets itself be thus shorn. At one of the great Stores, a director informs me, the hairdressers men are paid extra wages on the understanding that they get nothing beyond; but, when waiting my turn in that department, one day, I observed how nearly every customer, all the young men, slipped a copper or two into the hand of his officiant; and when I neglected this ceremony my change was banged down in a manner to let me know what I should think of myself. In this matter I feel with J. R. Lowell: I should not so much mind flinging twopences to foreigners; but it goes against the grain to degrade a fellow-countryman by gifts that curse him who gives as him who takes. In a pretty wide range of travel, I have observed how the prevalence of *bakshish* is always in inverse ratio to the standard of honesty and manliness; and it is no good sign of national health that John Bull seems relapsing into an Oriental weakness.

If one had to gratify only some man or maid with whom one had come into serviceable relations, that would not be so bad; but one resents owing tribute to overfed and overfeed personages, who pay large premiums for the right of taxing hotel guests. I can pride myself on once having exhibited great moral courage at a Berlin hotel, whose proud porter, all gorgeous uniform and insolent swagger, would hardly answer a civil question till it came to the point of departure; but when, gold-laced cap in hand, he cringed at the omnibus door, I dumbfounded him by a carefully composed address to the effect that I owed him nothing for civility, and for his pretensions would pay not one pfennig: my

FLOWER GIRLS IN THE STRAND

German fellow-travellers seemed to think me over bold as venturing thus to rebuke a man in such a uniform. In Austria, where already is felt a breath of the East, one pays for every meal at the time, and there are usually three waiters who levy a trifling tip, while one has done the work. This exaction became so troublesome, that some time ago, there was a movement of setting up "Reform" hotels, where tips were not to be expected: I know not if this reform has proved practicable. In Messrs. Lyons' Popular Cafe, a good example was set by what seems an honest and serious attempt to prohibit tipping; and in the Strand Palace Hotel, under the same proprietorship, we are assured that this rule is to be enforced. It is said that self-respecting waiters would gladly work on another system. It is also said that the waiters who protest against tips are those done out of their fair share of the tribute. Whatever arrangements may be made to abate this bad custom, it will be hard to hinder the British snob from commanding respect and attention by a paltry bribe.

Where tips seem most out of place is in a bath, yet there most surely pocketless customers have hands held out to them. I see that a bath-shampooer who has written his memoirs, puts as the climax of a good bather's qualities giving the attendants "their accustomed fee, whether the authorities allowed it or not"; and he gravely tells of one gentleman who, having omitted "the usual shilling", was so conscience-stricken that next time he made it a guinea by way of smart-money. If all clients were so open-handed, a shampooer, whose business at least puts him to small expense for tailoring, would make a good thing of it. This reminiscence draws me out of the Strand to where, beside the fruit and vegetable market of Covent Garden, we see one old name that has a history the "Hummums" Hotel, at which poor Thaddeus of Warsaw paid his last guinea for dinner and breakfast. So far back as Charles I.'s reign, it appears, a *Hammam* or sweating bath was set up, perhaps by some Eastern traveller, in the ex-Convent Garden of Westminster Abbey, then turned into our first square of gentility, surrounded by mansions and the piazzas that still in part remain.

An allusion in the *Spectator* shows how *hummums* became an English name for a hot bath; and Dr. Johnson told Boswell of his wife going to be cupped at this hotel, which seems to have long carried on some such hygienic or hydropathic practice, of which there is no hint in Miss Porter's novel.

It comes as a surprise to find the Turkish bath introduced among us almost as long ago as the slang word *chouse,* said to record the cheatery of an Ottoman ambassador's *chiaus.* At Brighton, when its Pavilion was still a palace, we hear of an Oriental who there practised some such treatment on a select body of patients. But the modern vogue of hot-air baths is due to a well-known character in his day, David Urquhart, M.P., celebrated for his vehement eccentricities, among them a constant suspicion of Russia and of Lord Palmerston, and his sympathy with what he lauded as "the Spirit of the East." This fanatic of Orientalism had a house near Watford, where he discomposed his visitors by receiving them in a bath at a temperature well on to boiling-point, himself and his family clad in turbans and gold-embroidered sheets. It was whispered that one of his children fell a victim to hydropathic discipline. His servants had to sweat in company with their master ; and his political admirers found their faith oozing at every pore when kept waiting an hour or two in a hot-house till the prophet could receive them.

Urquhart found a disciple in the Irish Dr. Barter, who about sixty years ago used the Turkish bath at his Hydropathic Establishment at Blarney, near Cork. Thus it may be that in some parts of the Continent such baths are known as "Irish-Roman." Not long afterwards the Hammam in Jermyn Street was started by Urquhart himself, then the new practice soon began to spread. In the sixties, I remember another Turkish bath in or about Marlborough Street. This, I fancy, was the scene of Trollope's amusing adventure in *An Editor's Tales,* where he describes himself as followed into the bath by a would-be contributor, spending his last three-and-sixpence on a chance of more than barefaced introduction to such a patron. What seemed like a real Eastern bath than our luxurious Hammams, was a shabby, stifling den in Leicester Square, frequented by Levantines and others to the manner born; this became taken over and much improved by Mr. Bartholomew, who perhaps did more than anyone to popularize Turkish baths in different parts of the country. Since then many have sprung up in other quarters of London; and most of them seem to flourish in a way showing how they supply a felt want; but one notes that the most frequented have lately added the Russian vapour-bath to the hot-air rooms.

We have passed by without notice the oldest bath in London, filled by Romans from the Holywell or some adjacent spring. This Roman Bath, one of the most interesting relics of Old London, may still be seen down the narrow turning of Strand Lane, beside Somerset House. It belongs to a large draper in New Oxford Street, whose staff, I am told, have the privilege of refreshing themselves for business in its cryptic pool, now known to few Londoners ; but in my youth it was open for a bracing dip in hot weather, while also the water-drawn from a separate basin, *bien entendu* was in demand for hotel tables. The bath habit came to us, as no doubt to Rome, from the perspiring East; and to Anglo-Indians we chiefly owe the daily tub that now seems a characteristically British institution. Our time has seen also the opening of many public baths, mainly due to that bogy of individualists, Municipal Enterprise. Some of us can remember how only here and there could be found a small swimming-bath, while in hot weather unabashed youth had more freedom as to washing in the Thames or the Lea. *Washing* is the significant word in old books, before London houses of any pretensions had bath-rooms, and before young University men, like Pendennis and Warrington, began to set up shower-baths in their chambers, to the disgust of grimier Templars in the floors below. But one kind of bath has not taken root here, such floating basins as line the bank of the Seine at Paris. Such a one was placed in the Thames, a generation ago, beside Charing Cross railway-bridge. The

charge was high, and in summer it seemed well frequented, yet it did not pay : I speak feelingly, as a share-holder. Before long it was towed down to Southend, where now, with the help of the tide, it laves East-end trippers.

To return to the head of hotels: one wonders if these new palaces that seem to raise the *dernier cri* of luxurious living away from home, will ever come to be looked down upon as behind the times. We know how once famed hostelries have fallen out of favour and fashion. Captain Gronow tells us how in his day the fashionable hotels were such as the Clarendon, Grillon's, Long's, and Limmer's, which last a poet rhymes with

> Brimmers.
> For gallant young gentlemen, burdened with care.

Long's still holds out in Bond Street, and some of its contemporaries thrive more or less profitably ; but others, through one cause of decay or other, have lost even their name. Nerot's, where Colonel Newcome put up, is now the St. James's Theatre. Only the other day the Star and Garter at Richmond, once renowned as scene of not austere hospitalities, came to be shut up, perhaps only for a time ; and two other chief hotels of the place have also retired into private life. The riverside hotels that once netted much custom for fish dinners, seem not to keep that fame fresh. For such decay of suburban houses of entertainment, motoring is blamed, that carries pleasure-seekers so much farther afield; then, of course, many once noted hostelries have gone off with the coaches for which they made a starting-point.

It is about Charing Cross that in our time has sprung up the thickest banyan grove of millionaire bivouacs ; but this now sends out suckers westward, into Piccadilly and Mayfair, where some old houses, like Claridge's, in which crowned heads have been able to sleep at ease, take fresh root and expand themselves by new buildings. And in this quarter's side-ways there are some modest-looking havens of high rank, not so well known to the man

IN THE STRAND: WAITING FOR ELECTION NEWS
*During an election the Daily Graphic exhibited at its office cartoons of Lord Salsbury and Mr Gladstone,
each mounting a ladder; the rungs above each statesman represented the seats he had won.*

in the street, but familiar to *habitués* who shun the more sumptuous caravanserais: we remember the quiet hotel at which Lord De Guest entertained Johnny Eames. Bachelors, like Mr. Eames, when their means allow, may live hereabouts in small establishments that are a sort of cross between an hotel and a lodging-house

Farther west, out Kensington way, we have a new class of hotel that seems to be frequented by visitors making a long stay, verging indeed into high-class pensions. And a great smartening has come to the more modest boarding-houses of this quarter, shy as they are of that name, "stained with all ignoble use." Some of us know, if only from novels, the frowsy boarding-houses of the last generation, refuge of old maids, young men in offices, and odds and ends of not always solvent humanity. In less choice quarters one might find such a home as Johnny Fames had with Mrs. Roper in his early days; but the "paying guests" of Kensington and Bayswater need not complain of what they get at often moderate terms. As for "Todger's," now that rents in the City are so high, and fares to the suburbs so low, it has long vanished, or taken off its customers to some roomier and airier site.

Another class of hostelry that has much improved in our time is the Temperance Hotel, a name once of some reproach, often denoting nothing more moral than a house that could not get a license. A number of good hotels of this order have been opened in the Bloomsbury quarter, about the British Museum, where their accommodation at a moderate fixed charge recommends them to modest American visitors, at home not used to ordering wine with their meals. And, indeed, at all British hotels Boniface, in whose eyes teetotalism used to be a scandal, has had to adapt himself and his charges to the fact that a good many customers can and will dine without giving him a chance of making cent. per cent. profit on the "wines of commerce."

In the City, naturally, are busy hotels hiving men of business; and here, too, in out-of-the-way nooks, some cramped old inns of Dickens' day still

keep a connection with foreigners. But foreigners, for the most part, notoriously drift to the Soho quarter and the purlieus of Leicester Square, where their tastes are catered for at many houses of entertainment, including some surprisingly cheap restaurants, sought out by British customers also, if only to get a relish of Continental ways. It is forty years ago that I, vainly taken for a man who knew his "town," was trusted to guide certain young Oxford dons to a real French dinner in this petty France. To get up an appetite for the choice feast, we walked far afield in Surrey; then as the shades fell, I had to betray quite rustic ignorance by leading my friends to a very ordinary hotel, where we had a very ordinary dinner at a very ordinary price, and felt as much disappointed as the would-be fast damsel, who, having screwed up her courage for reading a French novel, worked with grammar and dictionary through George Sand's *La Petite Fadette*, to find it not so unlike a tale that would pass muster in any Sunday-school. Since then, it has become less hole-and-corner work to nose out a foreign dinner in or about Soho.

The present writer, as reviewers modestly style themselves, has a confession to make which will show how ill-qualified he still is to speak of the many tables spread in central London for his fellow-citizens according to their tastes and means. I grew up to think it unmanly to make much fuss about eating and drinking, nor have I seen cause to change that philosophic opinion. Having sometimes found myself in places and circumstances where I was glad to get anything wholesome to eat, I can say a perpetual grace over the plainest fare, and am apt to be somewhat contemptuous of both *gourmands* and *gourmets*, especially when they affect turning up their noses at food for which many would be thankful. So I am behind the fashion of my time, which the most unobservant bystander must note to have grown less greedy, but more nice, not only as to the kickshaws of the West-end, but as to the sardines and tinned salmon that seem the luxuries of the East. One observes, moreover, that restaurants, of the class that considers quality rather than quantity, have become more showy, more cheerful, and more varied in their fare than they were under the consulship of Plancus; also, that the best hotels now lay themselves out for tempting rich people to dine away from home. It should be observed, with concern, that people who have already too much to eat fall into the way of taking another meal in the middle of the night, at resorts lying handy to their scenes of pleasure; and it appears that not even Sunday now makes a Sabbath truce in the perpetual war upon ennui among feasters who would be all the better of fasting once a week on domestic cold mutton, as was oftener the practice of their austere fathers. But if I say much more on this subject, I may be silenced by a hiss and howl from Harley Street. Doctors must live, as well as waiters and the shareholders in hotels and restaurants, who are all concerned in encouraging the pecunious public to "do itself well."

Being no good judge of such matters, I have taken counsel with a friend versed in the science of gastronomy. He informs me that there is not much to choose between the restaurants in vogue from time to time; that most of their customers will be well content so long as the charges are high enough; and that, once a name is won for luxury and fashion, the snobbish sheep come flocking in to fatten beside the "best" society, that so willingly exhibits itself in a glow of electric light. Another friend of mine, simpler in his tastes, has a humorous tale of how, seeking to restore nature on a modest chop or suchlike, he strayed into one of those "smart" restaurants, how he opened his eyes at the bill of fare, and how he was able to "get out for" a sum which may be left to the reader's imagination.

It would take too long, even if one were able, to describe all the eating-houses of London, from its public tables of Lucullus to its humblest cocoa-rooms and the suburban "pull-up for carmen." The sourest stoic must admit that, in certain departments of this province, there has come about a marked improvement, thanks mainly to foreign influences brought to bear upon John Bull's monotonous and wasteful cookery. The stuffy old chop-house, in which he was wont to box himself up with his heavy meal, is being smartened and ventilated out of all recognition. Now British firms take a lesson to expand our shabby tea-rooms into popular cafe's, that want only sunnier skies to flourish as on their native boulevards. Another innovation is vegetarian restaurants, at least one of which has grown almost into fashion within a stone's-throw of Charing Cross. Till lately such resorts of a peculiar people resembled rather the Manchester "Fruit Parlours" at which David Grieve had his economical meals. I can remember what was perhaps the first vegetarian eating-place set up in London, by Dr. and Mrs. Nichols, who found a wide sale for their booklet *How to Live on Sixpence a Day,* its success rivalled only by a contemporary publication, *How to make Fowls Pay.* That American couple came over here as reformers in various lines, which seemed to make rather a tangle of their activities: they were missionaries of Catholicism and of Spiritualism, as well as of Vegetarianism and other exotic principles. Mrs. Nichols claimed to be the first woman who, in this generation, had taken a medical degree; and she tried to set up at Malvern a school for teaching girls some sort of esoteric medicine akin to what has since become known under such names as Faith Healing and Christian Science; but I fear this pioneer never made such a good thing of her mysteries as did Mrs. Eddy. Nor did she succeed as a prophetess, for her familiar saints had revealed to her that she was to be the instrument of my conversion to Rome, as seems now out of the question, unless ghostly persuasions can avail.

The Nichols professed to live according to their own precept on sixpence a day; but their guests were well served with the obnoxious ox and the pernicious pig, as I can testify, who once enjoyed their hospitality, when the lady's first question to me was, delivered in a solemn Yankee drawl: "Sir, do you devour the corpses of dead animals?" Though bound to confess that bad habit, I asked them to let me share with them their sixpenny fare, being never unwilling, once in a way, "to sit a guest

THE BELL INN, HOLBORN

with Daniel at his pulse." I can report that we had two dainty and appetizing meals, the *pièce de résistance* being some preparation of crushed wheat, still sold, I believe, as "Dr. Nichols' groats." My hosts ate only at ten and three o'clock; but out of consideration for British weakness, they sent up to my bedroom half a slice of bread, three plums, and a glass of water, to which I added an indulgence that displeased the mistress of the house. At this time she had lost her eyesight; but on my appearing before her next morning, she rebuked me thus: "I see, sir, or rather, another of my senses instructs me, that you use, or, to speak more truly, abuse the herb called tobacco. Now, you go right away up the hill to the well of the blessed St. Anne, and vow to her that you will never smoke again." I went to the well, but I made no vows; and this may be mentioned to show that, if critical on other folks' cakes and ale, the reader's humble servant is not beyond reproach by more austere Philosophers.

The restaurant started under Dr. Nichols' name was carried on in Oxford Street till quite recently, but of late years took to propagating the new vegetarianism that makes a special cult of nuts and other fare found digestible by our Pithecoid ancestors. Having strayed off so far into reminiscences, I come back to the Strand, passing many theatres, that prompt me to fix the date of my first appearance on the stage of London by Sothern's Lord Dundreary, as the dramatic sensation of the day. Between the acts, I had come out to air what must have been my first dress-coat at the Portico of his theatre, when, to my surprise and confusion, a strolling damsel accosted me. "Well, Charley, how do you like London?" To this generation Charley's Aunt will be more familiar than Lord Dundreary; and it is not every Playgoer of today who in *Babil and Bilou* has heard the once Popular song, "Spring, Spring, Beautiful Spring," that, if I err not, was the work of mine host of the Exeter Hall Hotel. One's first coat goes threadbare hardly sooner than one's illusions. I wonder if I should now scream with laughter at Dundreary's stammering epigrams, or be moved to hum that chorus flattering the

"loveliest season of the year," whose east winds come to make themselves felt by old fogeys as its most striking quality. My first disillusioning in stage enchantment must have come early, for it was at the time of the Fenian troubles, when an Irish actor-manager starred it in one of Dion Boucicault's Irish plays, I forget whether *The Colleen Bawn* or *Arrah-na-Pogue*. In his part as a patriotic hero, he sang "The Wearing of the Green" with such effect as to bring tears into some eyes of the audience. Soon afterwards I met him at supper, where he was asked to sing, and, like Tigellius and other *cantores* of all ages, gave much ado before letting himself be pressed, but at last obliged us with that song which current political excitement made a topical one —

Sure it's-the most distressful country that ever yet was seen,
For they're hanging men and women for the wearing the green.

So he sang with all pathetic tenderness, but shocked me by adding in a comic aside "Serve them right, the blackguards!" The Orangeman had dropped the actor's mask.

That reminds me of meeting J. L. Toole at a social gathering where he was asked to sing. Without any *façons*, he began successively three songs, one of them about "The Speaker's Eye," which he was then singing every night in his theatre; another "An 'Orrible Tale," which he must have sung thousands of times all over the country. But this time he broke down in the words of each one, explaining that on the stage he had certain points to give him a cue, without which he here stood at a loss. In place of a song, then, he volunteered to tell us a story, a somewhat "edited" version of which I have more than once seen in print, so I will only relate that the heroes of it were himself and Buckstone, and the scene that same portico where I was put to shame by being detected as a young man from the country.

Were it my cue to dwell on dramatic matters, I could wish to have better borne in mind the talk of two men in whose company I used to sit a generation ago — Jonas Levy of Gray's Inn and Kingsgate Castle, known for his collection of theatrical books and for his liberality to the Dramatic Benevolent Fund — and Thomas Spencer, one of the practical inventors of electro-plating, who lived well on towards the end of last century. For one keenly interested in the subject as, to tell the truth, I was not — it would be a treat to hear those seniors jogging one another's memory to recollections of all the famous plays and players that had appeared in London during half a century. What I best remember from Mr. Levy's lips is the story of how he embarked at Newhaven for the Continent — once, as the lady in the *Overland Route* says when asked if she had ever tried So-and-so's tea —how his sufferings were so acute that he used his authority as Vice-Chairman of the Brighton line to make the boat put back, and how he never again attempted to leave his native shore, though any day he might cross the Channel as a distinguished deadhead.

Of Spencer also I have a tale to tell, that became a legend in the club which was the scene of it. He was a Tory of the school of Strafford and Laud, as hot on politics as on certain grievances he nursed about inventions for which he had failed to secure a profitable patent. One day I came into a room in which he had been at fierce controversy with a Liberal editor. The disputants having reduced one another to fuliginous silence, I felt that a moral window should be opened, and cast about for some neutral theme likely to relieve the tension. I had just been buying a newly-introduced filter which I thought might interest Spencer, not aware that this was one of the patents as to which he thought himself defrauded. On the mention of that sore subject, the legend makes him burst into a torrent of "language" that would not be licensed by the Lord Chamberlain: as a matter of fact, he simply sat and gasped at me. Another tradition of the club represented these two rich men as lighting their pipes one night with £1,500 worth of I.O.U. paper from fellow-members, who were mostly less fortunate authors, artists, and the like, so among them such

patrons had a good chance of having their anecdotes well received.

Now, had I listened more dutifully to those reminiscent worthies, I might here tickle the reader's attention with matter that deserves to appear in print. But, indeed, I have left myself little space to speak of that other kind of entertainment, the high places of which are thickly set in this quarter. Within a radius of half a mile or so, may be counted more than thirty theatres, and new ones coming on to swell the list. Would the "good Lord Shaftesbury "not turn in his grave if he knew how half-a-dozen of them stand side by side in the street named to honour his memory? Old and new, the theatres about Charing Cross reckon themselves as the aristocracy of the stage-world, whose voucher gives a play the right to go on its travels as a Metropolitan success. But while trains and trams fill them from all parts of London, nearly every suburban region, too, has now its theatre, some of these hardly "minor" in pretensions, and most of them likely to be visited, sooner or later, by whatever piece has pleased a central audience. In all, London's theatres are some three-score, commissioned according to our insular want of system. Drury Lane and Covent Garden hold letters patent from the Crown, in old privilege; the majority are licensed and controlled by the Lord Chamberlain, whose censor has been a thorn in the flesh of certain dramatists; the rest, in outlying parts, stand under the stern eye of the County Council.

The theatrical profession has risen in the world as its standing-places have widened. It claims social recognition, aspires to titles, and off the stage hides marks of the dyer's hand under the best of kid gloves. Its leading gentlemen and ladies draw salaries that would astonish a Crummles or a Fotheringay; some pets of the public in their day of popularity may be better paid than a Bishop or a Cabinet Minister; while one fears that the rank and file of a troop never wanting ambitious recruits, have often still to experience such bouts of poverty as play a part in old novels. And as in other professions it is not always the best practitioners who get the largest fees, so here also fortune seems not always fair in the distribution of motor-cars and diamonds. As for successful dramatists, the chorus of common authors declare them scandalously over-paid. We must console ourselves by considering how hard it is for them to get themselves put on the stage; and how often, when they hope to bear their blushing honours thick upon them, as a once prosperous actor-author has it, the very first night "comes a frost, a killing frost." But if their fruit do set and ripen to the public taste, it finds such a profitable market that more than one playwright of our day is credited with an annual income to set Shakespeare up for life.

The heels of theatres become jibed by innumerable music-halls, developed from such humble "Caves of Harmony" and "Back Kitchens" as were known to Thackeray's heroes. In these spectacular chapels of ease, the service of pleasure is said and sung with less formality and restraint, but not with less *mise en scène*; and the most sumptuous Opera-houses can no longer look down on some of those showy rivals. Even as dissenting tabernacles now ape the architectural pretensions of the Establishment, the Halls have been growing into Variety Theatres, whose visitors sit at more freedom, pipe in mouth, if not beaker in hand. The chairman, with his refrain of "Give your orders, gents!" who once made the mainspring of such entertainments, has run down in our time; and decorum is wound up to a higher-point as well as decoration. Ladies are not ashamed to be seen here, who, if I remember right, visited "Evans's" rather by stealth, peeping down from a grating like that of the House of Commons Gallery; and this was only in its latter days, when Paddy Green had grown so respectable as to engage cathedral choir-boys as a chorus. The moral atmosphere of such places must have become less smoky and beery since the days of tbe "barbarous conviviality of the Cider Cellars," and the *Judge and Jury* burlesque where a living caricature of Lord Brougham pleaded before an unrevered chief Baron, whose name was writ in much gin and water. On the other hand, one suspects a decline in the mental tone of

such amusements, pitched to the low note of intelligence struck in much of our popular literature. Music-hall "turns" seem much of a piece with the snippety "tit-bits" of a press that strains itself to furnish topical sensations and exciting novelties. I could never understand a queer kink in the nature of a friend of mine, else a man of austere morals and of somewhat priggish manners — R.I.P. Among his few indulgences was an earnest devotion to music-halls, where he took me in a missionary spirit, and when I was moved to yawn or smile, he would frown sternly as at one misbehaving in church. But most of our fellow-countrymen seem to take this pleasure not too sadly nor thoughtfully. Even at temples of the legitimate drama, when any serious masterpiece has a long run, it is most often as turned into a gorgeous spectacle with limelight always poured upon some popular favourite.

The stage, on one side indeed, affects to take itself very seriously. Besides holding the mirror to nature, it sets up a pulpit for preaching on social problems, and has lessons of topsy-turvy ethics to exhibit as well as Punchinello somersaults. One comes across grave revolutionists who frown at such works as the Bible and Shakespeare as "anti-social," while they hail a new gospel in plays with a purpose, which to greybeard critics seem more like a revolt against old commandments. This is not the place to judge such pretensions; but one observes that still in no small proportion of our palaces of pleasure, the main attraction is seeing women do what few of the spectors would for the world see done by their wives and daughters. In most of us there are chords that will thrill to the piping of some "Fifine at the Fair"; and it is a story older than Shakespeare's 'round O" on Bankside that theatres are apt to be closely neighboured by houses of less placarded fame.

Yet vice has been learning here to pay homage to virtue. There are said to be still dens of London, where one can sneak in to see such shameful sights as are more open in Eastern cities. But all the memorizing old fogies are in one tale as to the higher standard of propriety which half a century has brought to the public amusements of London. The plays of Congreve or Wycherley could hardly be put on the stage now, when importations from the boulevards have to be much dressed to pass muster with what the *esprit gaulois* sneers at as our prudery. Our lively Latin neighbours, too, through the eyes of their most thoughtful authors, begin to recognize the modesty of the Teuton as a valuable asset of national life, so we need not be sorry or ashamed if our more honest laughter is given to dramatists that durst not too openly snigger over the frailities of human nature.

But that London has still much to learn from both moralists and sociologists, may be seen when the seamy side of it is turned out into certain streets, lit by midnight glare of folly and sin. That is called seeing life, where a thoughtful mind sees death rather, painted and bedizened to parade a false gaiety under the electric lights of civilization. In this quarter of entertainment for man, and for the beast in man, British frredom allows a scandalous licence to the solicitations of vice, better cloaked and masked in some capitals that make less profession of decency: thus foreigners are led to exult unduly over a display of social evil that at the best is London's shame. Nor is it only the forlorn "daughters of joy" who touch an honest heart with sadness: beside their flaunting forms go slinking shadows of crime and misery. When the theatres and music-halls have put out their illumination; when respectable citizens have gone sleepily home from business or pleasure; when the hotel and public-houses have closed their doors, and belated wanderers must content themselves for refreshment with coffee-stalls and hot-potato cans; when the poorest guests have huddled up in their doss-houses or charitable shelters, there are still many to whom London streets offer but stonily cold harbour for pinched stomachs and downcast faces — penniless outcasts lurching and limping in search of some dark arch to creep under, some shivering — place on a bench along the Embankment or in Trafalgar Square, perhaps some solitary corner from which to leap into a last bed in the black-flowing river" —

Anywhere, anywhere
Out of the world!

VILLIERS STREET

CHARING CROSS

CHARING CROSS stood a mile out of old London, when it began to stretch its "Liberties" beyond the walls. From Ludgate a road, in time bordered by mansions and gardens, ran along the Strand of the Thames to the village of Charing, that long made a station on the way to the Palace of Westminster, and was no doubt well provided with inns, where many a cask of ale would be tapped for the attendants of courtiers and suitors, or for strolling citizens. By Edward I. a monument was erected at each resting place of his beloved Queen Eleanor's body on its funeral procession from Grantham to Westminster, the last of the series being at Charing, for which name *Chère reine* has been fancifully suggested as origin; but it occurs also in Kent. On the border of Middlesex, the roadside Eleanor Cross at Waltham stands restored by a more reverent generation than those Puritans who destroyed Charing Cross as a relic of superstition. The modern memorial of the latter has been placed in front of Charing Cross Station; but it is believed to have stood where Charles I.'s statue now looks down Whitehall towards the scaffold upon which he stepped from a window of his palace, and towards the Parliament-house that has overlaid his throne.

This hamlet was bound to grow when taken under the wing of royalty. Wolsey's York Place, appropriated by Henry VIII., came to be rebuilt under the name of Whitehall, from which Queen Mary could catch sight of Wyatt's straggling band as it passed through Charing to attack Ludgate. The noble palace designed here by Inigo Jones was never completed; and Charles II.'s seraglio, no longer suburban, Dutch William deserted for the more modest Palace of Kensington. Of the magnificence of Whitehall, mainly destroyed by accidental fire, nothing is left but part of one wing, the Banqueting Hall, a building long used as a Chapel Royal, but now as the Museum of the Royal United Service Institution, fitly neighboured by the new War Office. Across the street, the Horse Guards, where two mailed and booted sentinels sit living statues on horseback, to the admiration of strangers, seems to have made a gateway of the palace leading out to St. James's Park. The Cockpit, used in Pepys' day as a theatre, is understood to have been on the present site of the Prime Minister's Downing Street residence. The Palladian style of the structure is represented in the new Government offices that line a great part of Whitehall, and may one day make a complete avenue of public palaces between Trafalgar Square

UNDER HUNGERFORD BRIDGE

and the Abbey.

It is only within the last century that Charing Cross became centre of Greater London, the boundary mark between East and West. At the date of Nelson's crowning victory, a narrow, dirty lane of mean houses led by the Church of St. Martin's, that once could be rightly described as "in the fields." "Hedge Lane," too, ran north beyond the site of the National Gallery, not begun till 1832; and about this time the square came to be cleared from unsightly buildings known as the King's Mews. The Grand Hotel belongs to the early part of our own generation, when Northumberland Avenue was opened by the needless demolition of Northumberland House and the suburban emigration of that ducal lion that, according to a hoary Cockney jest, wagged its tail as often as it heard twelve o'clock struck. There are Londoners still alive who remember how this fine site was bordered by a truly British jumble of dubiously pretentious buildings and very ordinary shops. Till 1830 an actual Hay Market was held not far off, now transferred to the Cumberland Market beside Regent's Park. Some aged citizens may have crossed the Thames by the Hungerford suspension bridge, whose second-hand frame went to span the gorge of the Avon at Clifton. Not so many memories will go back to the days when Charing Cross Station was Hungerford Market, and little Charles Dickens worked resentfully at a rat-riddled blacking factory factory on Hungerford Steps, a scene of real life transferred in *David Copperfield* to Blackfriars Bridge. Ever since, the area about Charing Cross has been undergoing a transformation, not yet complete. Only the other day was an opening made from the Square into the Mall, giving a vista towards Buckingham Palace. Now the ribboned sergeants will be going off their post at the corner of St. Martin's Lane, since the barracks behind are destined to swell the *cadres* of the National Gallery.

Were Dickens alive to-day, he might tell us how the Tourist and Exchange Offices about this international rendezvous were humbly prefigured by a starting-point of coaches at the "Golden Cross," as, indeed, we know from the adventures of Mr. Pickwick. But not yet has the counsel of perfection taken form by which Charing Cross was to be a great central railway station, knotting together all the lines that come into London. Even Paris, that loves system and centralization as we do not, was fain to scatter her terminuses far apart in the suburbs. Surely it is time to banish the pedantry of *termini*, as to grant full right of naturalization to the vernacular *'bus'*, that reached us through France, as did cab, *cabriolet*, long ago shorn of its outlandish trappings. Did we not take from Italy an idea for the catacomb lines that now act as motor nerves to this ganglion of London communications? The name of the Underground Railway, at least, came from over the Atlantic as one of those jocular metaphors our cousins are so quick to coin. In very early days of railroad enterprise sprang up a philanthropic secret society for helping runaway slaves, and Levi Coffin got the nickname of its "President," when some baffled slave hunter is said to have declared that there must be an underground railroad to Canada from that sly Quaker's house, as his pursuers could never hit on further trace of any fugitive who gained it.

How did Londoners get on without their "Underground," which began to break out through the streets as London became familiar to me? This convenience is supplied by two companies, the Metropolitan and the Metropolitan District, the one, as some of us know too well, paying but a small dividend, while the other, I understand, has returned to its shareholders only the consciousness of being public benefactors, execrated if ever they try to raise the fares on some vain excuse of carrying passengers at a loss. Roughly speaking, the Metropolitan takes the north side of the system, the District's domain being on the south, both of them with long feelers into northern, western, and eastern suburbs. Their rails are linked at Kensington and at Aldgate to form the Inner Circle, a joint main line,

on which frequent trains run round and round in either direction. The fact of two companies being concerned should make one wary which way one turns, as each may be more concerned to carry the traveller on its own metals than on the shortest segment of the circle. I have known country cousins who, living at Brompton and desiring to reach Kensington, innocently took an almost complete round under London to reach a point not a mile off. One hard winter, it was told how a tramp spent his last penny on a short-stage ticket, then passed the rest of the day in that snug roundabout. But only very cold and impecunious travellers welcomed the Stygian atmosphere of the Underground in its days of steam traction, when the northern stretch, from Edgware Road to King's Cross, had a specially foul reputation, and one drew a breath of relief on coming into the open-air reaches, where, also, the trains are gloomily walled out from all brighter prospects than a show of mendacious advertisements. In one such gap near Gloucester Road Station, a moving scene was once enacted, when marriages still had to be performed before noon. A block in the line had held up a train containing a bridegroom in gallant array. As twelve o'clock drew near, anxiety made him bold. Amid the cheers of his fellow-passengers, and the secret sympathy of protesting officials, he and his friends stormed the *glacis* to rush, begrimed and bleeding, to the altar at which a distressed bride awaited them.

The use of electricity has now purged the Underground caverns; and the suburban branches run mainly in the open air. Within the last few years the Circle has been ramified and transsected by deeper tunnels popularly called Tubes, which at many points are brought into touch with it by means of lifts and subways, sometimes so long that in all weathers one can here get a considerable amount of exercise under cover, and in atmosphere kept bright and clean by electrical apparatus, when fog or rain oppresses the upper world. New York, jealous of our "rapid transit," tried to go one better by its spidery Elevated Railway; but then took to burrowing underground after the mole model of London. Our first Tube was from Clapham to the City which for some time remained alone in its fuliginous glory. Then came the more renowned "Twopenny Tube," straight through the centre of London, so called because at first it was found possible to simplify the ticket system: one had the new experience of paying twopence for any distance, passing through a turnstile, descending by a lift, to be bustled into a long car, whisked through a longer hole and again lifted up into the open air. Now, several of these Tubes, the longest of them stretching from Hammersmith to Finsbury Park, are connected at several points; and through bookings between them have brought back the old ticket encumbrance. One can thus travel comfortably from almost any part of London to another for a few pence.

All these fresh aids to locomotion seem to call forth as well as to supply a want, for at certain times of the day they will be found inconveniently crowded. On the District Railway of a foggy evening, one must expect to travel in a mass of human beings literally packed like sardines; and we old fogies at all times may think ourselves lucky to get a seat, where the young and lively press in before us as to a pool of Bethesda. One has seen a Judge on his way to court standing buttressed by fellow swayers, while the bailed criminal he was to try might be sitting comfortably, for the nonce, in the same car. From America has been imported the art of straphanging, not to be done gracefully by all amateurs; and a point of manners arises which is said to have become rather honoured in the breach across the Atlantic. Courteous youth will take pleasure in giving up his seat to a lady; but one has also known a strapping damsel make place for a tottering greybeard. Some little time ago, I saw a scene in the Underground that was quite *fin de siècle*. A lady with a child pushed her way into a crowded carriage, to whom a tired looking City gentleman, since so it must be, gave up his seat. She thanked him, made the child sit down, and stood waiting till someone else rose up for herself, as did not I. Young John

Bull used to be taught more modest manners; but from Brother Jonathan he can learn how youth is the age of honour as well as hope, after which hoary old age must expect at the best to take a back seat. Another symptom of Americanization is the hustle and flurry of these impatient trains that have gone to cut short the lives of many weak-hearted citizens, in danger of being knocked off their legs by dashing youngsters. Hindoos who spread their bedding on the station platform below the unheeded time-table; Andean Indians who may have to wait a week for the next train; Spaniards, whose favourite time for setting out is *mānana* might all be the better of this smartening discipline, but we should seem already quite enough versed in the text "Time is money." Sharp Yankee critics, however, find fault that at every stop one or two seconds are wasted by Mr. Bull's inveterate want of spryness, the blame rather to be laid on Mrs. Bull's headlong eagerness to get into a carriage before other people have got out of it.

Trams are claimed as of Transatlantic invention; and the American G. F. Train lent his name to small jokes when he made a fiasco of introducing them into England, his street rails being indicted as a nuisance. But the first tramway on record was laid long before in Derbyshire, by one Benjamin Outram, who is said to have stood godfather to the name, but if so, only in the way of jest, as tram is a good old English word. Early in last century, a tram-line was laid from Wandsworth to Croydon and beyond, like the first railways, for freight rather than passengers; and in some parts of the country, on the edge of Monmouth and Hereford, for instance, may be seen traces of abandoned rails, remembered as in working only by the oldest inhabitant. I suppose that the *doyen* of our tram-lines in being is that from Swansea to the Mumbles, which has developed into a roadside steam-railway.

It must be admitted that our towns were slow to take up this device, denounced by the owners of free vehicles and by British Conservatism in general. They sprang up in the suburbs about a generation back, and since then have gone far.

St. Martin's-in-the -Fields

NORTHUMBERLAND AVENUE

Whatever we think of the principle of Municipal Trading, we must admire the improvement shown in the L.C.C.'s Electric Trams, hampered as they have been by variety of system and ownership. Some of these lines now run out for a dozen miles and more, ploughing up the country into fresh furrows along which London sows itself apace, as for instance, on the Edgware or the Uxbridge roads, that will soon be each one line of houses, broken by golf grounds and withering patches of market-garden. Still, in this matter London seems behind Lancashire, where a blotched pattern of towns is woven together by leagues of reticulated tramlines; while Uncle Sam, it is claimed, can now travel all the way from New York to Chicago on trolly-cars, in which, let us hope, he may sometimes get a seat. Electricity, either supplied by overhead wires, or by more expensive underground conduits, goes on everywhere supplanting other traction, except in the

City of Edinburgh, which sacrifices to its amenities by an inconvenient cable-system imported from the steep streets of San Francisco, so as not to shock the tourist eye, while to the stranger's ear the underground machinery keeps up a disquieting rattle through which the car steals upon him like a thief in the night. London's last bit of cable-line has lately been supplanted on Highgate Hill.

Trams are not yet suffered in the centre of London, though now they have forced their way across Westminster and Blackfriars Bridges, in vain defended by the House of Lords; and they have even stolen in a subterranean manner from the Embankment to Clerkenwell. Charing Cross is a noted haven of their rivals the motor-'buses, that make long cruises through the length and breadth of London, from Epping Forest to the Elephant and Castle, and from Shepherd's Bush to Ilford in Essex. For a time it seemed as if these privateers would beat off the tram-ways; but now the former have been losing the wind in their sails. Cursed by householders whose quiet they shook, worried by the police, cutting one another's throats by competition, constantly brought to a stand by the breaking down of novel machinery, themselves often the cause of accidents in their wild career, the motor-cars have fallen away from their "first fine careless rapture." Several lines, after indulging a district with the luxury of rapid conveyance, have abandoned this or that field to try pastures new. Whole fleets of earlier rigs, already prehistoric, seem now to be laid up in limbo. Other vessels of the kind venture forth only in summer, upon holiday trips, but shun the fogs and slippery streets of winter. It is understood that in future, no such heavy craft will be licensed to ply in the streets. A generation ago, I heard of a family from Peru taking lodgings in Brompton, where, on the first passing of a 'bus, they all rushed into the street under the impression that it was an earthquake.

As the swift motor halts on its panting course, up lumbers the horse 'bus again, the tortoise taken to be hopelessly beaten in that race. A few years ago a journalist from America, who is understood to have an interest in the sale of motors, made himself horns of iron, and prophesied that by now no horse would be seen in the streets of London. That millennium seems still to be prayed for, the horse dying hard as the dodo. I know several routes on which the old scotched 'bus has popped out alive and kicking, when the motor hid itself like the fine weather goody in a cottage barometer. Scared away by the machine, the horse-drawn vehicle had often to eat its head off, or to seek less beaten routes, on which it might glean wisps of custom; then again it stole back into the busiest thoroughfares, from which it was never wholly banished. Smaller owners may have been overwhelmed, while the large omnibus companies recognize the movement of the times by amalgamations and alliances with their crushing enemy.

Motor 'buses, it must be remembered, are no new thing, for some of the earliest public carriages through London were worked by steam till, after frequent breaking down, they came into collision with the law. As already mentioned, the idea of an omnibus came from France, where it is said to have been born in so illustrious a head as Blaise Pascal's. The first London 'buses, in the Reform Bill period, were run by one Shillibeer, who narrowly missed leaving his name on these conveyances, as Hansom, with less claim to immortality, did on the cabs improved out of his model. But Shillibeer had the bad luck of public benefactors: ruined by keen opposition, by oppressive taxes, and by the dishonesty of his conductors, he restored his fortunes as an undertaker, the name *Shillibeer* being transferred to funeral coaches, that gave it a sinister sound, as a hearse has lent itself to a grim play of words. "*Fortuna lavet fortibus!*" sighed the doctor at a funeral, to be corrected by the parson "Don't you mean the next example: *Mors est communis omnibus?*"

The omnibus world seems at present in a state of transition, so we had better put it that of late years there were two main fleets of 'buses that navigated the streets of London, besides smaller squadrons, and the ruthless "pirates" which sought to steer clear of the law in their petty exactions. The London General Company long reigned paramount, its once profitable shares held largely in Paris, so that when the Road Cars entered the field of competition they distinguished themselves by flying a Union Jack as appeal to British patriotism and patronage. The Road Car Company deserved well of the public that owed to it the improved omnibus, on which no rheumatic gentleman is now asked to go outside to oblige a lady. Time was when only a very "advanced" woman would venture herself outside a 'bus; and, indeed, in former days to ride inside one was not the correct thing for a lady.

Before the coming of the motor, nearly seven hundred omnibuses were counted as passing Charing Cross in an hour. As the horse-drawn 'bus may soon be on its last legs, let us see how it struck a stranger, Mr. W. L. Howells, to wit, in his *London Films.*

"Except for the few slow stages that lumber up and down Fifth Avenue, we have hardly anything of the omnibus kind in the whole length and breadth of our continent, and it is with perpetual astonishment and amusement that one finds it still prevailing in London, quite as if it were not as gross an anachronism as the war-chariot or the sedan-chair. It is ugly, and bewilderingly painted over with the names of its destinations, and clad with signs of patent medicines and new plays and breakfast foods in every colour but the colours of the rainbow. It is ponderous, and it rumbles forward with a sound of thunder, and the motion of a steamer when they put the table-racks on. Seen from the pavement or from the top of another omnibus, it is of barbaric majesty; not, indeed, in the single example, but as part of the interminable line of omnibuses coming towards you. Then its clumsiness is lost in the collective uncouthness which becomes of a tremendous grandeur. The procession bears onward whole populations lifted high in the air, and swaying and lurching with the elephantine gait of things which can no more capsize than they can keep an even pace. Of all the sights of London streets this procession of the omnibuses is the most impressive, and the common herd of Londoners of both sexes which it bears aloft seems to suffer a change into something almost as rich as strange. They are no longer ordinary or less than ordinary men and women bent on the shabby businesses that preoccupy the most of us; they are conquering princes, making a progress in a long triumph, and looking down upon a lower order of human beings from their wobbling steeps. It enhances their apparent dignity that they whom they look down upon are not merely the drivers of trucks and waggons of low degree, but often ladies of title in their family carriages, under the care of the august family coachman and footman, or gentlemen driving in their own traps or carts, or fares in the hansoms that steal their swift course through and by these ranks; the omnibuses are always the most monumental fact of the scene. They dominate it in bulk and height; they form the chief impulse of the tremendous movement, and it is they that choke from time to time the channel of the mighty torrent, and helplessly hold it in the arrest of a *block*."

Most notable is the way in which horses allow themselves to fall into the orderly spirit of all this press of London traffic. A familiar spectacle, much patronized by street-boys, is a cab-horse helplessly fallen, till someone sits on its head, and other volunteers are ready with deft hands to release it from its harness. In London, slippery streets and worn-out legs often cause such a downfall, which you shall see a hundred times for once that you have to fly before a runaway vehicle. A friend of mine who brought a pair of skittish horses from the country, tells me that from the first they adapted themselves to their new environment, going quietly along past all sorts of novel sights and sounds, whereas on rustic roads a railway whistle or a donkey's bray would be enough to set their ears in agitation. Perhaps the fact of seeing so many other horses about them, taking all the din easy, goes to compose their equine minds. Another explanation was offered me by a discreet citizen beside whom I travelled on the top of a 'bus some generation or so ago, when cycles were not yet such common objects of the wayside: a procession of these then tall wheels, bearing lights, flitted ghost-like past our steady vehicle, when I, fresh from experiences of a provincial Bucephalus, admired that the 'bus horses took not the least notice of them. "The fact is," growled my chance acquaintance, "it is the same with the horses in London as with the people: they have too much to do to mind anything but their own business."

Cabs came into London rather before omnibuses, racing off their course the shabby two-horsed hackney coaches that date back to Stuart times, when their first public stand in London, 1634, is said to have been at the Maypole in the Strand. One fears, or hopes, that the cab-horse is on the way to be turned out to grass, its place taken by machinery, till the day come when one can call a balloon or an aeroplane from its stand in Piccadilly. The motor-cabs, popularly called taxis, which a few years ago came as single spies, are now among us in battalions, charging through the central streets at a pace that gives a new terror to crowded crossings. The dashing hansom, "gondola of London," seems like to sink in the collision with these ironclads; while the four-wheeled "growler" keeps afloat only by favour of nervous old ladies, and family parties with piles of luggage. For assurance of the public, these slow vehicles are now invited to equip themselves with the automatic register of distance, which is compulsory on the motor-cabs; though, if all stories are true, even such mechanical reckonings become infected by the notorious dishonesty bred about horse-flesh.

So hard hit have the horse-cabs found themselves, that many of them are now fain to accept the once despised sixpence a mile. For a falling-off in their fares, cabmen have their own stupidity to thank as well as the spread of tubes and 'buses.

Their idea of business seems to be spells of idleness broken by good, fat, easy jobs at not too frequent intervals; and they fail to catch the principle of small profits and quick returns, forgetting how many might-be patrons will not take a cab for a short distance in view of probable unpleasantness about the legal fare. As some excuse for "leaving it to you, sir," London cabmen may well complain of the complicated and rather inconsiderate regulations under which they are tempted to impose on their customers. A Parisian *cocher*, who earns extra payment at night, cannot then be forced to leave his own quarter, denoted by the lamp on his vehicle, whereas the London jarvey may at any hour be taken for his bare fare to the wildest outskirts of the radius area — four miles round Charing Cross — where he has small chance of another job, which might divert him miles farther from home.

THE HORSE GUARDS

The radius system is an absurd one: you may take a cab to Camberwell or Bethnal Green for sixpence a mile; but on the genteel edge of Kensington, from High Street to Hammersmith station, the fare comes to two shillings for little over a mile. When the White City Exhibition rose like an exhalation upon a stretch of ignored rubbish-heaps behind Shepherd's Bush Green, it was discovered that the entrance stood a few yards beyond the radius, to the profit of the old-fashioned Jehu, while the taxicabs are so far under police control, that for them the authorities could "make it so" in correction of an original mistake as to the precise distance. Anyone who has lived close to the radius, can speak of the demoralization it works on suburban cabmen, always on the lookout for a job outwards for which they get double fare, but apt to be "engaged" if the sixpenny area come in question. In the central parts, they learn to be more accommodating, but everywhere the fare becomes often fixed by a compromise between the conscience of one and the open-handedness of the other party. The worst of it is that, when the passenger remembers how the letter of the law may make a tight fit for the driver, the latter is very ready to take a bonus as sign not of bounty, but of innocence, and to grow extortionate in proportion to his customer's generosity. The stranger should know that in any case of dispute, he has a right to be driven to the nearest police-office or police-court, where the matter will be settled; and the mere hint of this procedure is usually enough to silence an unreasonable demand, if not to smooth a sulky look. Miss Tox, we remember, in sending for a cab, always had the man told that the fare was a shilling, and the lady's uncle a magistrate.

Our cabmen might count as angels of conscientious moderation beside, for instance, their *confratelli* of Naples, where the ex-brigands now seek congenial employment as drivers and railway porters. Egyptian donkey-boys are hard to beat for impudent extortion. But the most shameless *wallahs,* in my experience, are those who handle the reins in India, where their gentle beggary has to be repressed by the high-handed curtness of the *sahib*.

I once took a carriage to a railway station in a certain native state, and after having been carried through the narrow streets at a break-neck pace, stirred up in my honour, I felt bound to make the driver's face to shine with special bounty, so I gave him enough to live on for a week, with the result that all the rest of the day, he had nothing better to do than encamp outside of the station, sending in petitions for more.

Foreigners, it is to be feared, are all the world over looked on as fair game by the vulgar. A Belgian visitor told me how, taking a cab from Fleet Street to the books, he inquired the fare beforehand, which was stated at twelve shillings, "and it was usual to give the driver something to drink halfway". Our drivers, indeed, are not averse to so translating the *pourboire* custom of the Continent. But sometimes the supposed stranger turns out a Tartar, as when once from an early train at Ludgate Hill a fur-coated gentleman desired to be driven to the *Daily Telegraph* Office, some hundred yards or two as the crow flies. This was, in fact G. A. Sala, but the cabman, taking him for a distinguished foreigner, treated him to a long and leisurely round, up Farringdon Road to Pentonville, along the Euston Poad to Paddington, down Park Lane to Piccadilly, and so at last by Charing Cross to Fleet Street. Sala, whose most pressing business at the office was to get a nap, made no objection, but took his sleep out in the cab, then, on arriving, handed the man his legal shilling with the remark, "You funny fellow." One takes the story to be apocryphal of Bishop Temple's giving a cabman eighteenpence for a ride to Fulham Palace, and on being satirically questioned as to St. Paul's probable conduct under like circumstances, replying, "St. Paul would have been at Lambeth, and the fare would be only a shilling!"

From the multifarious vehicles whose endless roar and rattle are drowned in this whirlpool, let us turn our attention to the currents and eddies of foot-passengers or loungers that swell the moving flood, from idle boys dabbling on the edge of the fountains, to open-eyed visitors from all ends of the earth, drawn here on business or pleasure. About Charing Cross, an ex-President, or a reformed King of Cannibal Islands, may any day be found rubbing shoulders with our own notabilities, hardly noticed in the throng. I have seen Disraeli tottering over this pavement, like a dressed-up skeleton, with lack-lustre eye and chalky face; and about the same time I encountered Gladstone hurrying alertly through a side-street, his coat-tails flying in the wind. A curious experience comes to my mind. Lunching at a club beside Trafalgar Square, I spoke with my host of three persons, one of them for the moment much before the public eye. On going out, within two or three hundred yards of Charing Cross, I met all those three persons, drawn from different classes and quarters, among a population of millions. What were the odds against the long arm of coincidence gathering such a chance handful, even at the heart of London's whirlpool?

Of the varied crowd swirling round Charing Cross, how many Britons stop to consider what place this familiar area holds in the world? Trafalgar Square is the centre of London, that is the heart of England and contains within its boundaries the meridian from which we measure the world. Still closer at hand, in Downing Street and Whitehall, throbs the administrative pulse of an Empire on which the sun is understood never to set. Some modern geographers have shown cause to take this island as in a sense the centre of the earth. Older philosophers were clear about our globe being the physical pivot of the solar system, as morally it still is for us; and a contemporary pundit of science has gravely maintained that this petty star of ours should rank in the centre of the material universe. These things being so, it seems not doubtful that the Nelson Column stands out the visible hub of creation, even if the Bunker's Hill monument at Boston be allowed as its antipodes. Many years ago I visited Bunker's Hill with no less a cicerone than Oliver Wendell Holmes, to whom in complaisant ignorance I posed as a humbled enemy, forgetting that this was, in fact, scene of a British victory, and that Brother Jonathan

had here no more to be proud of than making a good stand against the red-coats. A British defeat might be taken as a mere spangle to history, a passing bubble on the smooth course of events, when British victories seemed so much matter of course that one suspects the hysterical fervour with which this generation piles wreaths about the memorials of its heroes. Perhaps foreigners are less enthusiastic in looking up to Nelson, high perched above his lions, even though not a few of them owed to Trafalgar more than they know. In this connection I recall a polite fellow-traveller in France, who, having occasion to speak of an English disaster in battles long ago, made haste to show me in what direction lay, many leagues off, one of those famous fields on which we are better able to echo Napoleon's *"Ca toujours finit de même!"* In the same spirit, William Black's' courteous Highlander would not wear his tartan trousers before a young lady from France, for fear of stirring painful memories of Waterloo. The stolid Saxon is apt to be less considerate, and more blatant in his patriotism, like that old Scotswoman making light of the fact that our enemies, too, offered up prayers for victory: "Puir bodies! but wha could understand them?"

With respect, or otherwise, the trophies of our national pride are here surveyed by strangers born under all flags of the earth Parthians and Medes and Elamites may at every hour of the day be found in Trafalgar Square, along with the pig-tailed Chinaman, the negro, unheeded even by street-boys, the Red Indian stolidly dissembling his amazement, the mild Hindoo jostling sahibs with a new-found strut, the almond-eyed Japanese Jack on shore knocking up against a burly Russian tar, the Egyptian wondering at monuments where no one pesters him for *bakshish*, the Italian sighing for the sun of *dolce far niente*, the Alpine mountaineer lost in admiration of so many tall chimney-pots, the Parisian twirling a critical moustache, the German professor studiously conferring with his Baedeker, and, conspicuous among the throng, the frequent figure of Uncle Sam, one eye cocked in complacent comparison with his own sky-scraping Babels, the other moistened by sentiment for the old home of his race.

Apart from its magnetic character, in Trafalgar Square more foreigners are likely to turn up than in other parts of London, since close at hand, about Soho and Leicester Square, is the headquarters of our Continental colony. I take this to be a somewhat recent settlement, though that cosmopolitan scoundrel Casanova, when he favoured London with a visit, sought his first lodging in Soho. In the great emigration of the French Revolution, Thaddeus of Warsaw is the only exile I recall as having a garret in this vicinity. Châteaubriand, when he lived in London as Minister of France, could revisit his attic home in the New Road, looking out on the churchyard of Marylebone. The Manchester Square neighbourhood, it appears, became a sort of Faubourg St. Germain *in partibus* for the more distinguished exiles, so long as the funds lasted which they might have been able to smuggle out of France. The Count d'Artois, as head of this society, held his court in Baker Street, which contends with another for the honour of having been Tennyson's "long, unlovely street." Some lucky refugees were able to tenant villas at Richmond or Hampstead ; and one notable colony made a co-operative household at Juniper Hill, near Leatherhead. But the poorer exiles had to be content with humbler lodgings, congregating thickly about the then raw suburb of Somers Town, and round old St. Pancras Church, where many of them would lie, never again to see that sunny land on which their mind's eye was always fixed through the fogs of exile and the storms of revolution. When this graveyard came to be broken up by the Midland Railway, thick layers of coffins were taken out for reburial; and one of our best-known novelists could, if he would, tell a grim tale of his own experience in superintending that resurrection work, now recorded by a conspicuous memorial to the disturbed dead, towering above clumps of idle tombstones for almost obliterated names.

That must have made a strange leaven, fermenting with hopes and fears, in the midst of London. Gently-born men and women, with no habit of earning a livelihood, found themselves at once thrown on their own resources, and had to make a gallant shift at self-support by the accomplishments of happier days. Many became teachers of French, of music, of fencing, of drawing, of dancing. Some found a home as tutors and governesses. Others, like our Sedleys and Micawbers, turned their attention to coals, or more naturally to wine. One nobleman set up as a tailor; another stooped to shoemaking; a Countess opened a shop for the sale of ices and other dainties; an accomplished gourmet exercised his skill as a salad-dresser for parties. Ladies turned their hands to embroidery, to flower-painting, and to dressing dolls. In some cases faithful servants started restaurants, from which they fed their ex-masters. Young folks were put upon making straw hats, which found a ready sale, when it was the fashion among our aristocracy to assist and patronize the loyal *émigrés*. A West-end concert, got up for their benefit, is said to have realised the sum of sixteen thousand guineas. Some of them had the good fortune to marry English heiresses, as at Juniper Hall General d'Arblay won the heart of Fanny Burney, whose pen kept them both, while his sword had to lie idle. For the utterly destitute, there was a Government allowance of a shilling a day. Châteaubriand, for one, seems to have managed to make money as an author; and he had a friend who lived not so ill on the proceeds of a French journal printed in London, where the Abbé Delille was head of a small literary colony. Newspapers would be eagerly read by exiles who any day might thus learn of husband, wife, or child brought to that devouring guillotine that for a time was in vogue at Paris.

From memoirs like Châteaubriand's and Vicomte Walsh's, we know in what a gay spirit such unfortunates met their adversity. But there were frowns among them, too, and heartburnings between fellow-sufferers, for the first flight of exalted devotees to the throne looked askance upon the Constitutional Royalists, Girondins, and other Moderates, who had to follow their example when

STATUE OF THOMAS CARLYLE

reform grew to a revolution terrorizing its own children. It was all the Count d'Artois could do to gain a show of civil toleration for the sons of the detested Philippe Egalité. Priests and *philosophes* had mutual reproaches to exchange. Some of the exiles had served in arms against each other; yet we find them all half-disposed to join in sly exultation over French victories that seemed like to adjourn the hour of their return. There were defeats, too, to mourn; and we hear of a ball being put off at news of a French fleet's disaster which illuminated the rest of London. It is amusing to note how complacently the poorest French people took their superior qualities for granted, pluming themselves as missionaries of dress, deportment, taste, and elegance, and of course orthodox religion, to pagan John Bull. "The English," Walsh tells us, "who spend so much money to live on spleen and tea, often looked with envy on our French society, where we were able to enliven our days and evenings." The same writer quotes Burke as declaring that Britons, driven from home under similar circumstances, would have been ready to commit suicide.

One wonders how many of these impecunious strangers spent their spare hours in learning our language. Among later fights of political refugees who have elbowed one another on a hospitable soil, it is matter of common remark how the German loses no time in acquiring English, sometimes to the point of lecturing us on it, while the Frenchman may spend years among us without troubling himself to master *un traître mot.* I once had a private view of the tragedy of such an exile, when I lodged in the same house with a certain Count X., a political refugee of the Second Empire. He and his wife occupied the drawing-room floor, giving themselves airs of rank and fashion, but, I fear, paying our landlady only in coin of compliments and flattery. They professed to despise our *cuisine bourgeoise,* so went out to take their meals "at restaurants," which impressed the hostess as a mark of superiority, till it transpired that those *diners en ville* might be translated as a morsel of bread and a bundle of sprats. Since "French of Paris was to

her unknow," and her foreign lodger was equally unilingual, I served to some extent as interpreter between them, and soon guessed that the unfortunate couple were actually starving, as they would not confess for a time. Presently they decamped, leaving in pawn for their unpaid bill nothing but a very ill-tempered monkey, which would have tried the temper even of a *mont de piété.*

For many years I heard no more of that chance acquaintance, and had quite forgotten him, when one evening, in a street off St. James's Square, I met a distinguished-looking gentleman, well dressed, and apparently as much at ease as any of those bloated aristocrats that suck the blood of the people. My first impression was of the late Duke of Cambridge, to whom he had a superficial resemblance. To my surprise, he stopped me, speaking in French, nor was I less surprised when I found him simply begging in most courteous style. As politely as my blunt British manners would allow, I referred him to a charitable agency of his own countrymen, and passed on, much puzzled what to make of him. His voice seemed familiar to me, though not his looks; then, a few minutes later, there flashed into my recollection the personality of Count X. Since our last meeting his face had been disguised in white hair, and by the gas-lamp he would not recognize me, whom he addressed as a stranger. How had he been living all these years ?

I never saw or heard of him again. But I have not yet touched the point of my instructive anecdote. On coming out of St. James's Square, I had been accosted by a beggar of commoner mould, a woman with a decoy child in arms, who, after a whine or two, gave me up as a bad job. I turned round to see how she would treat that portly gentleman in the Inverness cape and white silk muffler, who presented himself as a more promising subject for her art. Sure enough, so long as I could keep him in sight, she was following him round the Square, not aware that they were two of a trade that here spent its skill in vain.

Now, if any sentimental reader denounce me as hard-hearted for turning a cold face to the outstretched hand, let me tell him that when I was younger and more innocent, also with more time on my hands, I never met a street-beggar without listening to his appeal, going into it, often at some trouble, and being prepared to help in any deserving case. I never once hit upon a case that bore examination as deserving, though often led on far by glib and plausible stories that excited my professional admiration by artistic touches of fiction. The Charity Organization Society and other agencies, making it their business to investigate such stories, have the same report to give. The professionals appealing to one in the streets are impostors, who make a more or less easy living by it; and if one have money to give in charity, one is really robbing the poor by worse than wasting it on such worthless humbugs, who drain away and poison a stream of benevolence that, rightly directed, might cleanse all the true distress of London. These people prey upon the weakness of human nature. A woman, dressed for the part of starvation, hires for fourpence or so a baby, if she have none of her own, and such an actress has been caught pricking the child with a pin to prompt its part in the squalid comedy. The full-fed reveller gets a glow of complacent self-satisfaction by throwing her a sixpence he can well spare, then goes his way, thanking the electric-lit heaven that he is not as those publicans of the Charity Organization Society, some of whom, if he only knew it, spend their lives as well as their means in trying to mend social evils which such as he only botch anew by their lazy donations.

So long as there are soft-hearted people who make a conscience of giving a copper to anyone who asks them with apparent marks of poverty, so long will there be beggars in the land. Beggars are not a striking feature of the London streets, but the most artful and thriving of the fraternity may be looked for about Charing Cross, where hotels full of well-fed visitors make the coverts of their hunting-field. There is the out-at-elbows scholar, who earnestly begs a total stranger to recommend him on the spot for a tutorship. There is the insinuating foreigner, who inquires if you can speak his language, and

from this indirect flattery goes on to confidences as to his unfortunate position. There is the respectable young working man, who has just come out of hospital, with a frail basket of tools over his shoulder to show him ready for a job. There is the neat and modest damsel driven to sell bootlaces for the support of a disabled father. There is the whole gang of "confidence men," who now and then amazingly find dupes. All these I counsel the stranger not to trust without careful examination into their story; and he would in most cases save time by at once referring them to the police.

Here is struck a note that resolves all the caterwauling of foreigners into harmony. They loudly criticize our constitution, our institutions, our national character; they grumble against our climate; they groan over our cookery; they shrug their shoulders before our architecture; they hiss at our drama; they shriek about our manners; they yawn through our Sundays; they sniggle at our prudery; they snarl at our *morgue*; they even jeer at our Lifeguardsmen; but all of them join chorus of admiration for our police-constables. Citizens of liberalescent empires and subjects of Republican bosses alike envy us the stolid figure that, without visible weapons, without official pride, without fuss, stands visibly controlling a maelstrom of traffic, living statue of British respect for law and order.

The London police-force, indeed, makes a model to the world, copied, helmet and all, in miniature, so far off as Siam, and so near as Paris, in spirit. No agent of oppression could enjoy such credit at home, testified to by the very jests and nicknames fastened upon him by the vulgar. "Peeler," now almost extinct, and "Bobby," are, of course, from Sir Robert Peel, under whose Ministry he came into being; while his later *sobriquet* "Copper" seems to be of much older origin, perhaps akin to the German *Caper*, a pirate or catcher. He is accused of too much familiarity with area-doors and the back-entrances of public-houses, but that is mainly our coarse fun, which we poke at the gravest and most popular statesman. The manner of his being banged about and hoodwinked in the pantomime is but the gargoyle burlesque that makes the seamy side of unruffled faith. If ever, being but mortal, he exceed his commission, we are the people to let him hear of it; but in our hearts we recognize the patience, good-nature, moderation, and common-sense with which, as a rule, he does his duty to the general advantage.

Of late, his temper has been sorely tried, yet he has emerged triumphant from all ordeals, even at the hands of hysterical Maenads too vain and foolish to understand what might come of their fumbling efforts at disorder. Even Sunday shines for him less of a Sabbath than other days, since on that day of rest cantankerous busybodies, sore-headed malcontents, loud-lunged agitators find it easiest to draw together mobs of idlers, among whom some are always ready to be stirred up to violence, but for the presence of the police. Everyone understands what these amateur politicians mean to say, except sometimes themselves. "We don't quite know what we want, but we want it bad, and we want it all, and we want it right away!" The only place where it may be said with effect is in the councils of a nation long ago risen above the need of having its laws made by excited mobs. There are lands where public opinion has no better safety- valve, but such is not ours.

Thanks to a disciplined police, in part, our mob assemblies are mild indeed compared with those of former generations. But not so long ago certain mischievously irresponsible windbags were able to raise at Charing Cross a storm that smashed windows and had almost broken loose to the wreckage of shops. One leader of that uproar has since learned better, who then went into the thick of the fray, and got his head broken like a man by police truncheons, while some of his allies were content with sitting safe at a window and hounding on the rioters by applause as from a private box. But when these sedition-mongers were for repeating their dangerous experiment, it was brought home to them how violence is a game all able-bodied citizens can play at. Trafalgar Square was packed with volunteer constables, and as the would-be rioters marched up it was a treat to see how weedy public-house politicians and noisy hobbledehoys went down before the firm ranks of the police, who would rather deal thus with ten times their number of men than have to do with scratching and screaming women eager to force themselves upon mock martyrdom.

It was on the day of the first Trafalgar Square riot that I heard of a party of country cousins, who, visiting the National Gallery, remarked that there seemed to be a great many people about, but took such commotion to be nothing out of the common in the centre of London. My lot was to pass by one of the last meetings in which this agitation fizzled out. Some score or so of undersized and out-at-elbows patriots, chiefly foreigners to all appearance, had gathered in a corner of the Square, head and shoulders above whom stalked their most chivalrous champion, a man as warm-hearted as he is wrong-headed on one or two points. This hidalgo, ever graceful and humane even in his perfervid grudge against the order of things, was minded to be courteous to those foes who had shed his blood and cast him in a dungeon. To a police official who stood by watchfully observant, I heard him say: "Very sorry, Mr. Inspector, to give you all this trouble; but you know it isn't our fault." The officer of the law's answer was to turn on his heel with a *H'm!* as expressive as Lord Burleigh's nod. Here, I reflected, were in presence the two elements of our national character: the stiff dough of Teuton common-sense, that bakes so well when mixed with not too much yeast of Celtic fervour, also with more or less wholesome adulteration and flavouring ingredients from foreign parts.

The aliens whom we have received by thousands yearly are hereabouts found so thickly lumped that in some streets they seem to have banished the native inhabitants. The main colony appears to be French, with a large sprinkling of Italians. But the Italians, who are counted at over twelve thousand, have another settlement of their own, on the farther side of Holborn, with Leather Lane as its narrow avenue; and this swarm, as coming chiefly from the hot-blooded South of Italy, bears not so good a reputation in our land of law and order. There are also outlying rookeries of organ-grinders in Battersea and Hammersmith, where they are said to find daughters of the soil willing to adopt their costume and to serve their artillery of torture, as it may be to a refined ear, while it brings a touch of Southern grace and gaiety to the children of stuffy courts, to make up for the cheap poison hawked about in ice-cream barrows. The Italian Church in Hatton Garden may be taken as a moral centre of the colony. I think it was in Tottenham Court Road that Samuel Butler describes a raw emigrant from the Mediterranean on his knees before a dentist's show-case, conceived by him to contain relics of a saint; but when I once pressed this humorous author as to the authenticity of the fact, he would not swear to having seen it with his own eyes. There are many legends that would as ill bear cross-examination. One would like to bring out some points kept obscure in De Quincey's account of his hungry trampings of Oxford Street and Soho, which he declares to have been solaced by such jingling airs as stir well-fed authors to fury.

As for Germans, they are *überall,* every second baker's shop in London bearing a name that looks as if it hailed either from the Fatherland or the Land of Cakes. In this central quarter Latin patronymics are most in evidence as connected with what seems its chief trade of cookery and provision supply, but Teutonic ones also stand over shop doors, mixed with Slavonic, Magyar,and other outlandish names, not seldom anglicized by that international race that is content to thrive in our modern Babylon. But the Jews, of course, have their head-quarters rather in the East-end than in the West. Soho appears to have been morally as well as materially aerated by its opening up in Charing Cross Road and Shaftesbury Avenue; and even before the clearing of these new thoroughfares the most dangerous elements of foreign outlawry had been overflowing across Oxford Street, to hide their explosive aspirations in streets near Tottenham Court Road that were a haunt of artists.

In a recent year over forty thousand aliens arrived at the Port of London, of whom only a small proportion were rejected as manifestly undesirable, caught in the meshes of a new Act that seemed to infringe on British traditions of hospitality to all and sundry. It is not always possible to say for certain how many of these may have been mere transmigrants, perching here on the way to other lands of promise. Then the whole body of strangers within our gates may be divided between those who have taken up their abode among us for good, or otherwise, and the numerous birds of passage like hotel servants, come to learn our language, along with fowls of prey, who have reasons for a temporary absence from their native jurisdiction. Another division is suggested by manifest foreigners who look to be down on their luck, and those apparently thriving in our foggy air. The police could tell queer stories about some of those more or less voluntary exiles, among whom are occasionally enacted obscure tragedies, believed to be the work of political secret societies. But either because too well watched, or because not so ill-advised as to quarrel with the law that gives him shelter, the reddest anarchist is shy to *faire des siennes* in London, and contents himself with airing his principles in the smoky atmosphere of certain cafés, or in still more secret resorts. Most of the foreign colony, indeed, set an example of law-abiding industry and quiet thrift. Not a few of them marry English-women, and bring up their children to be patriotic John Bulls, who in a generation or two are no longer to be distinguished from the mass of the community, unless by their name, and not always thus, when Disraeli, Goschen, and Labouchere soon become as familiar to us as Walsh or Waddington are in France. Perhaps the chief industry of Soho may be taken to be the manufacture of British flesh and blood out of raw material drawn from far and wide to this magnetic pole of humanity. Long before Charing Cross was set up, indeed, London had been absorbing Flemings, Frenchmen, and other foreigners, who still filter in to make it an epitome of the world.

WESTMINSTER

WESTMINSTER

NOT EVERY LONDONER could tell you off-hand the boundaries of Westminster, in which we have been ever since leaving the old City gates. In the thirty divisions of our Metropolis, the City of Westminster holds up its head among neighbour boroughs, remembering how it was once the independent seat of royalty, which gradually became welded into the mass of dwellings overspread by London's name. Nor do other cities bear such a rank as this one that grew up round what might be called the Cathedral of all England; and as an island of municipal life it has a peculiar official styled its High Bailiff. Its area stretches from the City to Kensington, and from Oxford Street to the Thames. With a population larger than that of most English cities, it makes three Parliamentary constituencies, the Strand district, that of Mayfair and Hanover Square, and the Abbey quarter, which last is the Westminster most familiar by name to a generation that has ceased to think of St. Paul's as its eastern minster.

The mists of early history rise off from a waste of riverside marshes and islets, one of them emerging under the name of Thorney Island, when a bar or bank thrown up by the silt of the Tyburn brook had been skinned over with matted vegetation. Here the Thames yielded a ford for that ancient road, paved by the Romans as highway from the north-western corner to the south-eastern coast of their British province. The rude Saxons were so struck with wonder at the construction of this road and its stations that they seem to have attributed such works to their mythical heroes, the Watlings, as elsewhere they gave a dark spirit of evil credit for the Grim's Dykes and Devil's Dykes of imposing British fortifications. When London Bridge came to be built, Watling Street was diverted towards it through the City, in which a fragment of this sideway still preserves the name. The original thoroughfare, holding on from the straight Edgware Road, took the line perhaps of Park Lane, then bent eastward to strike its crossing-place by Thorney Island, where the name of Horseferry Road makes a memorial of how Lambeth was reached in the centuries throughout which London had but one bridge.

Observing from Westminster Bridge how "ships, towers, domes, theatres, and temples" no longer "lie open unto the fields," we must stretch our imagination to picture the scene as it was in the days of Boadicea, whose effigy stands here, looking as if her chariot should be turned round so as to give the plunging steeds a free course down the

Embarkment. On Thorney Island, tradition puts a church of St. Peter, built by an East Saxon king at the beginning of the seventh century, when the Apostle himself left heaven unguarded to consecrate this favoured shrine. Then rose a Benedictine monastery, whose Dane-ravaged walls gave place to the Abbey and Church finished just in time to be tomb of Edward the Confessor, who at Westminster had a "King's House," supposed to have been first built by Canute. The Norman kings dallied for a time with the fame of Alfred's capital; the Conqueror had been crowned at Winchester as well as at Westminster, to make assurance of conquest doubly sure. But the magnetic power of London drew them to the Thames, and they fixed their seat beside the Abbey, which was rebuilt by Henry III., to be completed under the first Tudor king, all but the incongruous western towers added in Wren's time. Windsor, Sheen, Hampton Court, Greenwich, Whitehall, Kensington, St. James's, in turn became favourite residences with successive groups of sovereigns; but the Palace of Westminster was long royalty's official seat, as it now enshrines the modern majesty of the people.

Such, in brief, is the history of the group of historic fanes in which Church and State have been throned together for a thousand years. The oldest of the secular buildings is Westminster Hall, first erected by William Rufus, enlarged and dignified to be a meeting-place of Parliaments, and a theatre for state ceremonies down to the Coronation banquets of George IV. Many famous trials have been held here, among them those of Charles I., of the Seven Bishops, and of Warren Hastings. Till the new Courts of Law were built at Temple Bar, this Hall made our chief temple of justice, whose shrines have now been cleared away, and the spacious Norman structure, with its rich oak roof and show of royal statues, is restored as a monument of the past, and as a befitting anteroom to the Houses of Parliament. At one time it was allowed to be littered with tables of money- changers and scriveners; then for long its outside walls were blocked up by the shops of booksellers, wig-makers, and other hangers-on of the law.

This is not the only clearance made in the last generation or two, for G. A. Sala could remember how the most sacred monuments of English history were neighboured by a *cloaca* of "malodorous streets" and "felonious slums."

The rest of the Palace of Westminster was burned down in 1835, to be replaced at a cost of three millions by Barry's imposing if much-criticized pile, containing eleven courts, a hundred staircases, hundreds of halls and chambers, not counting the private residences of officials of the House, and a prison for offenders against its privileges. The Clock Tower, over which flies a flag to proclaim when our legislators are at work, has a modern dungeon of no very severe punishment, that, coming to an end with the Session, would be nowadays an excellent advertisement for ambitious demagogues, who might ask nothing better than to have their duress famed by the tongue of Big Ben. Poor Guy Fawkes and his fellow-conspirators were more roughly handled when they proposed to move an adjournment of the House in a manner far from parliamentary. So conservative are we, that every year, on the night before the meeting of Parliament, its cellars must be formally searched to make sure that no store of explosives has escaped the eye of the police-force who keep watch and ward over this focus of national wisdom.

A quarter of a century ago certain Irish-Yankee miscreants attempted to revive the melodrama of Guy Fawkes in an up-to-date form, when in 1885 London became startled but not terrified by repeated dynamite explosions. I happened to be passing when the House of Parliament was thus shaken, and what struck me most was the absence of anything like panic in a commotion exaggerated to make copy for certain newspapers. I had reached the end of Westminster Bridge when the first explosion took place. A passing 'bus-driver waved his whip to another, with the cry, "Dynamite!" then both drove quietly on. I know not what put it into my head that there would be another explosion, so that for a moment I thought of crossing the road to get clear of the Clock

WESTMINSTER FROM THE RIVER

Tower beneath which I stood; but, on considering its height, I judged as well to stay where I was, and at once addressed myself to noting the demeanour of the crowd, no everyday chance for an observer of men and manners. After the first explosion, a number of passers by rushed into Palace Yard. When the second followed, they turned to scamper back, amid the jeers and laughter of those outside. The police were quickly on the spot to close all entrances, and after that no sentiment more agitating than curiosity was shown by the gathering throng. We had to wait for special editions of the evening papers to learn how, within, two policemen had been seriously injured amid the wreck of the empty House of Commons. It was on the same day that an explosion took place at the Tower, where the scoundrels succeeded in hurting some half-dozen children. Two of the same gang, it is supposed, had made an attempt on London Bridge, in which they appear to have been hoist by their own petard, nothing more being heard or seen of them. So perish all such traitors to humanity! Such was certainly the fate of the stumbling wretch who carried a bomb against Greenwich Observatory, seeking to blow up the very meridian, as would seem. On his body was found a scorched British Museum ticket for a chemical work, from which he might have learned the composition of his explosive; so in the Museum Reading-Room detectives were kept on sharp watch for the next reader who should demand that book. One day an excited assistant, according to orders, brought a ticket sent in for the perilous volume. The Superintendent, at that time a gentleman who had served his country in arms, hastily mustered a *posse* that with all due precaution closed upon the suspected malefactor; then he turned out to be the author of the book, who could not afford to buy it! At places like the British Museum, respectable citizens were subjected to inconvenient suspicion. One eminent scholar was arrested by a zealous young constable as carrying a black bag, which on cautious examination turned out to contain nothing more dangerous than proof-sheets of the "Oxford Dictionary," that ever since has been exploding in numbers. But the public soon got over its first fit of scared excitement after the blowing down of Clerkenwell Prison wall, when four people were killed and forty injured by reckless ignorance, helped by police bungling.

The tooth of time is an enemy against which no policeman can guard the most sumptuous pile. The new Palace's outer coating, though carefully selected, is found too soft to be weather-proof. Whether the smoke of London be to blame, or, as has been suggested, the fumes from Doulton's Works wafted against it by the prevailing wind, this stone wears away so as to need constant repairs. The Abbey, too, seems to have decayed faster in the last few decades than in all its previous centuries; and one of its canonries has to be suspended to meet the cost of constant patching, which puts it in debt like any brand-new temple of gingerbread Gothic. Not far off, Cleopatra's Needle has in one generation of sojourn among us lost more of its sharpness of

outline than through ages under an Egyptian sky. Sir W. B. Richmond puts the blame on the sulphuric acid with which, from one source or other, London's air is now loaded. A silica wash has been applied in vain as a tonic. But if any New Zealand artist, when he comes to make his sketch here, find nothing but ivied ruins, there is no fear for the fame of our "Mother of Parliaments," wherever it may be housed by that day.

We may have to look abroad for models of stately palaces, but the British Constitution, built up in our rule-of-thumb fashion, without regard to style or symmetry, proves as yet the most solid structure that ever kept a people's freedom storm-proof. All over the world it has the flattery of envy, and of imitation in some most uncongenial climes. The Czar is fain to let a Duma come together. The very Turk puffs at hubble-bubble electioneering. The Shah has played to his peril with representative institutions, not so easily broken as toy-soldiers

THE ABBEY FROM WHITEHALL

might be. The King of Tongataboo sits among tawny M.P.'s. India cries out for National Councils to vindicate liberties of which she knows nothing but from English books. What those apes of our good-fortune may still have to seek is the public spirit and practical temper, without which their representative chambers will be but as sounding brass and tinkling cymbals.

One need not expatiate on the mixture of keenness and fairness with which here is played the great game of Ins and Outs. To an outsider, the rules of this game seem by no means ideal, devised as if to give chance undue weight as against skill and principle. Constituencies of various sizes have the same voice in the choice of Government. Electoral districts like Romford, Harrow, or Wandsworth speak no more loudly from tens of thousand throats than do Rutlandshire or Kilkenny with their small troop of voters. And in any constituency the accident or trick of a confused contest may give it a member chosen by a minority, so long as a second ballot seems too reasonable, or troublesome, to fit in with our rough-and-ready arrangements. Then comes the question of how a candidate recommends himself to those sweet voices. In theory, their choice should mark him as the flower of his fellow-citizens. In practice it is not quite so, though, perhaps, more so than in any other country. In this country we have the immense advantage that still the best men, in every sense, are proud of getting into what has been called the best club in London, on which designation a certain member remarks that "the entrance-fee is far too high, and the annual subscription extortionately heavy."

Membership of the House of Commons is still what Disraeli judged it, "the greatest opportunity that can be offered to an Englishman." More and more, however, he must stoop to win this honour through an ordeal of heckling from organized caucuses, and of pledges to banded interests; while still luck comes sometimes into play, now that we have forgotten the rotten borough days when such statesmen as Macaulay and Gladstone stood upon the favour of a patron, and apparent nonentities like

Creevey in fact, and Phineas Finn in fiction, contrived to win their way to social success by taking a minor part in the councils of the nation. Local interest or popularity, the chance of a timely vacancy, the absence of a serious rival, go to account for many men getting into Parliament. Others have to lay siege to this ambition, pushing their trenches for years, perhaps to fall on the long-watched breach, perhaps to storm the place by fortunate assault at the nick of time. Some win by dogged perseverance after repeated defeats; some fail at the critical moment for want of the sinews of war. Though boroughs like Eatonswill are disfranchised, and great families no longer come to ruin by contesting counties, money has still too much weight in elections. Anyone could name Members of Parliament who, without being distinguished or gifted above their fellows, have practically bought their places by a judicious use of the root of evil. One such, whose success amazed me, I once fell in with on a tour of the kingdom for the inspection of seats soon to be vacant. He spoke quite frankly of such a one as too dear, and of such another as within his means, which he actually secured in due time, though a stranger, not only to the district, but even to the country, after earning a fortune at the other end of the world.

This greatness, then, some achieve by merit or other means; some are born with a fair chance of it; some have it thrust upon them; and when the rough sifting of an election is over, the six hundred and seventy seats are filled by as many gentlemen who fairly enough, perhaps, represent the wisdom, and unwisdom, of their electors. The majority proceed to make laws for us, more or less faithfully carrying out the mandate they have received from public opinion. Public opinion usually amounts to a few hundred thousand weathercocks, who have shifted their votes from one side to the other, partly in obedience to some popular cry, partly in impatience of the Government which has not made good such promises as are offered in turn by the Opposition. In this game the bowling seems always to have an advantage over the batting. But so long as the side that is in can hold together, it has the power to Oppress us with laws and taxes, a tyranny tempered by the moderation of the national spirit, by an eye on critical constituencies, and but there's the rub!—by the regulating pendulum of the House of Lords.

Here is a part of the machinery that looks more ill-contrived and indefensible than the other. In this deal of the game it is fortune that cuts and shuffles the cards. By services, glorious or otherwise, to their country, by weight of wealth won nobly or ignobly, by Court favour, by political intrigues, sometimes as an honourable form of disgrace, or as an extinguisher of guttering ambition, a citizen is raised to the heaven of the peerage, where he and his heirs are understood to lie calmly beside their nectar, careless of common mankind, in whose governance they have what is now practically the last word. What device could be more unpromising, which yet has worked not so ill? There are wise lords as well as foolish ones, and the latter may learn from the former not to take themselves for Solons. The most rakish heir of a once-noble name has a right to sit in judgment on the deepest questions, yet in practice he commonly abandons this responsibility to a few fit councillors. The House of Lords, recruited constantly from tried statesmen in the Commons, from the most successful professional men, and from men who have at least known how to make money, is not more inferior to the Commons in rhetoric than it is superior in experience and independence. Business men tell us they would rather deal with a Committee of the Upper than with one of the Lower House. It is the cream of the Lords who do most of their business. And if the worst comes to the worst, if dissolute dukes and impecunious earls and brainless barons are raked in from the turf or the bridge-table to vote against some measure demanded by the majority of the moment, why, this power of hereditary legislators cannot now in the long-run withstand the popular will, but will more or less gracefully bow to that opinion of the many, once it be clearly proved to know its own mind.

We may have had cause to thank Heaven for our House of Lords, so often and so easily pelted by democratic commonplaces. Yet prudent observers of the political sky foresee a time when the wind will not blow so steadily first from one quarter, then from the other, and warn us how the ship of State may soon be tossing on billows of popular agitation, exposed to gusty squalls, or even tornadoes long unknown in our temperate clime. Since these lines were written, such a tempest has gathered upon the horizon!—Gilded figureheads and gay bunting will then be of less service than a well-ballasted keel answering trimly to the helm. How would our Constitution be strengthened if we had a Senate of real senators, the cream and pick of all classes, interests, and talents, that might command the respect of every thinking citizen, and could not be belittled even by talking demagogues? Is it not time for a reform of the House of Lords, threatened with a revolution? There are forces at work more corrosive than the fogs and foul winds that sap the walls of Westminster. Some critics even ask if the corner-stone will always stand firm? Is it high treason to speculate how we might some day get a sovereign with a troublesome will and conscience of his own, not content to be the one man in the kingdom whose religion is fixed for him by law, and who has no open voice in public policy? He might even become a convert to Republicanism, which surely would be an ideal form of Government, but for the want of republicans.

In an out-of-the-way part of the country I once took tea with the holder of a famous title, fallen upon an old gentleman to whom it was of little use. He was singularly simple in his manners, secluded in his habits, and too poor to buy a coronet, instead of which he wore the same hat, on all occasions, for many years together, a social sin I envied, not abhorred, in one set above caring what his neighbours thought of him. For something to say, I asked him if he ever went to the House of Lords. "Only once," he replied. "They told me Gladstone was a dangerous man, and I went up to vote against him; but I caught a bad cold, and never

HENRY VII.'S CHAPEL

CHANGING GUARD, WHITEHALL

mean to go again." I am not sure how far he was himself playing the sly humorist, but a few weeks later this anecdote, "with a cocked hat and stick," made the subject of a picture in *Punch*. I might have taken it for a coincidence had not, the week before, the same paper given forth another experience of mine in the same sojourn — a lady meeting an old servant of hers, and asking where she lived now, to which the answer was: "I don't live anywhere, ma'am; I'm married." These two incidents had tickled me so much at the time that I communicated them to a friend, who was a friend of Du Maurier, and thus I became an unwitting contributor to *Punch*. There was another comic paper of those days named *Funny Folks*, for which also I supplied copy without meaning it. I had been travelling with a Parliamentary candidate, who was to take his stand on the temperance platform; so by way of practice, in the refreshment-room of a junction where we had

to spend half an hour, he asked a youthful waiter if any temperance beverages could be had. "Yes, sir; 'ock, sir, and claret, sir!" This answer I told as a good joke to the editor of *Funny Folks*, whom I met at dinner that evening. But when a few weeks later I was moved to trot out the same story before another friend, he winked at me derisively: "You got that out of *Funny Folks!*"

This apparently frivolous digression leads me round to the Fourth Estate of the realm, which some reckon now the most powerful of all, though it has no palace at Westminster. But the ministers of the Press, like the members of the House, depend upon the favour of their constituents. Fear of newspaper critics forbids me to follow out this theme; so I will only remark that perhaps the weakest point of our state is that, while electors of old were too often bribed and wheedled into voting Whig or Tory, too many in the present generation seem more easily moved by political caricatures and spicy paragraphs than by the soundest arguments or the most thrilling eloquence. Yet with all the faults of our much-mended Constitution, what other has as yet been so successful in making freedom and order dwell side by side? So, without more poking into the mortar of our institutions, let us pass from the State to the Church, that can no longer claim to represent the national voice.

Hard by, in a "temple of silence and reconciliation," lie the bones or stand the cold effigies of silent orators who once denounced and defied each other so hotly within the walls of Westminster Palace. Westminster Abbey is the most sacred spot in England, hallowed by centuries of worship among monuments of the past, where renowned rulers and their victims rest round the despoiled shrine of that meek Confessor whose heirs so seldom illustrated the Christian virtues. Oldest relic of all is the stone of Scone in the Coronation Chair, swept down by a glacier-stream of conquest from the Scottish hills, where it was fondly treasured as Jacob's pillow. On this stolen fragment of immemorial antiquity the Sovereigns of Britain sit to be crowned, making a public covenant with their people beside the tombs of their ancestors- a sight that has not always been seen in a generation, and which each generation may hope not to see.

The guardians of the Abbey look with dread on that rarely recurrent ceremonial, when its broken spaces must be lumbered up with galleries and other structures both disfiguring and damaging to the fabric. Did not theology as well as sentiment forbid, the new Roman Catholic Cathedral might with advantage be borrowed for such state spectacles. But for lack of dignity, the Albert Hall, that of Olympia, or the Agricultural Hall at Islington, would make a better theatre. Nor is Westminster Abbey well adapted for worship of a large congregation. It enjoys a peculiar ecclesiastical rank — shared, I believe, by St. George's, Windsor, and the humbler chapel of Christ's College at Brecon — in being under the see of no Bishop, so that its Dean is free to let any voice be raised in it. Under Dean

Stauley, a Presbyterian minister and even a layman held forth here, to the scandal of sound Anglicans. But when once I sought to stand within hearing of that mild heretic in his own church, all I could catch from behind a pillar were the words, *"Once more,"* hardly enough for edification. The Gothic fane is better suited for musical services, their sweetness enhanced by the natural gloom and silence that struck Washington Irving into eloquent meditation.

"The eyes gaze with wonder at clustered columns of gigantic dimensions, with arches springing from them to such an amazing height, and man wandering about their bases, shrunk into insignificance in comparison with his own handiwork. The spaciousness and gloom of this vast edifice produce a profound and mysterious awe. We step cautiously and softly about, as if fearful of disturbing the hallowed silence of the tomb; while every footfall whispers along the walls, and chatters among the sepulchres, making us more sensible of the quiet we have interrupted. It seems as if the awful nature of the place presses down upon the soul, and hushes the beholder into noiseless reverence. We feel that we are surrounded by the congregated bones of the great men of past times, who have filled history with their deeds, and the earth with their renown. And yet it almost provokes a smile at the vanity of human ambition, to see how they are crowded together and jostled in the dust; what parsimony is observed in doling out a scanty nook, a gloomy corner, a little portion of earth, to those whom, when alive, kingdoms could not satisfy; and how many shapes and forms and artifices are devised to catch the casual notice of the passenger, and save from forgetfulness, for a few short years, a name which once aspired to occupy ages of the world's thought and admiration..."

The sound of casual footsteps had ceased from the Abbey. I could only hear, now and then, the distant voice of the priest repeating the evening service, and the faint responses of the choir; these paused for a time, and all was hushed. The stillness, the desertion, and obscurity that were gradually prevailing around gave a deeper and more solemn interest to the place:

For in the silent grave no conversation,
No joyful tread of friends, no voice of lovers,
No careful father's counsel nothing's heard,
For nothing is, but all oblivion,
Dust, and an endless darkness.

Suddenly the notes of the deep-labouring organ burst upon the ear, falling with doubled and redoubled intensity, and rolling, as it were, huge billows of sound. How well do their volume and grandeur accord with this mighty building! With what pomp do they swell through its vast vaults, and breathe their awful harmony through caves of death, and make the silent sepulchre vocal! And now they rise in triumphant acclamation, heaving higher and higher their accordant notes, and piling sound on sound. And now they pause, and the soft voices of the choir break out into sweet gushes of melody; they soar aloft, and warble along the roof, and seem to play about these lofty vaults like the pure airs of heaven. Again the pealing organ heaves its thrilling thunders, compressing air into music, and rolling it forth upon the soul. What long-drawn cadences! What solemn, sweeping concords! It grows more and more dense and powerful — it fills the vast pile, and seems to jar the very walls — the ear is stunned- the senses are overwhelmed. And now it is winding up in full jubilee — it is rising from the earth to heaven — the very soul seems rapt away and floated upwards on this swelling tide of harmony.

The Abbey makes London's sight of sights, which few can visit unmoved, by its illustrious memories, if not by its solemn ritual. Of one young Australian, indeed, it is told that he would not allow himself to be roused to admiration for a structure so little up to date. "My word, you should see the Scotch Church in Ballarat!" But even gold-grubbers from Johannesburg and pork-butchers from

Chicago might fain stand hushed in such a scene, where gentler spirits dread their own footsteps as a sacrilege. So popular a sight, indeed, is this in the tourist season, that the spirit of the place seems exorcised by so many hasty stares, and the parties conducted through its storied chapels must carry away but a confused impression of monuments whose congenial atmosphere should be twilight silence.

Few visitors have such a chance of communion with its shadowy inhabitants as did Châteaubriand when he had so spun out a lonely day-dream as by accident to get locked up here for the night. All his shouting and beating upon the gates being in vain, he had to resign himself to sleep with the dead, among whom nothing seemed alive but the hammer of a clock striking the long hours. As from one world into another, there reached his ears the muffled roll of wheels and the cry of the watchman outside; and into the Abbey's solemn spaces stole the Thames fog and London's smoky breath to deepen the gathering darkness. Since better might not be, he groped about for a resting-place, chosen on a cold sarcophagus, shrouded in marble and curtained by emblems of death, where, like Charles v., he had a sensation of rehearsing his own burial. There, he says, he was in a front seat for beholding the vain pageant of time, and did not fail to indulge congenial reflections on the littleness of mortal life, however illustrious for a moment. "Bacon, Newton, Milton are as deeply buried, as much passed away for ever as are their most obscure contemporaries. Myself, exiled, vagabond, poor, would I agree to be no more the forgotten and sorrowful nobody that I am, on condition of having been one of those dead men, once famous, powerful, glutted with enjoyment?" Also, in this chilly hall of funereal spectacles, he could not but let his flesh creep for half-tickling, half-appalling imaginations. When at last a faint ray dawned out of one of the blackest corners, he fancied it at first an emanation from the spirits of the young York Princes, murdered by their uncle. But this light proved not at all ghostly, a paper-shielded candle in the hand of a girl

VIEW OF WESTMINSTER

coming at daybreak to take the place of her sick father as bell-ringer. She might well be frightened to encounter among the tombs a polite stranger wanting to be let out.

The adventure ends *à la française,* with a cryptic allusion to a kiss, the point of which is made less clear than the fact of this reflective genius being so little overawed by his night's experience that presently he was conspiring with a friend to court emotions by again getting themselves shut up in the Abbey. I knew a less illustrious foreigner who had the chance to be locked into the organ loft of one of our English minsters, but his experience was not so prolonged or so edifying. "I prayed the Virgin to open me," he related in his imperfect English, which petition could be translated as a summoning of the verger. Another nocturnal intruder on the Abbey tombs was the sacrilegious burglar of tradition, so scared by Roubiliac's realistic sculpture of Death brandishing a dart at Lady Elizabeth Nightingale, that he is said to have dropped his

tools and fled from that moonlit terror.

Many authors have here mused on an obvious moral, which Francis Beaumont put into verse, as Addison into prose :

Think how many royal bones
Sleep within this heap of stones;
Here they lie had realms and lands,
Who now want strength to stir their hands,
Where from their pulpits sealed with dust,
They preach *In greatness is no trust.*
Here's an acre sown indeed,
With the richest, royalist seed,
That the earth did o'er suck in
Since the first man died for sin.

No pilgrims have been more eloquent on this theme than Americans. Washington Irving's meditations might be thought too well known for quotation, while another transatlantic visitor of our own day, Mr. William Winter, serves us with a catalogue of great names:

WESTMINSTER ACROSS THE RIVER BY NIGHT

You cannot long endure, and you never can express, the sense of grandeur that is inspired by Westminster Abbey; but, when at length its shrines and tombs and statues become familiar, when its chapels, aisles, arches, and cloisters are grown companionable, and you can stroll and dream undismayed "through rows of warriors and through walks of kings," there is no limit to the pensive memories they awaken and the poetic fancies they prompt. In this church are buried, amidst generations of their nobles and courtiers, fourteen monarchs of England beginning with the Saxon Sebert and ending with George the Second. Fourteen queens rest here, and many children of the royal blood who never came to the throne. Here, confronted in a haughty rivalry of solemn pomp, rise the equal tombs of Elizabeth Tudor and Mary

Stuart. Queen Eleanor's dust is here, and here, too, is the dust of the grim Queen Mary. In one little chapel you may pace, with but half a dozen steps, across the graves of Charles the Second, William and Mary, and Queen Anne and her consort Prince George. At the tomb of Henry the Fifth you may see the helmet, shield, and saddle which were worn by the valiant young knight at Agincourt; and close by — on the tomb of Margaret Woodville, daughter of Edward the Fourth — the sword and shield that were borne, in royal state, before the great Edward the Third five hundred years ago. The princes whom Richard murdered in the Tower are commemorated here by an altar, set up by Charles the Second, whereon the inscription — blandly and almost humorously oblivious of the incident of Cromwell — states that it was erected in the thirtieth year of Charles' reign. Richard the Second, deposed and assassinated, is here entombed; and within a few feet of him are the relics of his uncle, the able and powerful Duke of Gloucester, whom treacherously he ensnared and betrayed to death. Here also, huge, rough and grey, is the stone sarcophagus of Edward the First, which, when opened years ago, disclosed the skeleton of departed majesty, still perfect, wearing robes of gold tissue and crimson velvet, and having a crown on the head and a sceptre in the hand. So sleep, in jewelled darkness and gaudy decay, what once were monarchs! And all around are great lords, sainted prelates, famous statesmen, renowned soldiers, and illustrious poets. Burleigh, Pitt, Fox, Burke, Canning, Newton, Barrow, Wilberforce —names for ever glorious! — are here enshrined in the grandest sepulchre on earth.

As well as not always reverent sight-seers, a hindrance to devotion seems the mob of statues and other memorials of worthy mixed with unworthy names, their claims to remembrance seldom equal to the pretension of their monuments. Yet this incongruous jumble not unduly represents the various phases of our national life. Mailed crusaders lie near their descendants in the softer garb of cavaliers, and these are succeeded by the sculptured allegories so oddly fitted to an age of wigs and ruffles, which in turn give place to the revival of purer taste that marks our own day. But we could well spare not a few pompous epitaphs and sprawling classicalities that crowd into obscure corners some of our truly illustrious dead.

The idea of making Westminster a tomb for English heroes seems to have been Cromwell's, whose own corpse was so shamefully expelled from its precincts when dawned "the golden age of the coward, the bigot, and the slave." During the next century or so admission was granted somewhat indiscriminately, being, to the dead as to the living, mainly a matter of fees. There was more room here when Johnson quoted to Goldsmith a line which the latter slyly whispered back, as anon they passed under the rebel heads on Temple Bar: "*Forsitan et*

nostrum nomen miscebitur istis !"

Now the scrimped space is jealously guarded, as it need be, when notoriety's trumpet gives forth such noisy blasts. Our great men, or big men, loom out through a haze of paragraphs and puffs, enlarged for the eye of public curiosity by journalistic art, so that it is more than ever difficult to cast their true proportions, while nothing but good may be said of them. If such a man's opportunity be to die at a season when no exciting cricket-match or moving political debate or sensational trial be stirring, our ticklers of the public's long ear seize the chance of "booming" this fresh memory, and soon work themselves up into shrouding the celebrity of the day in a fame measured for all time; then more paragraphs can be made of outcries against the authority that should not let itself be lightly moved to fill the few graves still left in the Abbey. In the case of authors, this outcry becomes loudest, as they have the widest constituency of applause; but it is just in such cases that renown may well wait for its due estimation. Our age would be more judicious than its predecessors, could it always pronounce infallibly which of its favourites were worthy to lie beside Chaucer in the Poets' Corner, that already shows scant room for abridged memorials to enchanters of the English tongue, born on both sides the Atlantic.

Royal burials ended here with George II., and before that the Stuart kings lay unrecorded in this roll of carven fame, though James I. erected tombs both to his mother and to her foe, Elizabeth. His own grave was identified only in our time. Charles II. has no memorial but the gruesome wax effigy which once made part of funeral pomp. Several of these effigies are now exposed to view above the Islip Chapel, but some are in such a state of hideous decay as to be kept locked away. The oldest shown seems to be that of Queen Elizabeth, with staring eyes and pinched lips. Buxom Queen Anne and sallow William, overlooked by his Mary, look as if they had been restored. The most lifelike figures are those of the elder Pitt and of Nelson, the latter dressed in his actual clothes. How many of the marble statues below had been better made in wax, and, instead of figuring through centuries of sculptured nakedness, clothed in perishable silk and lace such as padded out their imposing figures to the bleared eyes of contemporaries!

Some more precious ornaments of the Abbey have been less carefully preserved. The golden shrine of the Confessor's tomb, with other treasures, were melted down in the first blaze of the Reformation. The Puritans, very unreasonably, wrecked that younger Edward's tomb, who was the most Protestant of our kings; and by them also were destroyed some artistic emblems of superstition; yet not so much havoc was then wrought as might have been feared. Just before the Revolution, a prying chorister was able to handle the bones of the Confessor. Private cupidity or vandalism may be blamed for the disappearance of jewels, mosaics, statuettes, and such portable bits of decoration. At one time visitors seem to have roamed at will over the structure, free to work the mutilations and dis-figurements that here and there are too apparent. Later on, the authorities went to the other extreme, when Charles Lamb complains of two shillings as an exorbitant charge for admission, while at St. Paul's it was only twopence. Always the Westminster boys must have had access to the Abbey, and boys at all times have been apt to mischief. Lamb half humor-ously hints at Southey, in his republican salad days, as author of an outrage upon Major André's monu-ment. In the Reformation time we have a record of more deadly mischief done by one of the school "children," who by throwing a stone that hit him under the ear, killed a boy selling books and papers in Westminster Hall, and had to take sanctuary in the Abbey, as often did more distinguished offend-ers, not always to find due immunity.

The quiet of the cloisters is enlivened by the laughing chat of these young gentlemen, whose time-honoured School adjoins the Abbey in which they pay their devotions, and they have also privi-leged entrance to the House of Parliament. The scholars, with their black gowns and white neckties, excite the respect or curiosity of foreign visitors,

who might see them more lightly arrayed in their Vincent Square playground, not far off, though they have been fain to give up the boating on the river that used to be one of their favourite pastimes. We know, if foreigners do not, how this foundation has long taken rank as one of our great public schools, a notoriously rough one from the old days when Busby's rod was plied on so many budding statesmen and prelates; yet it has had such a gentle pupil as Cowper, and such an uncongenial one as Zerah Colburn, the American calculating boy, whose school-days here had nearly been reduced to a fraction when he refused to submit to the truly British institution of fagging. Westminster's distinc-tion now is as the only one of the great London schools still clinging to its venerable walls, as well it may, when they incorporate some part of the monastery that was the core of the whole group.

The most notable fragment of the Confessor's building is the Pyx Chapel, now shown by electric torchlight, once the treasure-house of the regalia and crown jewels, in which came to be kept the *pyx* containing the standards of coinage, afterwards removed to the Mint. At the west end is the Jerusalem Chamber, a banqueting hall of the abbots, in which Henry IV. died, and it has been used for many gatherings both festive and funereal. Here, when Henry VII.'s Chapel proved too cold for them, the Westminster Assembly of Divines met to draw up a catechism that, even in its shorter form, has caused many tears and stripes to the young Old Adams of two continents; and here was hammered out that revision of the Scriptures that vexed some grown-up believers. In passing round the Cloisters, visitors will not neglect to turn into the Chapter House, which has served as a meeting-place for Parliament and as a store-house for Domesday Book and other musty records. It is now restored and lit by storied glass to the memory of Dean Stanley, long the loving guardian of a minster "which has been entwined by so many continuous threads with the history of a whole nation."

But this is not a guide-book to catalogue all the sights of our Christian Valhalla, coming to a cli-

PARLIAMENT STREET

max in Henry VII.'s Chapel. Before turning away from the Abbey, strangers should look into the church nestled beside it, like the tender of a man-of-war, St. Margaret's, "Parish Church of the House of Commons," notably rich in stained glass. The famous east window was intended for Henry VII.'s Chapel, but the Reformation barred it out of the Abbey, and not till the eighteenth century did it find a place in St. Margaret's, after moving adventures related in my book on *Essex*. Other windows make monuments to various worthies, more than one of them due to American liberality. The west window was put up by our cousins in honour of Walter Raleigh, without whom there might have been no British America. Another, the gift of Mr. George W. Childs, of Philadelphia, instigated by Dean Farrar, the then incumbent, makes a memorial to the poet whose song, "the common freehold" of since sundered nations, foresaw those

> Stained windows richly dight
> Casting a dim religious light.

My old club-mate, J.T. Micklethwaite, who lies buried in the Abbey of which he was the professional attendant and reverent devotee, used to chuckle over his tale of a cabman who, on receiving the direction, "Westminster Abbey," replied, "That's near the Aquarium, isn't it, sir?" About forty years ago spread the vogue of aquariums, whose glass was made excuse for miscellaneous entertainments. The Westminster one had its swim of popularity that ran dry in time, and its very name, hardly known to taxi-cabmen, begins to be forgotten by the rising generation of pleasure-seekers. It now makes way for a building that is to be the headquarters of the Wesleyan Church, an outward and visible sign how once humble Methodism has grown at ease in its fissiparous Sion. One wonders whether the Wesleys would be Wesleyans, were they alive to-day to find new life breathed into their Mother Church. And, when this building's turn comes to be demolished, one wonders what may have happened to Wesleyanism

and other *isms* that take themselves quite complacently for eternal verities.

Not far off rises the campanile of another pile, built by the Mother of Anglicanism, grandparent of such rebellious daughters, the Church that bids fair to outlive them all, after being driven from its old temples and schooled by persecution where it once held its head so proudly, with king and people on their knees beneath its hand stretched out to bless or to chastise. It can raise no controversy to state that in the last half-century the Roman Catholic Church has been winning back in England much of what was once its own, 'under leaders fiercely denounced or lightly mocked in vain —

> Go get you manned by Manning and new-manned
> By Newman, and, mayhap, wise-manned by Wiseman!

One of those English Cardinals, it is understood, was by the same poet made to say, "We ought to have our Abbey back, you Bees!" But since that might not be, the Roman Church set about building a cathedral for herself that should be not unworthy of her pretensions. The day had gone by when Catholic chapels did well to keep out of notice in holes and corners, where Protestant statesmen chalked up "*No Popery!*" but then ran away. Laughing in her sleeve at Ecclesiastical Titles Bills and such fizzling fireworks of modern Erastianism, this Church had been rising in the world till her prelates could present themselves in society with the halo of apostles to the genteel. Already, in the heart of fashionable London, had risen a conspicuous Oratory enshrining the memory of that convert who was a great English writer as well as an earnest believer. The site of the new Cathedral was chosen at Westminster, near enough to invite the *genitts loci*, yet far enough from the old Abbey to take an attitude of ignoring it, and the block of building here finished in the early years of our century has not failed to justify Rome's time-honoured title as mistress of architectural arts.

The Abbey seems inspired by English history.

The Catholic Cathedral looks farther back and wider into the world. The Byzantine style, the chequered colouring of red brick and white stone, have an exotic effect for judges forgetful that Christianity was not born on British soil. The arrangement of the structure suggests how this Church, while clinging to traditions of the past, keeps a clear eye for conditions of present life. Instead of its internal space being broken up, frittered away, blocked by shrines and monuments, the Cathedral has been adapted to the worship of such a congregation as can be gathered in the widest and highest nave of any English church, a vast open space from which thousands of eyes can be fixed upon the altar throned magnificently in the sanctuary where natural and artificial light are focussed upon the central act of Catholic faith. Behind is an apse looking south, for Rome stands so sure of her position that she can afford to smile at the pedantry of orientation affected by the Anglican Church. As yet, most of the interior shows the plain brickwork, its very bareness helping to bring out the noble proportions of the edifice; but these naked walls are gradually to be veneered with marble and mosaic, till the whole surface is smoothly and warmly clad, a consummation that may not long be devoutly wished, when this Church has the way of making converts among the wealthy, whose hearts she can turn to munificence. Already the scheme of decoration glows in patches upon the rough skin, carried out first about the High Altar, and in the chapels that open on either side along the whole length of the nave.

The first chapel to be completely invested with its tasteful ornament is that beside the Baptistery, on the right of the entrance, a memorial and posthumous offering of the late Lord and Lady Brampton. In this brand-new shrine, a heretic may well linger to admire the effect of graceful design and harmonious colour of rich materials; yet also he cannot but be moved to thoughts out of keeping with the text, *De mortuis.* The founder, better known as Sir Henry Hawkins, was not renowned in

his lifetime for piety and strict morality, either when he figured as *insigne mœstis prœsidium reis* or when he sat upon the bench with more sternness than dignity. One need not rake up unsavoury gossip that used to be thrown upon his doorstep. Shortly before his death there was published, at least with his approval, a book given forth as his memoirs. By this time at ease within the bosom of the Church to which he turned at the eleventh hour, he still chuckles over a cynical and worldly view of life, and lets religion appear rather as matter for pleasantry. He tells us as a good joke that in early life, when he had time to say his prayers, he sometimes caught himself addressing them to "Gentlemen of the Jury," upon which a bar-wit remarked how thus Hawkins showed himself so far orthodox as to be no Unitarian. He declares that in those days he was never so happy as when he had saved the life or liberty of some scoundrelly client by hoodwinking judges, bamboozling juries, and bullying innocent witnesses, as he explains without a touch of shame. By such arts he is said to have earned the largest fortune made at the Bar by any of his competitors, one of whom, noted for his sharp tongue, thus worded a contradictory boast, "I made the most money ever made at the *bar — honestly.*" A fellow-judge is credited with a blunt jest on what would happen in the next world to Hawkins's money, laid out after all with an eye to spiritual advantage. Law and justice this legal bravo seems to have looked upon as a profitable game, and the best thing to be said of him is that on the bench he showed zeal for the rules of the sport, turning to good account his long-sharpened experience as detector and defender of knaves. Is such a memory so easily transmuted into a sight of beauty, or an offering acceptable to Heaven?

But it is well not to be too curious in looking into the origins of sacred art. Money wrung from tortured Jews went to build Westminster Abbey; the masterpieces of Raphael and Michael Angelo cost many a son to the Church; and the

THE BLUES IN CONSTITUTION HILL

riches of the Anglican Establishment were often due to miserable sinners who made a bad bargain, since for centuries they have had never a prayer for their uncleansed souls. So let us leave the chapels of this new Cathedral to be hallowed in the years to come by pure and humble hearts better than by gilding and precious stone. The formal consecration of the whole fabric has been delayed till the present year by a canon, not observed in all Communions, that such a sacrifice should be free from the blemish of debt.

I must not lead the reader into crypts of controversy, but the stiffest-kneed heretic may pay toll of sixpence to ascend the campanile, for a prospect over miles of roofs, bristling with the numberless towers and spires that mark the broken ranks of Protestantism through which the Church of Rome, strong in her flexible armour and her firm discipline, seems to march like a Macedonian phalanx. This graceful tower, where St. Simon Stylites might have a pleasant time of it in summer, is nearly three hundred feet high, and by its slender isolation deludes one with an appearance of greater height than the Clock Tower's and the Victoria Tower's, both of them its superiors in fact. Other eminent structures, like that of Buckingham Palace and the huge block of Queen Anne's Mansions, give more variety to its view than to that from St. Paul's or the Monument. Now that the Great Wheel at Earl's Court has yielded to the whirligig of time, there is no better point of vantage for looking over the show side of London, greenly dappled by the parks of the West-end.

TOTTENHAM COURT ROAD

THE WEST END

WISE MEN, who are said to come from the East, may explain to us why the star of fashion, to which the rich and proud hitch their vehicles, tends to take its way westward. One of the commonest place-names in England, indeed, is Sutton, but Weston is also frequent, whereas Nortons and Eastons are much rarer. So strong is the tug of the West, that this end of any city seems aptest to win a repute as its choicest quarter, its Champs Elysee's, its Pera, cut off by a social gulf from the Stamboul of business. Even at our holiday resorts, witness Brighton, Eastbourne, and Hastings, it is the western horn that tends to be exalted as more select.

The growth of this side of London is an old story. Lords and prelates once lived snug within the walls of the City, then stretched their mansions along the banks of the Thames towards Westminster. Covent Garden and Lincoln's Inn Fields were the first squares of gentility, dating from Inigo Jones. Bloomsbury, Soho, and St. James's Squares arose under Charles II. Hanoverian princes, while waiting to occupy St. James's or Kensington, were still content to house themselves near Charing Cross. But by Pall Mall and Piccadilly the tide of fashion set westward, ebbing out of Leicester Square as in our own day we see the family mansions of St. James's Square dried up into clubs and offices. Berkeley Square was begun when Lord Burlington built his house as the last in Piccadilly, to have his view westward presently blocked by the Duke of Devonshire, who again was cut out by Lord Coventry at what is now Brick Street. Still farther west, where Apsley House in time came to stand, the tavern which welcomed Squire Western on his way from Somerset took the sign of the "Hercules' Pillars," as marking the end of a known world.

Mayfair, thus invaded, had been a rather disreputable neighbourhood, noted for its vulgar market, of which a fragment still holds out behind the clubs of Piccadilly, and for a chapel that, like that of the Fleet, did scandalous business in irregular marriages. But George III.'s reign saw this ragged outskirt reformed to become the most fashionable district of London, with Grosvenor Square as its new centre, while across Oxford Street, Portman Square made the lobe of other arteries that are not now so well filled with blue blood. Disraeli seems to have been at least a little "previous" when he put Oxford Street as a natural boundary like the Rhine, cutting off the true West End from "all those flat, dull, spiritless streets, resembling one another like a large family of plain children with Portland Place and Portman Square for their respectable parents." Not to speak of a royal princess, there are still half a dozen dukes and earls in Portman Square, where lived the head of the noble family with which Mr. Tittlebat Titmouse claimed kindred.

The City of Westminster is dotted, not so thickly as it might be, with tablets proclaiming celebrated occupants of this or that house, as, for instance, one near the corner of King Street, off St. James's Square, which lodged Louis Napoleon in his conspiring days. Many houses, of course, can be more or less authoritatively identified with real or fictitious personages: a friend of mine who lived in Curzon Street felt certain that Becky Sharp had been among his predecessors. Lord Beaconsfield certainly died at No.19, as he lived in his palmy days at 29, Park Lane. Gladstone is remembered in several homes, beginning with the chambers of the Albany, that have lodged so many celebrities in their youth. In one house of Berkeley Square lived Horace Walpole, in another Clive killed himself; and others could be pointed out as once the abodes of Lord Brougham and of Lord Clyde, if we cared for a complete directory of ghostly addresses thus distinguished. In Berkeley Square is a house long noted for the name of being haunted in our own time; but Lady Dorothy Nevill, in a position to probe this bad reputation, reduces its weird legend to a story of an eccentric tenant, disappointed in love, who let it go to rack and ruin for twenty years, during which he never went out, moving about the rooms only at night, when the windows showed mysterious lights in what was taken for an unoccupied building.

Nobody knows for certain how Piccadilly came by its outlandish name, at which doubtful guesses have been made. The names of its side streets often show how they were once the demesnes of noble families, whose mansions may still stand islanded among rows of unsecluded homes — Grosvenor House, Lansdowne House, House, Chesterfield House, and so on, beside the pretentious palaces recently raised by South African

millionaires and the like. The site of these houses must be a most valuable property in unearned increment; and if their owners cannot come to terms with an American heiress, they might always get new gilding for a coronet by selling such roomy town seats to be changed into blocks of flats. It is whispered, indeed, that the first crop of Mayfair flats has yielded a poorer harvest than was expected; so this new form of domesticity may be expected to flourish rather in the suburbs and in the purlieus of fashion, where it takes deeper root. People who can afford to pay hundreds or thousands of pounds a year for an apartment, may still prefer the old self-contained house, though, in the West-end, it is apt to be a model of inconvenience, especially in the bedroom and kitchen arrangements that will not meet the eye of guests, nor of passers-by admiring its fresh coat of paint and beflowered window-sills. Farther out, where fashion does not silver such discomforts, there seems a sad slump in last generation's homes of respectability, with their deep-sunk areas and long stairs, standing to let by hundreds in certain monotonous streets that hold desperately on to the skirts of gentility. Dear in proportion, and most difficult to get in the West-end, are small houses adapted to the failing supply of domestic service; and this explains the success of the flats that seek to add a new dimension to housing space.

I myself have long been on the lookout for a flat that would suit me, but find it rather hard to meet my modest requirements. I want one with nothing above it, and nothing below it, and no houses within a quarter of a mile of it, except a railway station, a police-office, a pillar-box, and a single shop to sell anything I may happen to need without delay. If ever I come across a flat that distantly approaches to such an ideal, the landlord and I have not agreed as to terms. One can't help suspecting that this kind of accommodation is too dear. When flats first began to rear their bulk in London, I occupied the dining-room floor of a small Kensington house, where "Chinese" Gordon, not yet the hero of Khartoum, was for a time my fellow-lodger in the drawing-rooms, and we were

SOUTH KENSINGTON STATION

BROMPTON ROAD ON A FOGGY EVENING

neighboured by lordly abodes like that of Sir John Millais, and a duke's *petite maison,* the rent of which was said to be £900 a year. Not far off, a too ambitious speculator built such a palace that no one ever lived in it, not even himself, as his house of financial cards fell to the ground before it was finished. It had to be demolished to make way for Kensington Court, having itself arisen on a nest of slums, where, to avoid unpleasant eviction, the shrewd owner was understood to have invited the occupants to supply themselves with firewood by pulling down their unsavoury homes about their own ears. The modest house in which I lived belonged to my landlord; but he informed me that its rent would not then be over £50 or £60 a year. When we came to be overshadowed by the first block of flats, I had the curiosity to price them, and found that less accommodation on the highest story would cost four times as much. This seemed disproportionate, considering that the heavy charge of ground rent is divided in the case of many-storied buildings. Flats were then an experiment; but still, in most parts of London, one gets more room for one's money, taking rates and taxes

into account, in the shape of a house than of a story.

It must be the constant worries and petty outgoings of the householder which help to make flats so popular that even "buildings," intended for the working-class, tend in many cases to be occupied by less horny-handed tenants. But as the rearing of "mansions" goes on apace, we may expect to find their rents falling, when the supply has gone beyond the demand. Mrs. Lynn Linton paid £140 a year for two rooms so high up that once or twice a year, as she could tell, her windows showed a clear view across leagues of London homes. This was in Queen Anne's Mansions, one of the first and the most soaring of such structures, a dozen or more stories high, which was to have been still more elevated, had the authorities not interfered, as they have been fain to do in Boston and Chicago, while New York strives to look down on the world from its towers of Babel.

As yet flat life is more at home on the other side of St. James's Park than in Mayfair, the spread of which westwards was brought up sharp by the edge of Hyde Park. Then fashion overflowed southwards into the newer squares of Belgravia, which was frankly Pimlico when George IV. had Buckingham Palace rebuilt on the skirts of this quarter, not all, indeed, to be reckoned in the true West-end, except as filling the pockets of very lordly landlords. But dignity revives again on the river bank, where the muddily-picturesque haunts of Turner give place to very elegant mansions. One most eligible site seems "ripe for development" as homes of wealth and gentility, when the Embankment shall be extended from Chelsea to Westminster Palace along what is at present an interval of chaos to draw sighs from any enterprising house agent. One can remember when an ugly prison stood opposite Lambeth, where now the Tate Gallery offers a promise of better things. "Boz" knew this stretch of the bank as a bathing-place of shameless youth; and it still shows some features not wholly out of keeping with the description in J. T. Smith's *Book for a Rainy Day*, a pen-picture taken from the site of the Tate Gallery.

"There are now very few trees remaining, and those so scanty of foliage, by being nearly stripped of their bark, that the public are no longer induced to tread their once sweetly variegated banks. Here on many a summer's evening Gainsborough, accompanied by his friend Collins, amused himself by sketching docks and nettles, which afforded the Wynants and Cuyp-like effects to the foregrounds of his rich and glowing landscapes. Millbank, which originally extended with its pollarded willows from Belgrave House to the White Lead Mills at the corner of the lane leading to "Jenny's-whim," afforded similar subjects to those selected by four of the old rural painters; for instance, the boat-builders' sheds on the bank, with their men at work on the shore, might have been chosen by Everdingen; the wooden steps from the bank, the floating timber, and old men in their boats, with the Vauxhall and Battersea windmills, by Van Goyen; the various colours of the tiles of the cart-sheds, entwined by the autumnal tinged vines backed with the most prolific orchards, with the women gathering the garden produce for

the ensuing day's market, would have pleased Ruysdael; and the basket-maker's overhanging smoking hut, with a woman in her white cap and sunburnt petticoat, dipping her pail for water, might have been represented by the pencil of Dekker."

"What I left open fields, producing hay and corn, I now find covered with streets, and squares, and palaces, and churches. I am creditably informed that in the space of seven years, eleven thousand new houses have been built in one quarter of Westminster, exclusive of what is daily added to other parts of this unwieldy metropolis." So grumbled Humphrey Clinker's master, who in Georgian days found that "Pimlico and Knightsbridge are now almost joined to Chelsea and Kensington." Yet where the Brompton Road and Cromwell Road stretch westwards, a contemporary tells me how he has shot over fields since covered by most eligible residences. When Lady Blessington moved to Gore House, seventy years ago, she spoke of herself as living "in the country," a mile from London, where now stands the Albert Hall; and her contemporary, Horace Smith, could more modestly take to "rusticating" at Elysium Row, Fulham. Soon the swelling tide poured on to submerge Kensington and Chelsea, which as insulated villages had gained social distinction of their own when the Court came to Kensington Palace. No quarter holds its head higher than the royal borough of Kensington, whose name is stretched on every side. "South Ken," as 'bus conductors curtail it, overlays the formerly more Bohemian Brompton; West Kensington would fain look down on its native Hammersmith; and far to the north the favoured cognomen tries to root itself afresh. Even the western annexe of Southend was once for advertising itself as Kensington-on-Sea; but that title stuck in the mud, as Southend itself cannot disguise its East-end connection by proposing the *alias* of Thamesmouth.

At the north edge of Kensington Gardens used to be worked Kensington Gravel-pits, a consignment from which to Russia was so royally paid for by the Czar, that the proprietor's gratitude took the form of naming Moscow Road and St. Petersburg Place, where the Greek Church should find itself at home. On this side, we strike another extension of the West-end, that holds on to it by the address "Hyde Park," growing a little shy of the more explicit "Bayswater," said to have been "Bayard's water," a watering-place when Bayard made almost a generic name for horse, like Dobbin in a less chivalrous age. This district was once christened "Asia Minor" from its population of Anglo-Indian officials; there is one corner of it that has been slyly styled "Jerusalem the Golden"; and not the least lordly part is nicknamed Tyburnia from that most vulgar Tyburn tree, set up at the crossways near the site of the Marble Arch. Park Lane — *horribile dictu!* — was Tyburn Lane, as leading to an arena chosen for executions so far back as Henry IV.'s reign. Much later, hangings were occasionally done in the most lively quarters, in the Haymarket, for instance, in the Strand, and in Pall Mall, for the sake of example, or as near the scene of the crime; but Tyburn long had such bed eminence in this respect, that a more modest place of execution, across the Thames, came to be known as Tyburn in Kent.

The Tyburn, like the Westbourne, has disappeared underground, their hidden streams degraded into drains; but the channel of the former is shown by the windings of Marylebone Lane, as by the very affix of St. Mary-le-*bourne*, and by such names as Brook Street and Conduit Street; a Brook field here was the scene of May Fair, that lasted down to George III.'s reign. Whitehorse Street, again, seems to mark its crooked bank, above the dip in Piccadilly that was this brook's course towards the original mouth, where its silt blocked the Thames with Thorney Island, the site of Westminster Abbey. The Westbourne, passing under its "Knights' bridge," fell into the Thames higher up, by Chelsea; and, now that it is cut off from the Serpentine, its channel appears no more plainly than in an aqueduct crossing the Underground railway at Sloane Square.

These natural drains of London rise, like the Fleet, in the sand-edged clay bank behind Hampstead, which nowadays has grown into such a sumptuous suburb, that it might almost be counted as morally belonging to the West-end, though cut off, like Austria from Germany, by the semi-Bohemian "groves of the Evangelist," bordered with what seems at least the stuccoed respectability of Regent's Park. People with more sense than money, know where to look for roomy houses at a fallen rent among the squares and Georgian streets of Bloomsbury, where such homes as those of Thackeray and Dickens, of Burne-Jones and Rossetti, of Lord Thurlow and Lord Mansfield, have come down to be much opened to "paying guests." I knew a man of means and position who unblushingly housed himself in Golden Square — where Ralph Nickleby lived and Matthew Bramble's party lodged — because he found this nook a smoky asylum from asthma. But Lord Bolingbroke's town house nowadays would be taken to the west of Bond Street.

Here, then, we have the quarters inhabited by Londoners understood neither to toil nor to spin, and the satellites of such, an area merging off into monotonous reaches of professional propriety, and islands of less conventional attraction. West-enders proper may be defined as those who live in London only part of the year, and having the best houses in town, make the least use of them. Certain corners and skirts of this province are notably affected by the dependents of wealth and rank. Kensington is the paradise of successful artists and authors. Dover Street, at the other boundary of fashion, is much given up to ladies' clubs and dress-makers, standing together like cause and effect. Savile Row is a centre of tailordom. Jermyn Street and its openings are in the way of letting lodgings. In Bond Street we look for jewellers and picture galleries, as in Baker Street for photographers. There was a time, not so long ago, when Finsbury in the City was a fastness of learned physicians. Now Harley Street, rather, has become a proverb for medical science; but doctors, of course, spread

ROTTEN ROW

themselves widely in the West-end. It is honey-combed throughout by mews, whole streets and lanes of stabling, that, though unsavoury, are said to make not unwholesome dwellings for the families thickly packed in their upper rooms. Will petrol have the same antiseptic effect as has been attributed to the ammoniacal odours of stables, which else might have poisoned the best part of London? But perhaps free flushing with water is the disinfecting agency; and somehow or other, whatever be the lot of human beings, good sanitation will be provided for the steeds of Plutus.

The sheeny angels of this Elysium are envied by many who see them driving or lounging in the Park, or passing on from one crush to another through the summer nights that, to more pensive minds, seem wasted on such revelry. Outsiders do not always guess how little those apparent favourites of fortune are to be envied in many cases: how black care can climb up behind the smartest motor-car;

how often an invisible sword hangs by a thread over the richest banquet; what fears and spites and jealousies may poison the sparkling cup of pleasure, or turn to ashes the most savoury fare. Moralists, indeed, have never been slow to proclaim that the passions and griefs of human nature gnaw but more sharply under furs and lace, a hard saying for ragged shiverers in the showers and blasts of life. Yet a very small experience might illustrate the troubles of those whose desires are multiplied by ever new needs; and a very little reflection should be enough to show the slaves of fashion bearing their own whips and scorns. How weary some of them must grow of an endless round of idle amusement, long before the gay throng gets leave to breathe fresh air at Goodwood and Cowes, and to wash out its over-loaded digestive organs at Homburg or Marienbad! The Season, it appears, tends to be a less well-marked period, broken up by week-end outings, frittered out by the long sittings of democratic

HAMMERSMITH 'BUS

legislators, and revived in moonlight glimpses of aristocrats stolen back to town, when perhaps they have been fain, like the proud Red Indians, to give up their hunting-grounds to strangers from still far-ther West. But still the blooming time of Society coincides with Nature's high midsummer pomps; and the harvest of marriages should be growing ripe for garnering in St. George's, Hanover Square, or other temples of fashion, before the West-end has earned its holiday.

> Good-night to the Season — the dances,
> The fillings of hot little rooms,
> The glancings of rapturous glances,
> The fancyings of fancy costumes;
> The pleasures which fashion makes duties,
> The praisings of fiddles and flutes,
> The luxury of looking at Beauties,
> The tedium of talking to mutes;
> The female diplomatists, planners
> Of matches for Laura and Jane;
> The ice of her Ladyship's manners,
> The ice of his Lordship's champagne.

Not every rhymer, like Praed, is able to take an inner view of this circle, on which so many authors, in prose and verse, have had much to say, among them the present poet-laureate, who began his career with *The Season, a Satire*. But for the moment the satiric pen has grown a little blunt in dealing with that old theme. In our time, Diogenes seems more indifferent, even more indulgent to the shows of society, perhaps as providing a pageant for the outside world; unless when stirred to a snarl at dukes and their demesnes, the esurient democrat appears often to turn less jealous eyes on the butter-flies of fashion than on the busy bees who store up envied provision of honey in the social hive. Even the most Radical papers, it will be noticed, provide their readers with glimpses into gilded life, and reports of the costliest chiffon blocks. I have met an industrious journalist living in a humble outskirt of "town," who confessed to me how, under the name of Lady X —, she wrote regular articles of fashion-

able intelligence at a remuneration of ten shillings per week. Since editors know their public, such articles must be trustfully read by middleclass and other patrons of the half-penny press, who thus, on paper, come into some tickling contact with the West-end.

Then there are always the novelists and dramatists, who set up for the crowd their peep-shows into those charmed regions. One does not wonder that story-tellers take by choice scenes on which there is more opportunity for decoration and stage effect. The heart of a duchess may not differ from that of a washerwoman; but the high-placed personage has a wider range of sensation and expe-rience, from which the artist can more easily weave a richer web of incident. The *roman bourgeois* needs stronger imagination to develop its possibilities of interest than does the cloak and sword drama; and hardest of all is it to distil pure tragedy and comedy from the elements of everyday common life. So less complaint is to be made of fabulists who pick out bedecked figures for their puppets, than of the pub-lic to please whose taste, it will be remembered, the characters in Mr. Pendennis's first novel were raised a step or two in the peerage at the suggestion of the publisher. To the humble reader, the West-end is a fairyland of romantic possibilities; the shop-girl's favourite hero or villain is sure to be that bold, bad baronet, or that virtuous lord who at last gives his hand as well as his heart to a lowly Pamela, in real life taken oftener from the stage than from the kitchen.

When we come to examine the glasses of this peep-show, we find them in our time as much clearer as are the plate-glass windows of Regent Street, compared with the leaded and small-paned casemates that served our ancestors. Authors are now bound to give a more faithful representation of the life of that class whose doings will be daily thrown in flickering cinematographs upon the sheets of our newspapers. But only of late do lords and ladies come to stand in such revealing light. The hungry novelists of the eighteenth century were dazzled when they cast their eyes upwards;

even smug Richardson and surly Johnson are ready to make allowances for a man of rank. So the imaginative pictures of fashionable life in that age must be taken as not very faithful, though, indeed, works of fact bear out works of fiction in showing silk-coated and lace-ruffled sparks of quality behaving in public places with an insolence that would now disgrace the plainest cit. Miss Burney was the painter of her time who had the best glimpses into high life, and the figure cut by royal princes and courtiers in her Diary makes less surprising the ill manners of her Harrels and Brangtons, not to speak of bears like her Captain Mirvan and Mr. Briggs.

The immortal Jane Austen, of course, is more at home in the country, or at Bath, than in "town," and her personages seldom rise above the upper middle class. But when she does give us a peep at higher ranks, one suspects her glasses of being a little clouded, unless manners have much changed for the better. Would any gentleman, nowadays, for very shame's sake, behave so rudely to a lady as did General Tilney to the romance-struck guest of Northanger Abbey? Surely no fine lady of our smartest set would be quite so insolently uppish as Lady Catherine de Bourgh. As for Mr. Darcy, his priggish pride would get him kicked out of the heroship of any novel, now that heroines no longer admire being treated *de haut en bas*. Miss Edgeworth and Miss Ferrier, for their part, deal very frankly with the big-wigs whom they bring on their scenes; but the former sometimes seems to overshoot the mark of comedy, as when she makes her Duke of Greenwich take mortal offence at a ministerial colleague for sending him a letter sealed with a wafer.

When the age of wigs had passed into that of powder, and that too had gone to dust, there came the days of the dandies, in which ladies and gentlemen of undoubted fashion took to writing stories of their own *monde*. But these can hardly be trusted, so much do they show conceit and utter want of sympathy or self-knowledge. What a haughty contempt has "Pelham" for all persons not of *bon ton;* how indulgent he is to the follies and caprices of his

equals; what unredeemed blackguards he finds in low life; and how ridiculous are the manners of the middle classes, as seen through the quizzing glass which Mr. Tittlebat Titmouse took for the sign of a complete gentleman! One can understand the grudge of professional authors like Thackeray and Tennyson against Bulwer Lytton, who in youth would endorse Byron's lordly sneer —

One hates an author that's *all author,* fellows
In foolscap uniforms, turned up with ink.

What seems less easy to understand is how the author of *Pelham* lived and learned to shine in historic romances, showing thought and research, then grew into the riper wisdom that bore fruit in *The Caxtons* and *My Novel*. Not incomprehensible was the puzzle of a Dutch reader who told me he could not make up his mind which of two English authors he more admired, Bulwer or Lytton. That misunderstanding makes the antipodes of another I once found in a travelled Italian, who, among the works of Byron, had been best pleased by certain burlesques he saw on our stage a generation ago.

For the personages of Lord Lytton's early novels, he found models in the circle of Lady Blessington, who kept up on credit a sort of London *Hôtel de Rambouillet,* more frequented, indeed, by dandies than by ladies of fashion. First in Mayfair, and then at Kensington Gore, her house, not without scandal, was practically the home of Count D'Orsay, that *Cupidon déchaîné,* who became a parasite of the Blessington family during their wanderings on the Continent, and ended his long London residence as besieged by bailiffs in Gore House. It seems strange how this self-exiled foreigner was able to succeed Brummell as our king of fashion, his reign marked by the same vanity and extravagance, if not by the same insolence. "Alfred," along with a fund of unfailing gaiety not to be extinguished by an always growing pile of debt, had accomplishments in the way of art that made him more than a lay-figure for waistcoats; his busts and sketches were as much in vogue as Lady

PICCADILLY

QUEEN VICTORIA'S FUNERAL

Blessington's *Books of Beauty* and other ephemeral works, out of which for a time she made two or three thousand a year. But now her novels are as the snows of yesteryear, like many others renowned in their day, whose fate may be taken to heart by some of our own popular writers. Her authorship, indeed, flourished chiefly through her salon in the West-end, where the critical Cerberus has often been soothed, by chicken and champagne, to let pass without a growl still duller stories than *Confessions of an Elderly Gentleman.*

This noble author had a dash of Hibernian cleverness, shown by the manner in which she was so long able to cajole her host of creditors, as well as the literary world. One smart *mot* I hope not to be wrong in attributing to her; but I cannot for the moment recall my authority. When the crash came, and she had to follow D'Orsay as a fugitive to France, she naturally expected some countenance from Louis Napoleon, newly installed as President of the Republic, to whom she had been hospitable in his days of adversity. He is said to have dryly asked how long she meant to stay in Paris. *Et vous, monseigneur?* retorted the ready Irishwoman. She soon died in exile; and Gore House was, at the time of the Great Exhibition, converted into a most ambitious restaurant, styled the "Symposium," by Alexis Soyer, that artist in cookery who is said to have been the original of Thackeray's Mirobolant, but he deserves to be better remembered for professional services to his adopted country in the Irish famine and in the Crimean War, when, in a gorgeous uniform of his own composition, he sought to refine our defective commissariat.

"Pelham" had the name of introducing sober black for men's evening wear. Another *habitué* of Gore House was Disraeli, who outdid even that dandy generation in his display of velvet, ruffles, waistcoats, rings, and chains, bedizening himself after an outlandish manner that makes his social success more of a mystery than his political career. His novels may be still read rather for their smart impudence, their scandalous indiscretions, and their curious mixed flavour of romance and cynicism, than for any deep knowledge of human nature; though, indeed, some good judges have been dazzled by works that seem often no better than flashy freaks of literature. For my part, at least, I like him better in his clever burlesques and his flights of Oriental fancy than in his pictures of a life into which he made his way as an "outsider." Unless we are to take him as having his tongue in his cheek when he presents great folk, this author is not ashamed to exhibit himself, beneath all his finery, in a most shabby character, "letters four do form its name." He meanly admired mean things, in love with the "splendid accidents of existence," with the upholstery and flunkeydom of aristocracy, as well as with its pride and power. There is, to be sure, a certain leaven of vague sentiment that keeps the affectation from going sour; and the cake is richly spiced with epigrams and personalities; but Disraeli's bounded outlook into a world given up to political intrigue and frivolous raillery, with interludes of young England masquerading, presents a mere artificial comedy of manners, which must have owed much of its success to the trick of bringing actual notabilities on the scene — Count D'Orsay, for instance, in *Henrietta Temple*, both as the pseudo-fictitious Count Mirabel, and under his own name in the dedication by "his affectionate friend."

Many other writers of Jeames de la Pluche's generation undertook to depict the West-end, who had less opportunity to observe its salons and banqueting-rooms. What are we to think of Samuel Warren, who thought so much of his own work? Is *Ten Thousand a Year* a faithful picture of life? Are the Aubreys of this world so compact of honour, dignity, grace, and other qualities to be at last rewarded by poetical justice? Are attorneys, linen-drapers, dissenting ministers and the like all so vulgar, scheming, and hypocritical? Was there ever

such a hateful little wretch as Tittlebat Titmouse, who, after turning an envious eyeglass on the fashionable world from afar off, finds himself fooled for a time by fortune to the top of his bent? What reader cares now to force his way through this once admired jungle of satire and sentiment? Arid our neglect of poor Warren's special pleading for gentility finds explanation in more than one novel of our time, where the same theme, a man of lowly birth suddenly embarrassed by wealth, has been treated with humour, sympathy, and truer insight. How a cheap draper's assistant may have the makings of a man in him is shown in Mr. H. G. Wells' *Wheels of Chance,* when for once the author deals with mere average human nature. How a raw clerk, conscious of dropping his *h's,* may develop a gentle soul under the sun of fortune, is brought out in the late D. Christie Murray's *Way of the World,* the moral of which, indeed, is rather marred by the ludicrous weakness of the hero, as also by the calumnious presentment of a comic villain, shown up from real life for his offence of having been once the author's friend and creditor. This novel, else hardly to our purpose, has a no doubt satirically exaggerated picture of the beginnings of "Society journalism," while its most lifelike figures are copied rather from Fleet Street than from the West-end. Another story of our time, Mrs. Jenner's *An Imperfect Gentleman,* gives a far fairer and more convincing account of what would happen through a head-turning inheritance, a question also well treated in Mrs. Oliphant's *The Wizard's Son* and *Harry Muir.*

In *Ten Thousand a Year,* many real persons are introduced under a very thin disguise of caricature: we can all guess who sat for Mr. "Quicksilver," afterwards Lord Chancellor "Blossom and Box"; Mr. "Venom Tuft "is said to be Abraham Hayward, without any hint of the qualities that must have gone to making him a trencher-fellow of the great; and the Marquis "Gants-Jaunes de Millefleurs" offers another presentment of Count D'Orsay, who figured so imposingly before that generation. In Blackwood's Tory Magazine, of course, nothing too bad could be said of Whig politicians arid of the great Bill "for giving everybody everything"; and it is noticeable how Mr. Titmouse's address to the electors of Yatton, intended for screaming farce, would now, with the omission of one paragraph, pass almost for electioneering commonplace. But this extravagant farrago of party and class feeling became the most popular novel of its day, undoubtedly relished by good, if prejudiced, judges, while on the author's own authority we have it that some of these voted Dickens quite eclipsed by a book which our generation cannot read without yawning. There seems reason to suppose that Warren made another attempt on public taste in the same style, half expecting it to fall flat, as it did. Mr. E. B. V. Christian, in his *Leaves from the Lower Branch*, points out that a novel entitled *Walter Hurst*, by "H. G. Pelham," published in 1854, to be soon forgotten, reads as if from the pen that wrote *Ten Thousand a Year:* if not by some writer who was trying to imitate him, I should guess at it as an early work of Warren's, kept in MS. for half his lifetime, as perhaps was Disraeli's *Endymion*, that came to be less timidly put forward by an author whose name had risen to be an advertisement for the dullest pages.

From such one-sided views, there was bound to be a reaction, which bounced to the other extreme. Dickens had the entrée to Lady Blessington's salon, but the society of kid-gloved scribblers seems to have been thrown away on him. We all know how his West-end folk appear either as fools or knaves, not to say mere puppets dressed up to be banged about by vigorous sentiment, whereas genuine honesty and true wisdom must be sought for among the poor and lowly, whose hearts are in the right place if not their *h's* and *w's*. Through this peep-show fashionable life is seen not steadily nor whole; as, indeed, most of Dickens' characters are exaggerated and highly coloured after theatrical models, to play their parts in what may be called the transpontine drama of fiction. It was perhaps a sign of wholesome stirrings in that generation that Dickens set copy lines for a new school of fiction.

Douglas Jerrold and a host of other popular writers, who could not at least be accused of snobbery, were all in the same tale of reviling the high and mighty, and proclaiming virtues that blushed unseen by the Coningsbys and Pelhams. This is the natural bias of the imaginative *maker*, who all along has been more in the way of rubbing shoulders with poverty, while the painter might get closer into touch with wealthy patrons. But democratic sympathy can easily be pushed too far, till a satirical humorist has to remind us —

> Hearts just as pure and fair
> May beat in Belgrave Square,
> As in the lowly air
> Of Seven Dials.

Was not Thackeray the first great novelist, after Fielding, who tried to hold the balance true? At the risk of being belittled as a "superior person," I avow my faith that Dickens, however excellent in philanthropic pleading, *qua* painter of human nature was to Thackeray as limelight unto sunlight, or pineapple rum-and-water unto wine. The moralist of *Vanity Fair* mocked at Bulwer's affectations and at the genteel life admired by Samuel Warren; but his satire of those in high places was not mere caricature. This satirist is a true humorist, with a tear seldom far from the laugh that sometimes seems overdone as a Punch's squeak; yet the still sad music of humanity may be caught even among the shrill note of his panpipes. Most of his characters are human beings, not mere lay-figures of virtue and vice. Becky Sharp has her moments of contrition; the duteous Laura Bell her twinges of jealousy; the wicked Lord Steyne is not without a touch of common kindness; Major Pendennis can for a moment forget his worldly selfishness; Colonel Newcome is none the less lovable for his dash of soldierly pride. The author's view of life is, indeed, limited, mainly turned upon the lower-upper and upper-middle classes, so that his novels would almost make a guide to the West-end and its purlieus, with excursions into artistic Bohemia.

Oxford Street by the corner of Bond Street

ST JAMES'S STREET, LEVÉE DAY

Hyde Park Corner on a wet day.

Humbler folk are here as much kept in the background as the inhabitants of mews hidden away behind the squares and lordly mansions to which he introduces us by the front door; but Thackeray has always a kind thought of honest poverty, unless when put into a flunkey's livery. In his early writings most plainly appears that tossing and goring mood to which plush was like a red rag. One can't help suspecting a shade of truth in Disraeli's bitter picture of "Mr. St. Barbe," with his jealous grudge against the aristocracy. The denunciation of snobs reads as a half-confession; and the masquerading part of Jeames de la Pluche seems studied with "the keen eye of an accomplice," who did not despise cards of invitation from "Lady Frances Flummery." But his early social uneasiness clarified into a rich vintage of moral wit and wisdom, which has been a most salutary tonic to the patients among whom he practised. He at least founded the school of

sympathetic realism brought to bear upon a life that had never yet been so truly painted. A prose Shakespeare might have been produced, had Nature but blended his genius with that of George Eliot, who takes a loftier outlook over scenes of rustic life, while her strength goes from her when she gets among the Philistines and Delilahs of the West-end. If it cannot be denied that the satiric novelist had a suspicious itch for scratching snobbery, let us remember how he gave a new and deeper meaning to the word. "Nobs and snobs," with Disraeli answer to "high and low"; it was Thackeray who taught us to call no man a snob, unless as meanly admiring the mean side of greatness.

Mrs. Gore, in her *Sketches of English Character,* is quite as satirical as Thackeray, without his sympathetic touch; and the *Chronique Scandaleuse* of their day shows how that *Vanity Fair* moralist had no need to invent puppets for

CHELSEA PENSIONERS

indignant belabouring. His "Gaunt House" was Hertford House, whose master, the "Marquis of Steyne," figured also as the "Lord Monmouth" of *Coningsby;* and everybody can put a real name to the "Wenham," "Wagg," and "Rigby" that played toadies and satellites to this ill-famed nobleman. The Marquis of Hertford belonged to a family which for two or three generations loomed out before snobs in a gilded haze of scandals; and he married a putative daughter of that other noble reprobate, "old Q.," who left the pair a large fortune. That dreary "town palace" was not his favourite residence; besides country houses in England, he had a *petite maison* in Regent's Park, and at Versailles a cottage of royal whim, built for the Comte d'Artois before the Revolution put French princes on their good behaviour. It was, indeed, Lord Hertford's boast that he kept a clean shirt ready for him in every capital of Europe; and in most of them he seems to have left much dirty linen for the wash. One noble taste he had, for the collection of pictures, which, when bought, he is said to have kept stacked up with their faces turned to the wall. Lady Dorothy Nevill relates that he once commissioned an agent to find him a picture which, it turned out, he had himself bought three or four years earlier. Such a voluptuary was sure to be on bad terms with his heirs; and on his death he left his collections with most of his wealth to an illegitimate half-brother, as is believed, who, brought up chiefly in France, came to be Sir Richard Wallace, when an English title was granted him for his services to humanity at the siege of Paris. He inherited Lord Hertford's artistic tastes, spending freely on old armour and bric-à-brac, as well as on pictures, but also on munificent charities which silver-plated his dubious origin; and his love of art was not so selfish as his benefactor's. Dying without an heir, he desired Hertford House and its treasures to be given to the nation, a bequest that took effect at the death of his widow; thus London gained one of its museums, haunted by a family history that is no masterpiece of nobility. Had Thackeray lived to moralize in "Gaunt House" as it now stands open to the common people!

An apt disciple of Thackeray was Anthony Trollope, who washed and stippled in his realism with such industrious pains, that he passes for a photographer rather than a painter of life. But the man must have had some high lights of imagination who portrayed Bishop Proudie without ever having come into contact with a Church dignitary; and most of the many peers and politicians who figure on his canvas could have given him only short sittings in the hunting-field or in the course of post-office business. One gathers that this voluminous writer, at once gently and roughly bred, had in youth little access to West-end society, and all along was in no danger of becoming a snob, inclined rather to bluster against his superiors than to toady them. But, within a certain range, he saw human nature clearly through his spectacles; and his method is simply presenting great folk as like other people, only a little externally changed by the conditions of their place in the world. In this he has been so successful, that his gallery of aristocratic full-lengths and sketches is certainly the largest, and, to my mind, the most convincing. I am not so sure about his shilly-shallying heroes and heroines, who have such difficulty in knowing their own minds. His rather rapid and mechanical workmanship has told against his fame; but that large output enabled him to present an extraordinary variety of types, from the old Whig Duke of Omnium, to his conscientious heir Planty Pall, from the straight-riding Lord Chiltern to the shifty Lady Eustace; then his way of re-introducing such personages, in the foreground or background of other novels, at different periods of life, gives him a chance of elaborating their characters through the shades added by time and responsible station. He seems, to be sure, more at home in country scenes; but his camera is so often brought to bear on the West-end, that never again can we believe it peopled by the genteel fairies and diabolic satyrs of the Minerva press, whose authors turned out their daubs for less than ten pounds a volume.

Our own generation's novelists are in the way of giving themselves out as quite at home among the smartest society, of which they treat us to so many and often so unflattering pictures. Sometimes, indeed, one can't help suspecting the pose to be on the side of the painter who takes his subjects thus much at their ease, or even in scandalous undress. There are some of these Paul Prys whose familiarity with the seamy side of high life things seems a mere affectation; others, who may or may not know what they are talking about, show up the West-end as marrying covetousness to frivolity; few present its denizens in any heroic light, who as often as not figure in current fiction stripped not only of wigs and *crachets,* but of bare respectability. But of these authorities I need say nothing, since they are in the hands of all readers.

A more trustworthy guide we have to social *penetralia* is in the memoirs that elbow one another out of the circulating library. Everybody who is anybody writes his reminiscences nowadays; and more than one of our *kaloi-kagathoi* has been moved to draw comparisons between "Society" as he or she knew it in youth and in age. Such contrasts we expect to turn out to the disadvantage of the present; but it is not always so with sunny natures setting softly amid honour, love, obedience, troops of friends, over and above comfortable homes in the best neighbourhood. From reflective and experienced autobiographers, then, with the help of novelists and journalists, we may come to some knowledge of what moral changes have passed over the West-end in the last generation or two.

The first observation to be made is that in our time "Society" has become more of a republic, no longer taking its laws from dandy dictators or dynasties of great families. There was a time of sharper distinctions and smaller herds of fashion, when the Court Directory might be known by heart to all privileged to have their names in it, who also would be known to each other at least by sight and by reputation, good or bad. Now the social sun shines down upon a jungle of coteries, standing stiffly upright or climbing eagerly as parasites, all striving towards some share of the light that will

expand their blossoms. The most gaudy of these growths, which forces itself into public notice, is not the most deeply rooted, nor bears the best fruit. As in other republics, wealth comes to overshadow claims of birth, and notoriety more easily passes for honour. Hard-and-fast lines tend to be rubbed out, as in the world of science; old barriers are thrown down, leaving a career more free to ambition and to talents, most effectually brought to bear in their literal sense of L.S.D. The constant bustle, change, and excitement that make the breath of life to a "smart set," are not to be compassed without money, come by honestly, or somehow or other. Only big fishes have a good chance to keep in the swim, where their rich scales are expected to be felt rather than seen. Mere vulgar ostentation is of no account; the golden rule is to spend for one's neighbour as he spends for others. Anything like originality, or the eccentricity for which Englishmen once had a name abroad, is now rather unfashionable, being, indeed, weeded out of our youngsters by the drilling to uniformity that is called their education.

One fence that in former generations divided Society into two opposite camps, seems now as dilapidated as the Great Wall of China. Whig and Tory mix freely in the search for pleasure, when the most crowded salons no longer fly the flag of a political party. Every now and then some heated controversy of class or interest may strain social relations; but our generation hardly understands the vehemence of party feeling that was nursed by our grandmothers as well as by their husbands. The most vehement Radicalism, if not too loud or hairy, is admitted into the world of fashion, sometimes even welcomed as a tickling novelty. The old orthodoxies, also, have ceased to be indispensable; Sunday is swallowed up in the amusements of a "weekend"; while everyday flirtations with novel religious fads are tolerated; and some fine folk show themselves ready to peep into shady superstitions, to make believe in any not too meddlesome or exacting creed, that makes a change from the old-

Old river wall, Chelsea

fashioned faith of their forefathers. Sound Churchmen, however, are still able to point to attendance at fashionable services and patronage of charities, as fitting into the press of social functions. It seems to be a current persuasion that the nineteenth ccentury cocks of positive science crowed too soon, so this generation feels able to turn round for another nap.

I am not qualified to enter on the subject of woman's clothes, as to which experts inform me that wider freedom of choice now reigns than in more strait-laced days. I will only observe that the dictates of female fashion can be inspired by no æsthetic principle, since the choicest *chiffons* of any season come sooner or later to the scrap-heap of vulgarity; and to a future generation, photographs of their mothers may look as absurd as now do their grandmothers from the age of pork-pie hats and crinoline. Men's attire certainly answers to the republican principle. D'Orsays and Disraelis would nowadays be stared out of their finery; and even such "swells" as used to make butts for *Punch* have passed much into the background. All Mr. Pepys' expense, if he sought to cut a figure in our haunts of fashion, would have to be on a studied plainness, distinguished only by cut and quality, or by the air of careless familiarity with good clothes, which to a sharp eye may mark off the real West-ender from *endimanché* visitors to the Park or Piccadilly. To tell the truth, it is often hard to tell the difference, when Tittlebat Titmouse, if he have mind and money to give to it, can on reasonable terms ape all the requirements of sartorial art. It is for the Tittlebat Titmouses of this generation, I take it, that some of our newspapers have lately taken to publishing dictates of fashion for men, seriously laying down the law on nice questions of ties, buttons, and boots, not without veiled advertisement of the shops where these indispensable decorations may be had at moderate prices. If any man has nothing better to do with his time than to read this sort of chatter, it is at least not such venomous stuff as spiced the *Sunday Flash,* in days when Ten Thousand a Year counted as boundless wealth.

To be well-groomed, rather than sumptuously caparisoned, makes now the ideal of a man's appearance; and the barber is as much a minister of fashion as the tailor. The shaven faces of gilded youth, who appear to take actors or priests as their model, are perhaps due to our want of respect for age. With his hat on, at least, the baldest senior is able to disguise the work of years, but for tell-tale wrinkles which no razor can smooth away. In the time of *Tom Jones,* a man was willing to sit down as old, or might hope to be looked up to as venerable, at an age when now he still contrives to play the part of a gay spark. In the working-class, we hear, grey hairs are looked on with dread as lessening a man's value in the labour market; but the more artful veteran of the West-end is able to keep a habit or appearance of activity almost to the age at which his grandsire was content to become a slippered pantaloon. This attitude of defiance to time, not only a superficial show, is no doubt due to the more athletic pastimes of a society that with garden-games, golf, and field sports strives to adjourn the process of petrification into alabaster. Such active habits are related to the present style of studious simplicity in male attire. Athletic games were clearly contra-indicated, as doctors put it, by the wigs, ruffles, starch, skirts, and other trappings of a more formal age — not to speak of hoops and headdresses.

It has been suggested that masculine supremacy is somewhat plucked by changes in fashion which eschew the cock-pheasant or the robin-redbreast as patterns for imitation. Since conspicuously fine feathers have been given up to the hen-bird, there can be no doubt as to woman claiming a position of more equality. I put aside a blazing question of politics; but it seems uncontroversial commonplace to insist on the freer tone of intercourse between the sexes, and the way in which girls take to the sports and games once monopolized by their brothers. The Georgian lady's charm of delicate languor is quite out of date, as shown by our heroines having almost forgotten how to faint away, a weakness quite common, indeed, with the

HANOVER SQUARE

THE DRIVE, HYDE PARK

heroes of older romance. When Belgravia was built, there and then, we are told, did fine ladies first venture to walk about unattended, a fact prompting the *mot* that in this new district "all the women were brave and all the men modest." Now women of all ranks have learned how to take very good care of themselves; and if some of our Amazons seem too free from the modesty once held to adorn their sex, we may set against them certain men not ashamed to parade affectations of effeminacy. These weaklings, indeed, are more in a minority than are the strapping damsels who poach on old preserves of manliness. But while far more athletic on the whole than were their grandparents, both sexes become unblushingly apt to think and talk a good deal about their stomachs, as well as about other matters that used to be tabooed in drawing-rooms. The cult of health even shows a tendency to take the place of piety, with doctors for its dogmatic priests, preaching in vain against a whole tribe of quack dissenters. Not the least flourishing of physicians, regular and irregular, are those who make a speciality of nerves and of the various obscure complaints bred by imagination, itself fed by excitement and over-stimulation.

Another symptom is a new love of publicity in high life. One of its recent annalists recalls the Duke of Wellington's indignation against a newspaper proprietor, who made copy out of being entertained at Apsley House. We have changed all that. The reporter no longer hangs in the lobby to pick up from Jeames or John Thomas a list of guests invited to ball or banquet. He, or she, would have us understand that they enter on so intimate a footing as to describe the dress, looks, and doings of the company, who appear to welcome such advertisement, as out of doors they expect to have their finery snapshotted for the admiration of the multitude. It is advertisement rather than information which fills the interviewer's paragraphs, now that the scandals, of old so malignantly handled in the *Sunday Flash,* are but rarely hinted at by our society journals till they bloom out in the Divorce Court. If it were the case that leaders of fashion, professional beauties

and the like, give some consideration for being kept before the public eye, they have a right to nothing but good words for their money. But if all whispers be true as to what goes on among our smart sets, one wonders at their willingness to live in glass houses, where, indeed, the throwing of stones might prove a dangerous fashion.

It is not only in play and pleasure-hunting that both sexes show themselves more keen. Of all the changes that have passed over the West-end in the last generation or two, the most marked seems the abandonment of that unconcerned attitude once held becoming to blue-blooded man, as well as woman. As the difference that struck him most, Mr. Charles Villiers told Sir Algernon West that, whereas in his youth "every young man, even if he was busy, pretended to be idle, now every young man, if he was idle, pretended to be busy." Notoriously the "best people" have given up their disdain for money-making. Your Pelhams and Mirabels had no idea of earning an honest penny; when the betting-ring or the gaming-table failed them, they let long-suffering tradesmen go into the Bankruptcy Court without a twinge of conscience, and only when pressed by debts of honour, or rude bailiffs, did they condescend to do business with sharp lawyers and extravagant usurers. Disraeli's "Armine," seeking to borrow £1,500, laughed to scorn the idea of taking more than half this advance in coals; but that hero's descendant might have seen his way to serious consideration of such terms. Hard-up scions of aristocracy began by dealing in wine, as a commodity of which they might be supposed to have some experience; and one can remember how eyebrows were lifted when a duke put his sons into tea and cotton. Now there is nothing which may not be sold, without loss of social credit, by the sons of peers who themselves perhaps are wholesale dealers in coals, dairy produce, game, jam-manufacturers, cab-proprietors, or what not. Why not, when our impecunious nobles think no shame to ape Nero on the stage, while ladies of title unblushingly exhibit themselves in public as nautch-girls? I quote the animadversion of a contemporary moralist who was born in or near the purple:

"Another quality which was formerly supposed to mark the Aristocracy was its contempt for filthy lucre. For my own part, I confess to some scepticism about this aristocratic trait. Some of the most penurious people I have ever known have had the longest pedigrees; and their contempt for lucre was only a contempt for the habit of acquiring it by trade. Money wrung from highly-rented land, or from the overcrowded tenements of great cities, has never stunk in the nostrils of "our old nobility." They drew the line at commerce, but that line has long since been obliterated. Dukes' sons rollick on the Stock Exchange and drudge at office desks. Sprigs of aristocracy tout for wine merchants and tobacconists. I have known one of the class who partly subsisted by recommending a bootmaker in the Burlington Arcade. Another was dressed for nothing by a tailor who said there was no advertisement equal to this youth's figure. Others, longer headed, pillage their friends at Bridge and Poker; and the more highly educated detachment subsist by writing social paragraphs for *Classy Cuttings*."

We are told that a comparatively low tone of commercial morality in Japan came from the fact that no nobleman or gentleman would soil his caste by concerning himself in trade. But now that our *daimios* and *samurai* stoop to enter the ranks of financiers and shopkeepers, what have they done to leaven the money-market with noble principles? The less apt of them lend their historic names as figureheads and decoys for companies promoted by sharper wits, cunning and dignity joining hands to fleece the silly flocks that often thus are brought to shivering repentance of their trust. Other well-born speculators have gone into the City to show themselves as smart as the proverbial Jew or Yankee, who in real life might often retort accusations of unscrupulous greed upon competitors titularly noble and honourable. A few years ago, a wretched gambler with other people's money sailed too near the wind, was

taken aback, and when convicted of fraud, by a dramatic suicide pleaded guilty to the crime of being found out. It was understood by those behind the scenes, that this notorious adventurer had partners in his schemes, all men of social standing, in one case of lordly rank, and that these associates brought him to direful wreck by the sharpness with which they took their opportunity to rat from the sinking ship. Even the conscience of the Stock Exchange was stirred by this treachery; and it was whisperingly noted how two of the selfish speculators were soon called to their last account. Their ringleader, or victim, as some held him, lies buried under the most sumptuous monument in his parish churchyard, bearing this eloquent inscription, *He loved the poor,* but omitting to mention that what he gave to the poor he robbed from the rich. His faithless associates might have as epitaph, *Japanese papers, please copy.*

And not only lords but ladies, it seems, are as keen about money-making as any *roturier* or *épicier*. Women of title, delicately wrapped in an *alias,* carry on milliners' shops in the West-end. Haughty dowagers gamble on the Stock Exchange as well as at the card-table. Blue-blooded damsels prove eager to play the shop-girl, in all but modest civility, at charity bazaars, the accounts of which, it is whispered, would sometimes ill bear auditing. Leaders of fashion are said to sell various favours for value received in "tips" from socially ambitious financiers. How should it not be so when some of our great nobles have been fain to restore their fortunes by marrying the daughters of wealth gained by mean cunning, sometimes not less cruel than the bold bloodshed and the adroit treacheries that went to win coronets in the good old days. Let America look up to the men who by "smart" and unscrupulous schemes have bloated themselves in ruining their competitors and "cornering" the necessaries of life; but if foul dollar notes are to plaster our tarnished titles, we should feel the need of a new nobility.

The faults of our own generation always stand out most clearly, of course bulkling but the

CHELSEA REACH

more largely when wrapped in a coat of whitewash. Other times had their own besetting sins and their share of ours. We have only to focus our literary telescopes on, say, a century back, and we catch the scandalous figures of the Prince flattered as "first gentleman in Europe," of "her frolic Grace, Fitz Fulke," of courtesans shameless in high places and noblemen at home in low company. Then we may draw the field of vision half a century nearer to see the Court and its purlieus purified and sobered by the influence of a sovereign whose life brought respectability into fashion. Most of the best equipped observers seem to agree that since Queen Victoria's retirement from the world, the tone of "society" has gone down in pitch, if its melodies be more intricate and varied.

The plain truth seems to be that many of those who style themselves the "best people" are, to say the least of it, no better than they should be. One need not look through the bloodshot eyes of a social democrat to find an "aristocracy" cumbering the ground when it chooses for its function to set models of folly, extravagance, self-indulgence, and greed. Perhaps the sign of deadliest rottenness is that it has little self-delusion as to its title to esteem. It lets itself be amused by its frankest satirists; it applauds plays in which its manners are held up to reprobation; and one of its most voluptuous thrills gained by listening to eloquent preachers against the "Sins of Society." To be naked of honour, and not much ashamed, seems the virtue of the fashionable congregations, whose sayings and doings are reported for us by half-censorious, half-envious pens, dipped in no such gall of indignation as served Juvenal. The common tone taken to the faults and follies of our own time is one of good-humoured amusement, tempered with critical clear-sightedness that winks on signs of a decadence not expected to grow too offensive in our time. Many will judge that what I am now saying is more or less

BEYOND HAMMERSMITH BRIDGE

true, but that it would be better taste in me to hold my tongue, and mind my own business, which at present, to be sure, is the observation of West-end men and morals.

Our preachers, if not our amusing moralists, make some converts indeed; and the West-end always houses many who have not bowed the knee to the Baals of the hour; while these do not so much pose before the cameras of our newspapers and novelists. To a social historian in another generation, their tell-tale photographs should be more useful than the highly-charged pictures of less realistic fiction; yet the future student must remember how the photographer, too, chooses his subjects and aspects; and how his taste may be warped by the spirit of the age to take more pains in fixing and developing its uglier features. Society is not all made up of raddled dowagers, of frisky matrons, and calculating maids, of Don Juans with one foot in the grave and precocious Talleyrands in their teens, of Barnes Newcomes as keen to swindle their neighbours in the East as to neigh after their neighbour's wife in the West, of Casanovas who have no itch to write their memoirs, and of Perditas who furnish copy for newspapers. But enough of such hothouse blooms! From the feverish scenes where they seem to flower too rankly, let us get out into the open air, if only into the Park.

CHILD WATCHING THE SCOTS GUARDS FROM MALBOROUGH HOUSE.

PARKS AND PALACES

THE WEST-END, as distinguished from the west side of London, might have been defined as the quarter environing a group of parks, nominally the pleasure-grounds of our royal palaces, but now treated as practically belonging to the sovereign people. For much of what is to be said about them, one may go to Jacob Larwood's *Story of the London Parks,* a quarry of historic slabs and fossil curiosities, out of which several authors have already built up their own pages. There, as elsewhere, can be learned how, like many other parks about London, these green spaces were originally demesnes of the Church that became the greatest landlord in Middlesex.

St. James's, name once a proverb for wealth and fashion, with St. Giles as its antipodes, began humbly as a leper-hospital, whose inmates were pensioned off by Henry VIII., and he turned it into a palace, making an annexe to Whitehall, already acquired from Wolsey. The swampy fields between them, stretching down to Westminster Abbey, he improved and enclosed as a park for this double residence. His successors sometimes lived in one house, sometimes in the other. Charles I. spent his last night in St. James's, before being marched to execution at Whitehall, where Charles II. died more

ignobly. Whitehall was accidentally burned, and William III preferred the quiet of Kensington Palace; but the first Georges lived a good deal at St. James's, till it came down to be rather the official headquarters of George III's royalty.

Under James I., St. James's Park contained an early "Zoo," for here he kept a collection of wild animals, including an elephant, a troop of camels, and foreign deer, as well as cormorants and other rare wild-fowl. At either end were the Spring Gardens and the Mulberry Gardens, which grew to be rendezvous for the polite public. But the Park was still the King's private pleasance; and even under Parliamentary domination, access to it seems to have been a matter of favour. It was then for a time docked of its saintly prefix. We remember how Roger de Coverley, as a boy, asked a Roundhead the way to St Anne's Lane, and was rebuked as a young popish cur; but the next passer whom he shyly asked after Anne's Lane, broke out upon him: "She was a saint before you were born, and will be a saint after you are hanged!" The St James's restaurant, which vanished the other day, had suffered greater ignominy among un-Puritan frequenters, too familiar with it as "Jimmy's."

Parliament, however, took care of James Park, and even had it restocked with deer, when the Lord Protector hoped to fix a new dynasty at Whitehall. Charles II., in his careless good nature, threw the Park more open to his loyal subjects, while trusting himself to walk about it, sometimes with little or no attendance. It was on the road beside Constitution Hill that he met his brother escorted by a troop of guards, and gave a smart answer to James's remonstrance on his own want of caution: "I am sure no man in England will take away my life to make you king." Loyal and curious subjects, like Pepys and Evelyn, could here see their anointed master strolling with his dogs, feeding his ducks, chaffing with Mrs. Nelly Gwynne and her like, or playing at *paille-maille,* a French game appearing to have been a cross between elongated croquet and hooped golf. When first introduced, early in the century, it had been played in an avenue that is now Pall Mall; but as this became disturbed by coaches, Charles laid out a new course farther within the Park, where it was kept strewn with crushed cockle-shells, to make a rebounding surface for the balls. The vogue of this game called forth other Malls in London, at Hammersmith and Chiswick for instance; Piccadilly also began fashionable life as a Mall; but that royal play-place in St James's was *the* Mall, which grew to be a chief resort of idle London, though now more thronged with hasty passengers making for Victoria Station. The Bird-cage Walk on the other side was so called as being actually furnished with prisoned songsters; and beyond this the enclosure seems to have extended over the site of the barracks and mansion-blocks that now hem it in.

In memory of his Dutch exile, Charles made a canal through this Park, on which he set an example of skating, a sport hitherto practised in England only after the rough street-boy manner. He took great interest in the wild-fowl caught and kept about Duck Island at the Whitehall end of the canal, where a decoy was set up in what should rather be called a group of islets. Duck Island had a governor *pour rire;* it was perhaps as a joke that George II.'s

queen bestowed this dignity upon her progégé Stephen Duck, the "thresher-poet," whom she afterwards raised to a more worthy post in the Church. There are probably descendants of Charles's pets among the wild-fowl that still may be admired in the lake, while of late years they have had greedy rivals for public favour in the gulls which winter brings up to hang in a screaming crowd about the bridge, swooping and snapping at morsels of food thrown to them. The Park in former days was peopled with deer so tame that they would eat out of anyone's hand. Also we hear of a herd of cows, kept to supply the visitors with milk. A survival of this enterprise lasted till the other day, when the owner of a milk-stall near Spring Gardens made a stand for immemorial vested interest, and had to be dealt with on the truly British principle of compromise, the cows being banished, but the stall granted another site not far off. The zoological attractions of the Park were renewed in George III.'s time by elephants and other animals presented to his queen, which made a show for country cousins on visits to town then as rare as the sight of an elephant in the flesh.

At the west end of the canal, near Buckingham House, was a sheet of water known as Rosamond's Pond, which acquired a romantic celebrity, not only as trysting-place of lovers, but, when the course of true love did not run smooth, despairing hearts were notoriously in the way of drowning themselves there. Under George II., the pond came to be drained and filled up; then some cynical wag fixed a notice to a tree that, whereas here "gentlemen and ladies cannot be accommodated as formerly . . . the basin in the Upper Green Park is a most commodious piece of water, in admirable order, and of depth sufficient to answer the ends of all sizes and conditions." The name of Rosamond's Pond was, in fact, transferred to another lakelet on higher ground, near Piccadilly; and thus certain writers have been led into some confusion of topography. The first pond had been railed in on account of accidental immersions, for even then London might be bewildered by fogs,

AZALEAS IN BLOOM, HYDE PARK

not to speak of citizens who befogged their brains with liquor.

Besides the occasional fishing out of "one more unfortunate" from Rosamond's Pond, loungers in the Park had no want of exciting spectacles from time to time, wrestling matches, hopping matches, and foot races in which men sometimes ran naked, to the shocking of well-dressed promenaders, who in one case showed their resentment by taking the shameless athlete at disadvantage, obliged to run a gauntlet of switches plucked from the trees. Eccentric wagers were now and then carried out in St. James's Park. It made a parade ground for the Guards, and, as during the Gordon riots, might be turned into a camp. For brutal tastes there was the diversion of soldiers stripped and tied up to be cruelly flogged in public. But His Majesty's Guards seem to have needed sharp discipline, if it

be true that they would play the footpad in dark corners of the Park. At an unfrequented side of it duels might come off, when the law had lost its edge that dealt sharply with bloodshed within the royal precincts. Larwood points out how the hot-headed Colonel Bath of *Amelia* would not draw sword in the Park; and when Alfieri fought with Lord Ligonier, they passed from Pall Mall into the Green Park, looked on as less sacred. Constitution Hill seems to have been at one time a usual duelling-ground. The Park also made a sanctuary in which bailiffs could not exercise their office, as must have been a matter of satisfaction to some frequenters, like Amelia's unlucky husband, when he durst not show himself in other resorts. An exception was in case of high treason; and treasonable utterances in the King's own park appear to have been punished with extra severity.

All through the eighteenth century St. James's Park, unless on special occasions, stood open as a public promenade, while the right of driving through it was guarded as a privilege. We can remember how, quite recently, the road by Constitution Hill was not free to all carriages; and still the Horse Guards' gateway is barred except to a favoured few. George III., who complained of being overlooked in his gardens at Buckingham House, had no mind to keep his people at a distance. Early in his reign a German traveller describes the Mall as crowded with people of all ranks, both by day and after dark, then lit by numerous lamps; and "when the sun shines, the ground sparkles with pins which have dropped from the ladies' dresses." Sir Richard Phillips could remember the Mall one moving mass of lovely ladies by thousands, with as many smart beaux, who, in a former generation, counted it an exploit to make handsome women blush by their stares and audible innuendoes, if we can trust Congreve's *Way of the World*. Before the end of the century chairs were introduced as a speculation. But then St. James's began to go out of fashion,

while for a time the adjacent Green Park became the choice resort. This, originally a stretch of meadows beside the road to Exeter, had been added to his grounds by Charles II., and was first known as the Upper Park. Much farther back it makes a momentary appearance in history as the open ground where Sir Thomas Wyatt's rebels, marching from Kingston to attack Ludgate, encountered the Queen's forces, and were split up into two bands, one of which trudged on to dispersal in the City outskirts.

The vogue of the Green Park did not last long; and the improvements carried out here under George III. were cut up by the fêtes at the peace of 1814, when a crowded fair and free passage of all sorts of vehicles ruined the turf, while the riotous mob treated itself to a huge bonfire before a showy building set up beside Constitution Hill as "Temple of Concord," and a Pagoda in St. James's Park was burned down in the display of fireworks. For a generation the Green Park seems to have fallen into neglect.

Professor Church, in his recently published memoirs, remembers it as no better than a big, ill-

KENSINGTON GARDENS

kept village green, traversed by straggling paths. In the early Victorian years, it became laid out much as we see it now, but for the broad walk converging with other approaches at the monument now rising before Buckingham Palace to the most lamented Queen of England. Perhaps this new vista of stateliness may bring it back into fashion; but at present, unless when a band plays here, it seems most frequented by grimy loafers and glowing urchins, with an occasional Robin and Rosamond too deep in whispers to mind the want of shade. It is shut at night, as I know, who in more active days have been fain to climb the railings.

As London spread westwards, Hyde Park had gradually come to be *the* Park but before passing on to it, let us have done with its predecessor. Frederick, Prince of Wales, shut out of St. James's Palace by his father, had several makeshift residences, one of them Carlton House in Pall Mall, that became what Marlborough House is now. It was given up to his mother by George III., who turned St. James's into a stage for State functions, while his London home was Buckingham House, bought at the beginning of the reign as the "Queen's House." We know how he loved to take his homely ease in the country, living much at Richmond Lodge and at Kew, both of which small and inconvenient houses he designed turning into stately palaces. When, after twenty years, he made Windsor his summer quarters, it was not the half dismantled castle he occupied, but a new building known as the "Queen's Lodge." Every fortnight the royal pair came into town to hold levées and drawing-rooms, halting for two or three days at Kew, where, according to Miss Burney's account, the royal idol was partly dressed out, the "tippet and long ruffles " being carried in paper to save them from dust, then the final touches were added at St. James's. The house now exhibited as Kew Palace made a mere dependency of George's favoured home, demolished when a grand castle at Kew was actually set on fire, which exists in pictures and plans, showing it to have been no great loss. The works were interrupted by the King's final state of

insanity, and he ended his days at Windsor, where Châteaubriand, for a shilling to one of his keepers, was allowed to stare at the afflicted monarch of three kingdoms.

George IV., who stopped his father's building, was extravagant enough in this way on his own account, as the Brighton Pavilion stands to testify. He rebuilt Carlton House as a long, low structure behind a colonnaded front, where now is the Athenæum Club and on the Park side a row of private mansions makes the finest terrace in London. A tall column rises here as monument of the generation to which "God bless the Regent and the Duke of York!" was a watchword of thick-and-thin loyalty; but of Carlton House, all that remains are the classical columns used in the façade of the National Gallery. There the Regent held scandalous state, while his unhappy wife had to shift for a wandering home at Shooter's Hill, at Connaught Place, and finally at Hammersmith. After coming to the throne, he had Buckingham Palace rebuilt by his favourite architect Nash; it was not ready before his death, and as William IV. took a fancy to St. James's, the new palace came to be completed in its present form only under Victoria, who latterly deserted it for more secluded abodes. George IV. also began to restore Windsor Castle; and the chosen retreat of his last days was the Cottage at Virginia Water. At the same time he had St. James's Park laid out much as we see it now, the formal canal being turned into a sheet of ornamental water. Under King Edward VII., some improvements have been made, the most notable being the opening of the Mall to Charing Cross through an archway giving a vista towards the Victoria Monument, set in a new stretch of garden before the Palace, over which flies the royal standard when royalty is at home.

Marlborough House, originally built for the great Duke, was bought for Princess Charlotte, then, sixty years ago, became the town house of the Prince of Wales, its obstructed front not offering much promise of princeliness, but its best face is turned towards the Park. The garden here, and the extensive grounds walled in behind Buckingham

Palace, are the only parts of the royal demesne now kept private, to be seen by those favoured with an invitation to some royal fête. Even the quiet court-yards of St. James's, for all their show of imposing guards, make a thoroughfare for all and sundry; and the Chapel Royal services are open to visitors by ticket when the Court is in residence — if they care to follow the little procession of gorgeously arrayed "children of the Chapel," who on Sundays are brought by train from their suburban boarding-house. The gateway, with part of the adjoining Presence Chamber, is a remnant of the old palace, said to have been built by Holbein; the rest was destroyed by a fire about a century ago. Some of the apartments are given as residences to officials or friends of the King, the blocks called York House and Clarence House being appropriated to Princes of the royal family.

Like St. James's, the Manor of Hyde was Church property, transferred to King Hal when Gospel light dawned upon him through Anne Boleyn's eyes. This stretch of woodland and mead-ow, dotted by marshy pools and cut in two by the West Bourne, Henry enclosed as one of his many suburban hunting-grounds, appointing a keeper or ranger, whose office soon became dignified enough to be held by a nobleman or even a Prince. The last generation was familiar with the signature of *George, Ranger,* to notices of Park regulations; and now the late Duke of Cambridge has no less honorary a suc-cessor than the King himself, while the management is discharged by the Office of Works, whose procla-mations take the place of those signed by the London County Council in the people's own parks.

James I. being the man to stand stiffly on his sporting privileges, had hanged some poaching trespassers here; but Charles I., who enclosed Richmond Park, made up for this unpopular encroachment by throwing open Hyde Park to the citizens, if they cared to stroll so far for an airing. It became an arena for horse and foot races, for archery trials, for May-day merry-makings; and now and then we read of a Cornish hurling-match car-ried out within its precincts, such as still may be seen at St. Colomb on Shrove Tuesday. I have come across no mention of football, which seems to have been played by choice in the streets, a turbulent custom kept up at Kingston, Dorking, and other towns till our own time. Sport and play would be interrupted by the Civil War, for the Park was turned into a camp, and at Hyde Park Corner was built one of a ring of defensive works to protect London against the royal forces, who once pushed so near as Brentford. Still, in quiet intervals, the Park made a pleasure ground, as we know from the Puritan Government shutting it up on Sundays, and from the fact that the Lord Protector had an acci-dent here when he undertook to drive six in hand, but proved not so skilful at this as in controlling the coach of state. Parliament went so far as to banish the deer and sell the Park to a private person, who, as Evelyn notes indignantly, was "sordid" enough to charge a toll for entrance. But the sale could be readily cancelled when the King came by his own again; and the citizens of London, to whom Richmond Park had passed, handed over it, too, with a courtly declaration of having acted as His Majesty's stewards.

Under Charles II. this Park bloomed out as a gay resort for coaches and horsemen, whereas St. James's, as we have seen, was open only as a prom-enade. What the Mall made there, became the Ring or *Tour* of Hyde Park, upon which it was the fash-ion to drive in a mill-horse round; this was on the higher ground to the north of the water, where some old trees appear to mark its position, and a refreshment pavilion has recently revived the Lodge to which wigged and hooped carriage-company resorted for syllabubs and mince-pies. A happy man was Samuel Pepys when he might gaze upon that circus of "gallants and rich coaches," and a proud man when first he could be seen there in his own coach, soon developing quite lordly contempt for the vulgar hackney carriages that now spoilt the whole show to his eyes. It was not till William and Mary's reign that hired carriages were barred, as they still are, from most roads of the Park. When William lived at Kensington, the Palace Gardens,

THE DRINKING FOUNTAIN IN ST JAMES'S PARK

By the ring, Hyde Park
The Ring was the fashionable drive of the seventeenth and eighteenth centuries

laid out by him in the Dutch style, were enclosed as private; and persons admitted on certain days in the absence of the Court had to present themselves in full dress.

To his suburban home William made a road lit by three hundred lamps, which, in course of time, became Rotten Row, but whether that name be a corruption of *Route de Roi,* is a disputed point. All those lamps could not clear the ways to Kensington from robbers; and the Park at night got a bad name, which it kept for long, in spite of the scare of Tyburn tree at its corner and of being patrolled by soldiers, who themselves were sometimes accused of playing the footpad. It was held safest when from time to time turned into a camp, as in the risings of 1715 and 1745, and again during the Gordon riots. Ever since our kings had a standing army, this made an arena for frequent reviews and military exercises. Duels, prize fights, and races were common, with the occasional shooting or whipping of soldiers, as

side-shows to the main exhibition of *beaux* and *belles* parading themselves in the successive monstrosities of dress that, had their day. Cricket matches make their appearance early in the reign of George II., played here by dukes and earls, though to exquisites like Lord Chesterfield, this seemed no sport for a gentleman. It would take too long to dwell on all the spectacles mentioned by diarists of their day as presented in the Park for public curiosity: now a Moorish ambassador and his suite, performing a *fantasia* before the infidels; now a solemn Persian riding in Oriental state; now a Highland regiment stared at in their unfamiliar garb; again a band of Red Indians trying to bear themselves with imperturbable dignity amid a gaping crowd, that kept a little shy of their tomahawks.

Queen Caroline, who had an itch for "improvements," extended Kensington Gardens, and formed the Serpentine out of the marshy overflow of the West Bourne, which had already been pressed into service of London's water-supply. She had in view an ambitious display of fountains to rival Versailles, while she seems to have been disposed to deal with the Parks in the highhanded method of a Louis. But on her consulting Walpole as to what would be the cost of turning St. James's into a private pleasance, the Minister dryly answered, "Only three crowns" ; and the prudent Queen took the hint. More than one sovereign had the idea of building a palace in such an inviting site as Hyde Park, which Londoners, once admitted to it on sufferance, came to look on as their own. By the end of the eighteenth century so much public money had been laid out here, that there was good excuse for holding it as quasi-national property. One well-wooded height near the north-western corner was kept enclosed as a paddock for deer, a shilling at one time being charged for admission. The Park deer remained on show till William IV.'s accession; but the last royal hunting, or rather, shooting, seems to have been early in George III.'s reign for the amusement of his visitor, the young King of Denmark, who turned out such an unsatisfactory brother-in-law. Larwood has to tell how half a century later a stray hare was started beside the Serpentine, to be hunted down by a fashionable crowd.

After the peace of 1814, London had here a variety of triumphant exhibitions, a show of conquering Cossacks, and also of royal guests, beginning with Louis XVIII.'s procession through the Park on the way to his restored throne. The Czar, the King of Prussia, and their followers, were so thickly mobbed, that Blücher had to take refuge in Kensington Gardens from John Bull's overwhelming friendliness. Later in the year both Parks were given up to a week's Fair and roistering fête in connection with the centenary of the house of Hanover, when in Hyde Park the bouquet was a miniature representation of the Battle of Trafalgar on the Serpentine, the whole French fleet being finally burned with a glare that paled the fireworks following. Unfortunately, drunkenness and disorder made the chief features of this national celebration; and

respectable people were scared away from a popular orgy not easily extinguished.

A few years later, a very different scene was enacted in Hyde Park, when the funeral of George IV's ill-used queen passed on its way to Harwich. London resented the hugger-mugger way in which the ceremony seemed to be hurried on; and, to avoid sympathetic demonstrations, the Government resolved to take the procession round the north side, keeping clear of the central streets and the City. But when the escort would have turned up at Kensington, Church Street was found blocked by a mob, so the way had to be held on along the south side of the Park under pouring rain that did not damp the popular feeling. Again the Park Lane route was defended in a hot scrimmage between the troops and the people. The cortège, driven back, turned into the Park and made a dash for the other corner. But the crowd got first to the Marble Arch, closed the gate, and held it against the Guards trying to clear a passage. Stones and bricks began to be thrown; the soldiers fired back, and several persons were here killed and wounded. To heighten the panic and confusion, a gang of thieves took to knocking down persons worth robbing in the name of the dead queen. At last the officials forced a way up the Edgware Road and along the New Road as far as Tottenham Court Road, where passage was again barred by a throng of carts and waggons, and an angry crowd, that pressed the hearse by Drury Lane into the Strand; so, after all, it entered the City amid an unfuneral tumult of exultation, jangling with the toll of bells and the boom of minute-guns. The Corporation having attended it to the City bounds, the funeral pushed on more rapidly to Chelmsford, while the mourners, worn out by their long day of exciting scenes, were fain to rest at Romford or return to London for the night.

Hyde Park saw a more solemn sight when the funeral of Queen Victoria passed by it in reverent silence and lamenting tears. At her coronation it had again been given up to the popular amusements of a Fair that gathered all the chief showmen of the country, among them "Lord" George Sanger, whose reminiscences go back so far. This time the conduct of the populace appears to have been less objectionable, for he tells us that the original term of a week was extended by gracious permission. Most of us can remember the martial displays that enlivened the Park at the Queen's Jubilee, and on the deferred coronation of Edward VII. But it will be a dwindling band that can look back to the great show of that reign, the Exhibition of 1851, when the Crystal Palace erected in Hyde Park was expected to prove a Temple of Peace among nations, for whom the gate of Janus too soon came to be burst open, once and again. Sir Joseph Paxton's giant glass-house, transferred to the heights of Norwood, was first set up on the south side of the Park, between the Serpentine and Knightsbridge, a space of late years often enlivened by Volunteer parades on summer evenings. The Exhibition of the next decade took ground farther to the south, where remnants of it still stand as annexes of the Victoria and Albert Museum. A sort of permanent Exhibition of the British Empire was here intended by the Imperial Institute, a design that did not take very thriving root; and part of the building is now used as headquarters of the London University.

Meanwhile, various changes had been going on in this double pleasure-ground, where Kensington Gardens is distinguished mainly by the exclusion of carriages and by the gates being closed at sunset. The "Ring" had been forgotten by the beginning of last century, when fashion found a longer career in drives round the Park edges, and Rotten Row became a display of horseflesh and horsemen:

> In trot or canter, on the backs
> Of ponies, hunters, chargers, hacks,
> Proud to display their riders' graces
> Through all imaginable paces
> From walks and ambles up to races.

But since Luttrell's dashing day, the police object to racing; while in our time this grew to be a place of careful hygienic exercise for the "liver brigade," who make not such an elegant troop as do the Amazons cantering at a later hour before admiring eyes. The hours of fashion are always liable to change, as also the places and opportunities of display that from time to time come into vogue. Some of us can remember when the Broad Walk in Kensington Gardens was a fashionable rendezvous, that seems now to have shifted, *toto cælo* across Hyde Park.

Old pictures of the Park and its surroundings show how much our ædiles have done for it in the last century, as our own eyes see how much they still might do. The toll-bar at Hyde Park Corner was removed in 1825, when also a railing took the place of the brick wall along Park Lane. To the opposite corner of the Park, the Marble Arch, an imitation of the triumphal arch of Constantine, was transferred from its original position at the front of Buckingham Palace; and quite recently it has been thrown out into the roadway by paring off a corner to give more room for traffic, as has also been done by the Green Park opposite Apsley House. All alterations and additions, of course, find critical censors. In our day of art-culture, it will hardly be believed what an outcry was made about the setting up of the Achilles statue, cast out of the cannon of Peninsular victories in honour of the Duke of Wellington. This classical monument, to be sure, does not seem a fitting one for the tight-strapped hero of Waterloo; but what then shocked the genteel public was that a nude figure should be put so boldly before their eyes, as for a time to scare away ladies from the new Wellington Drive. Popular discontent, again, was excited when a strip of waste ground at Hyde Park Corner, taken to belong to the Park, was enclosed in the gardens of Apsley House, whose master did not always remain a hero for all his countrymen. At the time of the Reform agitation, we know, he saw cause to fortify his windows with iron shutters.

London is not happy, as a rule, in its statuary. The Corinthian Gate at Hyde Park Corner had been topped by a ludicrous equestrian statue of the Iron Duke, so pelted by Punch and other critics, that at last it was removed to the seclusion of

THE THAMES FROM RICHMOND

A HOT AFTERNOON IN PICCADILLY, IN FRONT OF GREEN PARK

LAMBETH PALACE

Aldershot, there to inspire Tommy Atkins; and a more artistic memorial now stands in the opened space to the farther side of which the arch itself has been transferred. Not much admired is the statue of Byron looking over the Park where, as he said —

> ... the fashionable fair
> Could form a slight acquaintance with fresh air.

Even the ambitious Albert Memorial in Kensington Gardens is abused as a gilt pagoda with an idol inside; but it gets a good word from Mr. W. D. Howells as expressing no ignoble idea, if, indeed, "by stutters and stammers," and not standing mum like so many other "bashful columns . . . not able to say what they would be at." In a central glade of the Gardens is now placed Watts' *Physical Energy*, a replica of the monument sent out to South Africa

for Cecil Rhodes. Another recent addition is the statue of Queen Victoria before Kensington Palace, which should interest loyal subjects as the work of her daughter, the Duchess of Argyll, who has part of this palace as a town residence. German visitors may seek out rather, on the south side of the palace, a statue of William III, the gift of their Kaiser.

The best beauties of the Park are its own, helped a little by art, perhaps hindered, for it is thought that some of those grand trees have lost sap from the ground below them being swept too tidily, as is not the way of Nature. Like Horace, I once made a narrow escape, when, beside Rotten Row on a still evening, without the slightest notice, a few steps in front of me there cracked and crashed down an elm branch twenty to thirty feet long, barricading all the roadway. But that is a trick elms have in the best regulated avenues; and we must not question the gardening skill that gives us in their season such gay groves of hawthorn, such glowing banks of rhododendrons and azaleas, such bright beds of flowers beside such masses of dappled shade, where one may drown oneself from all the struggling life of the great city stretched for leagues around.

Many strangers finding not much else to admire in London, are taken by this oasis in its centre. Mr. Henry James, who has become hardly a stranger, was moved to wish himself a Government clerk who from a Bayswater home might walk all the way to his office on turf, day after day, by some fresh trackdown the Broad Walk, across the chase-like glades, and along the Serpentine, opening away river — like between its wooded and meaded banks. "The view from the bridge has an extraordinary nobleness, and it has often seemed to me that the Londoner twitted with his low standard may point to it with every confidence. In all the town scenery of Europe there can be few things as fine; the only reproach it is open to is that it begs the question by seeming — in spite of its being the pride of five millions of people — not to belong to a town at all." Then, beyond the Dell, with its rockwork and subtropical garden, would come for him the trim parterres about the Ring Road, through which he might pass on to the Green Park and the Mall, somewhere crossing or skirting Rotten Row, that in dull weather suggests to our fanciful author a circus whose lamps are out. "The sky that bends over it is frequently not a bad imitation of the dingy tent of such an establishment. The ghosts of past cavalcades seem to haunt the foggy arena, and somehow they are better company than the mashers and elongated beauties of current seasons. It is not without interest to remember that most of the salient figures of English society during the present century — and English society means, or rather has hitherto meant, in a large degree English history — have bobbed in the saddle between Apsley House and Queen's Gate."

It is only within the last half-century or so that the Park lawns have been so thickly edged with flowers. Dust rather than bloom is mentioned by eighteenth-century frequenters, when Kensington Gardens made a more richly planted contrast, under Dutch William much given up to a topiarian display of quaintly clipped shrubs, among which Tickell can report:

> Each walk with robes of various dyes bespread
> Seems from afar a moving tulip-bed,
> Where rich brocades and glossy damasks glow,
> And chintz, the rival of the showery bow.

The sunk fence separating the two areas was one of Queen Caroline's improvements, then a new device, as to which one knows not whether to take Horace Walpole seriously when he explains its name, *Ha-ha!* by a rustic's astonishment at being brought to a sudden stand. It now seems an emblem of the unobtrusive manner in which necessary restrictions are enforced, where the chief rule is public convenience and enjoyment. The Powder Magazine above the Serpentine makes an apparent exception to this rule; but it, carefully guarded, keeps itself in modest retirement, as does its neighbour the Police Station. Near the Victoria Gate, there is even a cemetery for pet dogs that could scamper freely hereabouts in their lifetime.

On the north side of the Serpentine a classical structure serves as station for the Royal Humane Society's aid in case of accidents. Liberty of bathing here is an old story, which in former days took scandalous licence; but is now confined to one stretch of the water at certain morning and evening hours. Any warm summer evening may be witnessed here a scene that has been painted as *Arcadia in Hyde Park,* and might make a gratis Life School for impecunious artists. Hundreds, thousands, of men and boys are sitting or skipping on the grass, many of them half stripped in their eagerness for the stroke of seven. Suddenly swells a cry of "All in!" Off go shirts of every hue, as if swept down by a hurricane, and in a minute the bank is alive with little Adams racing to be first into the water, followed more deliberately by troops of taller divers and swimmers,

BOATING ON THE LAKES

who have now to assume some minimum of costume before the eyes of envious strollers perspiring in frock coats and high hats. It seems a sign of changed morals that women come walking through this throng, even some who have the appearance of respectability. In my hot youth, these Dianas would have been hooted away ; but now no Actæon seems to mind them. My plunges into the Serpentine, indeed, were made in the morning, when the company was more select. A friend of mine who took to this practice when well over fifty, and kept it up all the year round to the benefit of his health, as he believed, reported that on the coldest morning he had seventeen faithful companions of the bath, nearly all of them elderly men, the youngsters of our day being more Sybaritic or keeping later hours. One of the sights of the Park, for spectators fit and few, is a swimming race held here on Christmas morning, that last Year brought together some fifty competitors to be baffled by ice. I must own to never having seen this Spartan contest; but time was when I belonged to a band

pledged to begin the year by diving into the sea at 6 a.m. by the light of one dip guttering at the end of a pier.

The Serpentine is also used for boating, an exercise frequently complicated, one observes, by the fact of young men and maidens seeing cause to keep their eyes too much in the boat, absorbed by a pastime that in all parts of the Park seems always in season. Skating is an amusement more rarely allowed by capricious winters and careful authorities. The Round Pond in Kensington Gardens makes a basin for miniature yachting, to the delight of juvenile mariners and some ancient ones. Close to this, paternal authorities have recently opened a children's playground, including a sand heap that gives bare-legged little Londoners the illusion of being at the seaside. Some years ago the idle state-rooms of Kensington Palace, adorned with pictures brought from Hampton Court, were thrown open by desire of the late Queen, whose home this was in childhood; and an exhibition of her toys proved more popular with the British public than Wren's

HIGHGATE

handiwork or the carving of Grinling Gibbons in the Orangery. It was in her early youth that Kensington Gardens had been opened to the public, where, for a time, clothes not stained by work were required as passport to the courtly precincts.

Foreigners complain of the dullness of the Parks, as of all London, on Sunday; but in this respect some change has come about, which I, for one, call an improvement, since I worked for it as a Vice-President of the National Sunday League that championed this relaxation all along. A few bold spirits were the real motive power of the Sunday League, which got less credit than it deserved for bearing the burden and heat of the day, because another society stepped in at the eleventh hour to share the honours of victory. When we began our agitation, the public-house was the only place of

amusement open on Sunday, and that naturally too well frequented. I remember a man getting into an omnibus one Sunday forenoon, who explained to the conductor that he did not care where he went: "put me out anywhere as soon as it is one o'clock," when he could find hospitable doors open in every quarter. The Sunday League fought steadily against this state of things; it obtained a series of legal decisions by which its coach was driven through two obstructive Sabbatarian Acts, of Charles II. and George II., one really directed against conventicles, the other against disorderly houses; it took halls for lectures and concerts, which a judge pronounced not incapable of being registered as religious meetings; it financed these undertakings, since no charge for admission could be made; it started Sunday bands in the Parks, where they are now supplied by public authority; it ran Sunday excursions to the

St James's Park Bridge

THE GROVE AT HIGHGATE

seaside; it won over Broad Churchmen and clergy-men, some of whom volunteered to act as door-keepers and attendants for the national collections on Sunday afternoons; and at last the justice of its cause moved Parliament — the obstructive House of Lords sooner than the chapel-ridden House of Commons — to open our museums and galleries on the one day when most of our fellow-citizens have a chance of visiting them. There are still Sabbatarian laws, falling more and more rusty, as they can be put into action only by a common informer, who, except for some meddlesome fanat-ic here and there, has ceased to come forward since magistrates have docked him of his fees. Most of the small shops open on Sunday could be prose-cuted, if anyone cared to prosecute them, though certain perishable articles of food have always had licence of sale, as we know from the poet—

> The feathered race on pinions skim the air
> Not so the codfish, and still less the bear :
> *This* roams the wood, carniv'rous for his prey;
> *That* with soft roe, pursues his watery way :
> *This*, slain by hunters, yields his shaggy hide;
> *That,* caught by fishers, is on Sundays cried.

Sunday, of course, is the popular day in the Parks. A century ago, it appears that on other days it was almost abandoned to fine folk, who on Sundays had to put up with unpleasant staring and crowding. It was not for half a century or so later that, in Mrs. Proudie's period, the aristocracy set an example of Sabbath quiet, and only their servants might be seen driving here. Now, it is to be feared, the children of fortune drive farther afield ; but in Hyde Park, after church hours, a most select crowd may be seen gathered on foot for a Sunday parade near the Grosvenor Gate, where it is whispered that some prayer-books carried as phylacteries have not been opened in any church; and, indeed, the reporters of cheap papers are more concerned to note how Lady This wore white *toile de soie* and a sloping hat of black crinoline, while Mrs. That looked very smart in sage green with a lovely ermine mantle, but her daughter was all in black, relieved by one long white plume. Such a show of pride aping humility does not go so far back as Tittlebat Titmouse's day, whose Sunday delight was to gaze on the equipages of fashion. In 1855, Lord Robert Grosvenor's Bill for curtailing popular pleasures on Sunday, roused a mob to riotous protest, which took the form of hooting and pelting the carriages of Sabbath-breakers in the Park; and that demonstration may have helped to prick lordly consciences.

Modern riots have been tame beside those recorded of our hotheaded forefathers. The most serious one this generation can recall is in 1866, when, the Reform League's meeting having been shut out of Hyde Park, an excited mob threw down the railings, and a Home Secretary was moved to tears by the risk of collision between the troops and the people, most of whom, as usual in such cases, hardly knew why they were gathered together. It was my chance to witness a later disturbance in the Park, which might rather be described as an ebullition of the exuberant patriotism that in democratic states makes a more serious menace to the peace of nations than does the ambition of kings or the cautious machination of statesmen. Bruin was the bugbear of that day, when the Russian Ambassador was insulted in the Park, and saved from hustling only by the interference of some gentlemen. Others ran to protect a humbler victim of popular feeling, an odd-looking little fellow, waving a flag, against whom went up the cry that he was a partisan of Russia. A crowd of some hundred or two closed upon him, whom he kept off gallantly, swinging his flag *à la moulinet* as he retreated; but presently he was knocked down, and the flag snatched from his hands; then *solvuntur tabulæ risu,* for it turned out to be the Union Jack! Later in the afternoon I saw Gladstone's windows broken in Harley Street, and Thomas Carlyle turning away from the senseless throng, with what thoughts one could imagine.

Since the attack on the Park railings, our rulers have seen well to throw open the gates for public demonstrations, held usually on Sundays, in the openest area on the north side, with much braying of brass bands, fluttering of emblematic flags, and popping of gingerbeer bottles, as accompaniment to blatant oratory that is for the most part lost on the mass of the crowd, packed round perhaps half a dozen rostrums. Suffragists, Licensed Victuallers, philanthropists, democrats, here meet in turn to proclaim their wrongs or sympathies; but it is only the inner ₁circles who seem to take the cause very seriously, as a rule, the long processions fringing off into a more or less good humoured picnic in fine weather. When enthusiasm is damped by our sullen skies, the audience will have to make up in earnestness what it lacks in numbers; but, however hoarse the speakers can shout themselves, no threatened institution seems to be one penny the worse, except our patient police, on whom falls the burden of such a show.

At the north-eastern corner, nicknamed the "Tyburn Oratory," eloquence is always flowing on a fine summer evening, and most loudly on Sunday afternoon. Here religion, or irreligion, is the common theme over which open-air preachers, Salvationists, socialists, anarchists, teetotallers, and other more or less well-meaning conversionists and cranks strive to outbawl each other at such close quarters that sometimes the heated elements run together as an explosive compound. More often, indeed, their hearers show an impartial indifference, sauntering from one doctrine to another in the way of pastime, but now and then the flock falls to arguing or jeering against the volunteer shepherd, to whom, poor man, is forbidden that one most Catholic rite, the making a collection. Such miscellaneous congregations are gaily dappled by uniforms of Guardsmen and other heroes, who on Sundays frequent this corner, not so much with a view of edification as because it makes a sweetheart exchange. It is said that Mars here comes into somewhat mercenary relations with Venus, who is expected to pay for the honour of parading herself in scarlet company.

SAILING BOATS ON THE SERPENTINE, HYDE PARK

I have even been told, but do not answer for it, that the tariff differs according to the arm of the service to be leant on; that a Life Guardsman's fee is half-a-crown, while your plain T. Atkins has to be content with a shilling; that a smart Hussar or a stalwart Highlander also comes expensive; but I am not informed how Territorial khaki stands in this market. A more authentic fact, which, if they were aware of it, should shadow the holiday spirits of our defenders, is that this corner of the Park once made a place of military execution, perhaps chosen for the *genius loci* of Tyburn tree!

The best of those preachers I have heard, so far as elocution went, was a German who used to hold forth in his own language, not, indeed, at the Marble Arch, but in Regent's Park, near the entrance to the Zoo, where is another such bazaar of divers counsels in politics and religion. This gentleman appeared to be much in earnest, and his

organ was worth listening to as a lesson in German; but I fear it was *vox* and little else one caught some way off, usually trumpeting against the Pope in a style that would have delighted Orangemen. *Peter war nimmer in Rom — das ist eine Lüge!* one heard long before coming in sight of a 80 vehement Boanerges, who would go on repeating such statements till his own backers felt the need of changing the subject. But when they pulled his coat-tails as a hint, he would turn round with *Ein Augenblick!* then pour on as fluently round his in-exhaustible point, till at last they were fain to silence him by striking up a hymn long before his testimony had run dry.

Thus unawares I have carried the reader into Regent's Park, so called as laid out by George the Magnificent, who designed treating himself to another palace here, and Regent Street was to have been an avenue connecting it with Carlton

House. This, originally known as Marylebone Park, was also Church land turned into a Tudor hunting-ground, then "slighted" under the Commonwealth, when Cromwell marked its timber for use in his navy. Allowed to fall into fields, till restored as a royal Park, it came to be opened only at the beginning of Queen Victoria's reign. It measures more than Hyde Park by a hundred acres or so, but is cut up by several private enclosures, such as a Baptist College, and St. Dunstan's Lodge, where the clock of St. Dunstan's, Fleet Street, with its automaton strikers, was transferred, as was the name of St. Katherine's, a hospital shamefully demolished at the East-end.

The best known of these encroachments is the Gardens of the Zoological Society, containing the London sight dearest to children and country cousins, unless it be Madame Tussaud's waxworks, near the south side of Regent's Park. Even when they cannot pay for admission, youngsters may hear from without the fearsome roar serving as a lion's dinner bell; and happy are those treated to a chance of feeding the monkeys or mounting the elephants, that by sober attention to this business earn many a tit-bit. The elephants are perhaps first favourites; and a loud outcry was raised when the Society sold Jumbo to America, its officials knowing, as the meddlesome protesters did not, that his temper was not to be trusted. Every amateur, indeed, is apt to have his own fancy, like that incomplete zoologist who demanded to be first taken to the *dangeroos*. In vain the kangeroos were exhibited to him; and it was only by accident that he came upon his cynosure in a cage labelled, "These animals are *dangerous*." But, over and above being a garden of marvels for children, the "Zoo" contains a good all-round collection of animals to give it rank as a public institution, the father of which was Sir Stamford Raffles, remembered also as founder of Singapore.

On the other side of the Park, the Inner Ring drive encloses the Botanic Gardens, an institution that does not flourish so well, perhaps as not having been so fully opened by its Fellows to the public, though often made the scene of lively fêtes.

Beside it is the ground of the Toxophilite Society, aiming to represent the archers of Old London. There is room here for cricket and football and for such displays as the Cart Horse Parade on Whit Monday. Regent's Park has not the same stamp of fashion as Hyde Park; but its Broad Walk, its Italian Garden, and its Lake are praiseworthy features, set amid a rim of most respect able terraces in the stuccoed classic style affected by Nash and his royal patron. The branching water has one tragic memory, dating from 1867, when forty skaters were drowned under broken ice, as need not happen again in a depth shallowed to four feet. On the north side the Park has sunk into it a canal of business, beyond which rises Primrose Hill, an Alplet some two hundred feet high, to be ascended for a wide view of London's smoke.

But how is one to describe and compliment all the parks of London? Battersea Park, with its sub-tropical garden and fine landscape features, which Besant called the most beautiful of all; Victoria Park, with its lakes and its turf trodden by the hobnails of three boroughs; Southwark Park, hidden away behind a wilderness of docks; Finsbury Park, so far from Finsbury; a mere catalogue of them might be spun out into a chapter! Almost every suburb has in our time bought or had given it some private park caught by the tide of building, to be turned into a play-place, often around an old mansion that proves rather a white elephant to the new ownership, wasted in mere tea-rooms, unless it can be adapted as a public library. Bits of once village green or common have been dressed up for the same service. The Archbishop of Canterbury and the Bishop of London have followed royal example in handing over to the public part of their palace grounds, where already, indeed, they had not much privacy of enjoyment. Many of our old churchyards, too, bloom for a living generation less disposed to be gloomily reminded of the dead. Among recent acquisitions may be mentioned Springfield Park at Clapton, laid out on a high bank of the Lea; the Ruskin Park, formed from that lover of beauty's Herne Hill grounds, not far from Brockwell Park, distinguished by its old-fashioned flower garden; and the Gladstone Park of Dollis Hill, so named in honour of the statesman who here spent quiet week ends at Lord Aberdeen's modest mansion, now standing on the edge of London.

What capital has such a ring of paradises, natural and artificial, as surrounds London, many of them once princely or prelatic parks? We will not boast of the Lea Marshes nor of Wormwood Scrubs, that, among his friends, fitted a rude nickname on Carlyle's beard; but we may ask all the cities to match Hampstead Heath, with its kite-tail of playflelds stretching across almost to the Waterlow Park of Highgate, so finely looking over London. Then in a wide circle come Stanmore Common, Harrow Weald, Ealing Common, Hampton Court, Kew Gardens, Richmond Park, Wimbledon Common, and a whole string of others in South London, passing on by Peckham Rye to Blackheath, Greenwich Park, Woolwich Common, Bostall Wood, from which we jump across the river to Barking Level, where it seems best merely to look and pass on. But in the far East is one of London's largest open spaces, Wanstead Flats, at the end of which Wanstead Park with its lakes and avenues, designed to rival Versailles, and still nursing one of the noblest heronries in England, is hardly known by name to most Londoners. This playground of the Essex boroughs once made only a corner of Epping Forest, preserved for the public by the spirit and liberality of the City Corporation. The adjoining Hainault Forest has now been added as a picnic place, ten miles out of London. Still farther afield, the sumptuous City holds pleasure grounds for its children, West Wickham Common in Kent, the Farthing Downs in Surrey, and Burnham Beeches in Bucks, while in Berkshire the holiday citizen finds Windsor Park as freely open to him as are St. James's and Kensington Gardens.

SPRING TIME IN THE PARK

The George Inn, Southwark

THE SURREY SIDE

WHILE WESTMINSTER distinguishes itself as a City, Southwark bears for title *the* Borough, as oldest of all the swarms sent out from the London hive. Nay, according to one theory, of which my friend Mr. Loftie is advocate, or at least suggester, Southwark might claim higher dignity as the original London, if the bulk of the Roman buildings were first set up there, with a fortress on the north side as *tête de pont*. The chief argument for this is Ptolemy's putting Londinium in Kent. But Ptolemy and Pausanias were the fathers of guide-books, and I have some reason for knowing how liable that class of writers are to err. Anyhow, these pages keep clear of controversial matter, so, with a respectful reference to Mr. Loftie's own scholarly writings, I will take leave to stick to the commonly received view of Southwark's origin.

This is that when a town sprang up on the northern gravel bank of the Thames, the south side was an almost uninhabitable marsh, broken by ponds, ditches, and channels, mostly over-flowed by the tide as far as the low, heathy heights now known by such names as Denmark Hill, Brixton Rise, and Lavender Hill, below which Lambeth Marsh and Brook Street tell as plain a tale of their past, while Bermondsey and Battersea suggest islets on the amphibious shore. The first inhabitants of this shore would be fisher-folk or prowling outlaws, who might prey upon the traffic passing from the ford at Thorney Island. Some sort of road there must have been across the marsh, even before the Romans raised and paved a way on from the bridge they built over the Thames. Hint of their construction survives in the name Newington Causeway; and it is believed that Roman roads might come to light below the foundations of Surrey suburbs, which have yielded bits of antiquity enough to bear out that theory of a Roman city on the south side.

If London stood on the north bank, the other end of the bridge had to be guarded by some work of defence, about which, sooner or later, would grow up such a transpontine suburb as appears in so many cities. Seldom can this "Bridge End" aspire to equality, as in the case of Buda-Pesth. Rome has its Trastevere; Calcutta its Howrah; Warsaw its Praga; Cologne its Deutz; New York looks condescendingly over to New Jersey City, but cannot, indeed, belittle its Brooklyn. So London got its Surrey side, which it long inclined to treat with good-natured hauteur as a poor relation, that has indeed thriven to count two-thirds of a county's population in its metropolitan precinct,

BARGES BUSY ON THE THAMES

besides urbanized men of Kent. Southwark still owns a certain dependent position in its nominal wardship under the City; like Westminster, it has a High Bailiff, who in this case is a City official.

The first extra-city borough began meanly enough, outside the *South-work* by which the bridge head was fortified on the Surrey side. Its best houses would be along the road that is now its High Street, to which we shall come presently. But on each side, along and behind the river, and notably westward by the early embankment still known as Bankside, there grew up nests of doubtful characters taking refuge beyond the reach of strict City discipline; so that this suburb came to bear some such reputation as the *subura* mentioned in passages of Horace and Juvenal which schoolboys are allowed to skip. A writer for our modest public must follow such example; and it will be enough to say that medieval prodigals were more famliliar with the Borough than would be the steady citizens who

through industrious apprenticeship rose to wealth and honour. In the Reformation time we find this a scene of popular amusement, when amusement was not always innocent. Theatres, banished from the City's bounds, were set up here among pleasure gardens to which there was much resort by ferries, as well as by London Bridge, so that on fine summer evenings Bankside must have been like a permanent fair. It is now a narrow, muddy, and malodorous wharf, littered by rubbish, overswung by cranes hoisting bales from stranded barges to the line of warehouses behind, through which run hidden passages like the dismal Love Lane walled in beside the City of London Electrical Works, and the not less belied Moss Alley. Yet, as Besant points out, it is not without a squalid picturesqueness, and has a noble view across the river to the dome of St. Paul's, if its usual frequenters cared to look at anything more inspiring than the splash of a rat or the tricks of a mudlark. The prospect must have been pleasanter when the Thames was gay with swans, and rowing-boats, and state barges like that in which the Lord Mayor made his annual procession till not so long ago, or that royal one preserved in the Victoria and Albert Museum, which is hardly sixty years out of the water.

The name of the "Bear Garden," borne by a Bankside alley, recalls how the most popular amusement, when drink would not be lacking and tobacco had become obnoxious to King James's counterblast, was the baiting of bulls and bears, considered sport even for ladies, Queen Elizabeth for one, though they might cry and shriek at such "ill-favoured rough things," while your Master Slenders would have it believed meat and drink to them to see the bear loose. There are many allusions in Elizabethan literature to this brutal sport, and to Paris Garden, which made its most notorious arena, a resort as popular as the Crystal Palace or the Stadium in our generation. Further back in the good old times, we hear of boars, too, being baited before they became bacon. Then on Bankside flourished cockpits, which in other parts of London came to be turned into theatres. Such unedifying exhibitions were put down, along with the theatres, by the Puritan conscience, according to Macaulay, not so much by reason of pain given to the baited beast as of sinful pleasure to the spectators. Under Cromwell, seven bears belonging to Paris Garden were sentenced to military execution. After the Globe was pulled down at the beginning of the Civil War, its site seems to have been used for Richard Baxter's meeting-house and burial-ground; and John Bunyan also, it is said, preached on Bankside, who in our day might take one of the Southwark theatres for openly advertised sermons.

The bears, however, seem to have been restored with Charles II., for Mr. Pepys, after not having been there for years, in 1666 went to "the pit where bears are baited." The attraction on other visits of his was prize-fighting, not with fists but swords, an exciting duel that once ended in a general scrimmage; but that first time he saw a bull baited, when the way in which it tossed the dogs, one

of them "into the very boxes," made "good sport," though on reflection he voted it "a very rude and nasty pleasure." Fencing was long another favourite sport here; and Congreve uses a "Bear garden flourish" as a familiar term of swordsmanship. Again, Pepys appears at an alehouse on Bankside as a box from which to view the more thrilling spectacle of the Great Fire, till he went home to find it a case of *proximus ardet*, and had to spend the night in packing up his goods and burying away his money. The year before he had visited "Foxhall," to find no company there, for terror of the Plague. This resort Evelyn mentions as new in 1661; but not till next century did it become famous as Vauxhall Gardens, with its enticements of music, pictures, and statues, illuminated walks and dark thickets, and fireworks that fizzled out within living memory.

The "New Spring Gardens" at Foxhall — as Addison still spelt it — took their first name from the garden at the corner of St. James's Park, and flourished as a novel suburban resort, supplanting the coarse joys of the Bear-pit by prettier sights and sounds that were prostituted to pleasures by no means innocent. "When I considered the fragrancy of the walks and bowers," was Mr. Spectator's experience, "with the choirs of birds that sung upon the trees, and the loose tribe of people that walked under their shades, I could not but look on the place as a kind of Mahometan paradise." The novels of the eighteenth century have many scenes to show us what Vauxhall was, that from this side long blazed in renown, though eclipsed for a generation by the fashion of Ranelagh on the Chelsea bank; but the older lights shone on, as we know, down to the youth of Mr. Pendennis.

In Shakespeare's day several theatres were built behind Bankside, among them the Globe, in which the poet, as yet unconscious of his immortality, had the satisfaction to be a shareholder as well as an actor. He is believed to have lived on Bankside, with Bardolphs and Barnardines as neighbours, perhaps boon companions. In 1909 an artistic memorial tablet was placed on the south side of

Park Street, formerly Maid Lane, to mark what has been taken for the site of the Globe; then, Just before the ceremony came off, an American investigator, Dr. Wallace, rose, like the ghost of Banquo, to declare that it stood elsewhere, on the other side of the street, now as little parkish as it seems maidenly. Like so many other streets on the once gardened riverside, a sunless tunnel through grimy walls, it is reached by stairs from the south end of Southwark Bridge, and leads to Barclay and Perkins' huge Brewery, grown out of Thrale's, where Dr. Johnson, as his executor, played the man of business, pen and inkhorn at button-hole, helping to sell the "potentiality of growing rich beyond the dreams of avarice." Park Street got its name as having been cut through the grounds of a house belonging to Lord Desmond, whose own name in eighteenth century street nomenclature had been corrupted to *Deadman*. The Globe also stood near a very old thoroughfare, Stoney Street, which from the St. Mary Overies Ferry led into the road from London Bridge — its name now taken by the Stoney Street signal station at the end of the railway bridge.

We need not stop to make sure of the exact site of Shakespeare's theatre; but a melodramatic scene, quite after the Surrey-side school, may be recalled at this Brewery half a century ago. Among other visitors to such a truly British sight came Baron Haynau, fresh from the Hungarian revolt which he was believed to have put down with ruthless severity; and British indignation had been specially roused by a report of his ordering women to be flogged. No sooner had he written his name in the visitors' book, than its ill-savour spread like wildfire through the place; then out rushed the sturdy draymen, armed with brooms against the "Austrian butcher," who, to his amazement, found himself for once received by no means as an honoured guest. Assailed by angry cries pelted with dirt and grains, the victorious General was fain to fly with a threatening mob at his heels. He made his way to Bankside, and there took refuge in a public-house, whose landlady stowed him away in such a fright, that he is said to have cut off the

moustaches which in 1850 would betray him as a foreigner. The mob broke into the house, but, luckily for him, missed the room where he was hidden. Several hundreds of people had by this time assembled, worked up to such anger, that "General Hyæna" might well suppose them to be shouting for his blood; and if he had fallen into their hands, he might perhaps have been ducked in the water. But just in time the poor tyrant, with his clothes half torn off his back, was rescued by a body of police, who from a chorus of execration rowed him across the river to santury in Somerset House. He soon cut short his visit to England, where, to the Austrian Government's high displeasure, nobody was flogged or imprisoned for this demonstration, John Bull's verdict on it, as expressed by *Punch* and other papers, being "Served him right!"

The great Brewery, as beseems, stands near the Hop Exchange, and the narrow twisting passages beyond lead us on to a busy vegetable market, opposite which we are suddenly aware of one of the finest churches in London, half hidden away below the end of London Bridge. This is the ancient St. Mary Overies, re-christened St. Saviour's, and now adapted as Cathedral for the new diocese of Southwark. It was, indeed, a whole group of ecclesiastical buildings that once sanctified the taverns and stews of Southwark. There stood here a palace of the rich Winchester Bishops, whose successor in our time has still a castle among his seats.

But the peculiar note of St. Saviour's seems to be with the theatrical neighbours, whose parish church it was, not always neglected by them. The dramatists Fletcher and Massinger were buried here, as was Shakespeare's younger brother Edmund, with his associates in the Globe, Henslow and Burbage; and another actor-manager of the time, Alleyn, is honoured by one of the memorial windows. Edward Alleyn, like his fellow-player from Stratford, became a man of substance, for be bought the manor of Dulwich, and there founded his College, that has grown to be an important educational institution, while a bequest of valuable pictures turned the old building into a notable Gallery.

It is clear that some of those Thespians so far lived down the taint of the dyer's hand, as to pass for respectable citizens, not godless outcasts from the services of the Church, like Molière and Adrienne Lecouvreur in France. Alleyn might well grow rich, for he was not only part or whole proprietor of several theatres, but "bear-master" to James I., and at one time the keeper of Paris Garden, occupations that did not bar him from being on the parish vestry, and more than once chosen as church-warden.

As all London is buttressed by its railways, so the rise of the Surrey side depended on the building of the Thames bridges. We have seen how the first borough grew up at the foot of London Bridge, that for centuries remained the only one short of Kingston, round by which Sir Thomas Wyatt had to march, when he failed to carry the City Gate from Southwark and its inhabitants begged him to begone before drawing on them the cannon of the Tower. At the time of the Civil War a temporary bridge of boats had been thrown over the Thames at Putney; but it was not till the middle of the next century that wooden bridges were built at Putney, then at Kew, both now rebuilt more solidly. The second bridge in London was Westminster, opened 1750, in a storm of protests from watermen and vested interests expecting to suffer from public convenience; even so, under King John, the ferry-men had called out against London Bridge as dangerous opposition to their fare of a farthing for foot-passengers and a penny for man and horse. Blackfriars came soon afterwards, when a party of conntry-folk attended by Humphrey Clinker could speak of "the three bridges." Waterloo Bridge was to have been called "Strand" Bridge, and its date is marked by the changed name that has offended French visitors: one Parisian, not remembering his own *Pont d'Jena* and *Pont d'Austerlitz*, hotly calls on the English to forget Waterloo. About the same time rose the Southwark arches to make "the Iron Bridge" of *Little Dorrit*, who had to pay a penny each time she crossed; and the halfpenny toll on Waterloo Bridge may have barred many a poor wretch from thence flinging herself into the black flowing river. London Bridge, first built in stone by the generation that called for Magna Charta, and in the Middle Ages loaded with towers and houses like the poop of a Spanish galleon, was reconstructed, a little off its former line, in the Reform Bill era. Next came several bridges up the river, when also it began to be spanned by railways. It seems only the other day that on some of these bridges a small toll ceased to be levied. Still more fresh in one's mind is the prolonged rebuilding of Vauxhall Bridge, during which a temporary "Ten Year" bridge led over to the Tate Gallery. Blackfriars Bridge has lately been widened for tram-lines; and now there is designed a new St. Paul's Bridge, with trams as its *raison d'être*, while Southwark Bridge will be rebuilt beside it at a trifling expense of some couple of millions.

The last of our bridges, opened 1894, was the Tower Bridge, at once the lowest and the high-est of all, since looking up the river it looks down so commandingly from the lofty gallery open to pedes-trians, when the central drawbridges are raised to let vessels pass. But from the top only tantalizing peeps can be had on the river, the passage being closed in, as is undemtood, to shut out a temptation to suicide that overwhelms some troubled heads at such dizzy elevations. Below this the Thames must be crossed by underground passages. The Tower Subway has been shut up; and the once vaunted Thames Tunnel, with its subterranean fair, was not an endur-ing success. It is now used by a railway; but near it runs the new Rotherhithe Subway for all sorts of traffic, echoing fearsomely beneath thousands of electric lamps. The sub-fluvial passage from the Isle of Dogs to Greenwich is only for foot passengers; while farther down the Blackwall Tunnel makes a spacious carriage way. There is to be another subway at Woolwich, where the passage by ferry, in fog or snow, as yet helps us to understand how our forefa-thers might be put to it for crossing the river, unless when bridged by the frosts that seem to have been more severe in good old days.

COMING UP WITH THE TIDE

If London goes on growing at its present rate, another generation should see it transformed into a pile of tall barracks and workhouses, aerated by parks, squares, and ex-churchyards, opening out in long lines of populous road into roomy suburbs, whose spread will be checked only by the white cliffs of Albion, perhaps not even there when air-ships and tunnels have supplied rapid transit between the valleys of the Seine and of the Thames. Or is it London's destiny to suffer that fate which Macaulay foresaw through the eyes of a New Zealander, as before him Horace Walpole imagined a citizen of Lima wondering over the ruins of St. Paul's? Our rival political factions proclaim us to be at present making a choice of Hercules, on which will depend Britain's future, and with that the greatness of her capital. Are there children now alive whose bleared eyes may see London shrunk to its old bounds, perhaps huddled on some choice site like the heights of Highgate and Hampstead — which, according to Mother Shipton's prophecy, should become its centre — when for leagues, as about the walls of Delhi or Peking, the open country will be dotted with ruined temples and towers round the broken dome on Ludgate Hill, standing up in solitary state like the Kutub Minar? Can it ever come to lie squalidly deserted for a new city rebuilt by some conqueror, as at Bokhara and Samarcand? Are there generations yet unborn to whom this capital will be a show like "hundred-gated Thebes," a quarry of antiquities like Nineveh or Knossos, a mystery like the Cambodian Angkor or the Bolivian Tiahuanaco, an overgrown wilderness like the buried ruins of Yucatan? Is it possible that some distant age will know of London nothing but its name, when as yet undreamt-of structures have overlaid every fragment of the achievements on which we boast against the past, unconscious how our pride may point a moral or a mockery for the future?

Every vestige of the city, guessed alone,
Stock or stone —
Where & multitude of men breathed joy and woe
Long ago:
Love of glory pricked their hearts up, dread of shame
Struck them tame;
And that glory and that shame alike, the gold
Bought and sold.